RACIAL NEGOTIATIONS: POTENTIALS & LIMITATIONS

RACIAL NEGOTIATIONS: POTENTIALS & LIMITATIONS

W. Ellison Chalmers

Ann Arbor
Institute of Labor and Industrial Relations
The University of Michigan—Wayne State University
1974

This study was supported by a grant from the Ford Foundation. The opinions expressed are those of the author and do not necessarily reflect those of the Ford Foundation.

*Copyright © 1974 by the
Institute of Labor and Industrial Relations
The University of Michigan—Wayne State University
401 Fourth Street, Ann Arbor, Michigan 48103*

*Library of Congress Catalog Card Number: 74-78509
International Standard Book Number: 87736-321-8*

Printed in the United States of America

Contents

PREFACE   vii

1   **The Problem and the Approach**   1
   THE RESEARCH DESIGN   13

2   **The Participants**   17
   BLACK CHALLENGERS   18
   ESTABLISHMENTS   29

3   **Public Employment**   37
   MEMPHIS PUBLIC EMPLOYEES STRIKE   39
   CLEVELAND WATERWORKS
     EMPLOYEES STRIKE   44
   CHARLESTON HOSPITAL STRIKES   50

4   **Universities**   73
   UNIVERSITY OF MICHIGAN   74
   SAN FRANCISCO STATE   78
   DUKE UNIVERSITY   81

5 Public Schools **113**
    DETROIT SECONDARY SCHOOLS   116
    DETROIT SKILLS CENTER   120
    INTERMEDIATE SCHOOL,
        NEW YORK CITY   126
    CENTRAL CITY COLLEGE SYSTEM   127

6 Public Welfare **141**
    WASHTENAW COUNTY
        CLOTHING ALLOWANCE   144
    CAPITAL CITY WELFARE   149
    NEW YORK CITY SPECIAL
        GRANT DISPUTE   152

7 Construction **169**
    CONFRONTATION IN CHICAGO   180

8 Nonprofit Service Organizations **195**
    NATIONAL CONFERENCE FOR
        NEW CAREERS   196

9 Characteristics of Racial Negotiations **215**
    THE NEGOTIATING PROCESS   225
    RESULTS OF NEGOTIATIONS   233
    THIRD-PARTY INTERVENTION   242

10 Summary and Conclusions **251**
    BLACK AND WHITE ALIGNMENTS   254
    THE MEDIATOR'S ROLE   271
    CHALLENGING PROBLEMS   275
    CONCLUDING PERSPECTIVE   279

Preface

This research report explores some of the patterns of racial conflict in an effort, never before extensively pursued, to relate theories of race to theories of collective bargaining. The research design focuses on a new field of study although it draws on relevant theoretical constructs and the most appropriate scholarship and research tools available.

The choice of subject area, questions to be answered, and hypotheses to be tested in this project, as in all research seeking to explain social phenomena, developed from my view and set of values about America. In constructing and pursuing the research, however, I was guided by values that are shared with many others. Indeed, some of them appear to be the idealized social values of our whole culture.

Let me identify the relevant judgments and values underlying this research. I began with the common value assumption that America should not deny equal opportunities for self-development to its black citizens. Yet, one may wonder whether such an objective really motivates many white Americans. Ever since the first black slaves were imported, the people and institutions of America have imposed second-class status on blacks. The Kerner Report[1] accurately, although vaguely, described the "white racist" character of America as belong-

---

[1] Otto Kerner, et al. *Report of the National Advisory Commission on Civil Disorders* and *Supplemental Studies for the National Advisory Commission on Civil Disorders* (U.S. Government Printing Office, 1968).

ing not only to yesterday but to today as well. This second-class status and the limited opportunities available to many blacks have been, in part, the result of white prejudices. Even more, the consequences of those prejudices, when translated into institutional policies and procedures, have blocked blacks in their efforts toward self-realization. Thus, the publicly avowed objective of equal opportunity for blacks appears, at best, to be only an abstract and rhetorical goal for many, while discriminatory acts are prevalent and white perspectives and advantages continue with few challenges.

In contrast to this purely rhetorical position, I, along with many other Americans, want America to move toward the realization of that abstract goal. One step toward such a change is nondiscriminatory treatment of blacks. This objective is expressed by many whites as the achievement of personal attitudes and institutional practices that draw no color line. Under this standard, black Americans would have the opportunity to develop and to function like everyone else.

Because they are faced with discrimination and the failure of America to adapt in order to produce social equality, I wish that blacks were free to reject the objective of "noncolor" and to develop a group identity for themselves. While my personal values and goals are for complete equality, in practice as well as in theory, I am enough of an institutionalist to know that sweeping changes are not made overnight. The challenge is to explore routes that promise, realistically, the most extensive, rapid, and meaningful progress.

The Kerner Report fails to develop the meaning of its label of "white racist America," and to analyze existing dynamics toward nondiscrimination in this country. Furthermore, it gives neither a description of, nor a program for the development of black pride and black identity. It seemed to me that a scholar could help by developing analyses and guidelines toward those twin objectives. As an institutional economist, I could join others in exploring the potentials for governmental anti-discrimination programs. My particular specialty is the study of the processes of collective bargaining. With many others, I share the judgment that collective bargaining stabilizes conflict within the labor field and produces an acceptable accommodation of conflicting interests. Perhaps, I reasoned, institutions controlled by whites could use a similar negotiating process when confronted by blacks who challenged their programs, and achieve the same accommodation. Drawing an analogy to labor-management seemed to have additional relevant aspects. Since American institutions show little willingness to deal with black concerns adequately, blacks have to take the initiative in forcing changes. Using negotiations to achieve an accommodated result seemed to provide a nonrevolutionary route to eliminate discrimination and modify institutional functions to serve black interests.

As the research continued, my judgments became somewhat more realistic, although my values did not change. With the help of my black colleagues, I concluded that a simplistic assumption underlaid my early conceptualization of the usefulness of transferring experience from labor-management relations to racial conflict as a route to racial progress. The immediate objective of union-management negotiations is an agreement. This process is an acceptable instrument for labor because it produces advances for workers. Negotiations were tolerated and then accepted by management because they contribute to an accommodation with labor interests without endangering the firm's economic position. The public and the government supported the process because it appeared to produce social and economic stability at a minimal social cost. Thus, labor peace, the *settlement* of labor disputes through negotiations, became a desirable step for all participants.

It is obvious that one can apply a labor analogy to the search of racial progress only if blacks judge that the results of negotiations can be an important step forward. As the cases in this book clearly demonstrate, blacks have no reason to place such confidence in the negotiating process. Peace cannot be equated with progress. The crucial problem becomes not *whether* a settlement can be achieved, but *what kind* of a settlement it is. Therefore, I modified my earlier research focus. The revised questions became: (1) Can blacks use the negotiating process to overcome white resistance to institutional change? How much and what kinds of change can be achieved by their use of the negotiating process? In this approach, can they take advantage of pressures for change that exist either inside or outside the institution? (2) Can whites, operating within white-controlled institutions, use the negotiating process to reach an accommodation with specialized black interests and build these interests into institutional functioning? How can such changes affect the general objective of these various institutions?

As the research developed, it became apparent that the answers to these questions would come not from analyzing a racial negotiations process itself but from searching for the dynamics that affect conflict and confrontation as well as negotiations. Thus, the emphasis became how establishments define and face up to the racial components of their functioning, the objectives of black challenges, and the structuring of black pressures for such changes. As the research progressed, it also became apparent that the analyses of these data should distinguish among different sectors of American society and the different power relationships that appear when black clients or black participants challenge different kinds of institutions and white power structures.

There are no socially accepted rules requiring racial negotiations or defining how they should be conducted that are parallel to those embodied in the Wagner Act, and interpreted and enforced by the National Labor Relations Board. Thus, the perspectives of establishment and black leaderships, the real motivations activating white leaders and white institutions, the power structure of the establishment and its ties to the whole social fabric, and the attitudes and motivations of black leaders and the relevant constituencies appeared to be the crucial variables. Because this is a pioneering exploration of new institutional and racial relationships, the report emphasizes the tentativeness of the conclusions and indicates the areas that require further exploration.

The findings are presented in three different forms: abstracts of several incidents of racial conflict and negotiations, sector analyses of the common patterns in these cases, and generalizations about conflict patterns in America. The last chapter contrasts the limited results of the experience to date with the hopes of many black Americans. This format permits the material to be used in a variety of ways. Scholars and students can test current theories and develop alternative explanations for particular racial incidents and the patterns of conflict in schools, building construction, or other sectors, and focus on negotiations as a way to achieve racial adjustments. They may use one or more of these treatments to explore racial patterns in America and the more general theories of institutional change.

Practitioners will find different meanings in these reports depending on their roles. Establishment decision makers may seek to assess their positions as well as their negotiation techniques. Black leaders may assess whether to engage in negotiations at all and, if so, with what approaches and programmatic objectives. Third-party intervenors, particularly those with some labor-management experience, may be challenged to reevaluate the objectives and the techniques of their role.

Practitioners, however, will not find this a "how to do it" manual. As the research continued it became increasingly clear that participants must achieve a perspective on the reasons for the conflict, the probable objectives of each of the parties, and the probable results of alternative strategies. Practitioners must add data from their own experience and knowledge of the specifics of their institutional or leadership roles, and use the conclusions developed from this research to work out their directions.

Although the responsibility for this report is my own, my thanks are due to a great many who shared in its development. The Ford Foundation funded the three-year research period and The University of Michigan was the official sponsor. University assistance came from President Robben Fleming, Institute of Labor and Industrial Relations Codirectors Ronald Haughton and Charles Rehmus, and Louis A. Ferman, director of research at that institute. My wife, Thelma Fox Chalmers, served as editor throughout the three years with the assistance and support of Joyce Kornbluh; Joe A Miller and then Gerald Cormick participated as Assistant Directors of the project. Miss Betty Lu Ingraham performed more than her share of the secretarial duties.

I owe much to Louis A. Ferman for the original conception and for his continually helpful and critical ideas. Ronald Haughton provided important perspectives by drawing on his own experiences as a mediator and arbitrator in racial and labor disputes. Haughton and Ferman were primarily responsible for the original negotiations with the Ford Foundation, and continued to play an important role in the mutual adjustment of perspectives and directions of the project.

Many of the ideas incorporated into this book came from the black scholars who collaborated in the project either as authors of studies or as participants in conferences and discussions. I am particularly indebted to Jack Alexis, James Blackwell, Charles V. Hamilton, Tobe Johnson, Donald J. Roberts, Charles U. Smith, Richard Trent, and Preston Wilcox. As the case study references indicate, some of those black scholars shared responsibility with white colleagues including Arthur E. Antisdel, Louis A. Ferman, Charles Grigg, Marie Haug, F. Ray Marshall, Robert B. McKersie, Joe A. Miller, Jack J. Preiss, Michael J. Piore, Sumner Rosen, Herbert Semmel, and Don Watkins.[2]

I profited from discussions with Sam Jackson and Willoughby Abner, directors of the National Center for Dispute Settlement of the American Arbitration Association, and their assistant, Warren Taylor. Stimulating ideas, support, and critical comments came from Mark Chesler, James Laue, Joseph Smith, Will Smith, Don Straus, Simon Wittes, and many others.

Obviously, none of the above bear any responsibility for my analyses, judgments, conclusions, or method of presentation.

---

[2] Also participating in those studies were Arvil Van Adams, Tom F. Adams, George W. Bradshaw, Jeffrey Davidson, Robert Hall, Jeffrey Jacques, Chessie Jeffries, and DonCosta Seawell.

My debt is even greater to the major participants in each of the cases that are presented here. Without their confidential reports to the scholars who were analyzing their experiences, we would not have had the facts, perceptions, and insights upon which these individual reports are built. Obviously, not all of their differing views have been accepted in my general conclusions, but it is important to note that each, in his own way, contributed to the experiences from which these analyses have been drawn.

—*W. Ellison Chalmers*

PARTICIPATING SCHOLARS

Arvil Van Adams	University of Kentucky
Jack H. Alexis	Stanford University
Curtis C. Aller	San Francisco State College
Arthur Antisdel	Wayne State University
James E. Blackwell	University of Massachusetts
W. Ellison Chalmers	University of Michigan
Louis A. Ferman	University of Michigan
Charles M. Grigg	Florida State University
Marie R. Haug	Case Western Reserve University
James Hefner	Clark College
F. Ray Marshall	University of Texas
Robert B. McKersie	University of Chicago
Joe A. Miller	University of Michigan
Michael J. Piore	Massachusetts Institute of Technology
Jack J. Preiss	Duke University
Donald J. Roberts	Neighborhood Service Organization, Detroit
Sumner M. Rosen	Institute of Public Administration, NYC
Herbert Semmel	University of Illinois
Charles U. Smith	Florida A&M University
Emory Via	Southern Regional Council
Donald Watkins	Brooklyn College
Preston Wilcox	Afram Associates, NYC

NOTE: The affiliations listed for participants are for the positions they held at the time of the study.

CHAPTER 1

The Problem and the Approach

The nation has experienced serious conflicts between black protest groups and white-dominated institutions that are likely to continue and even intensify. Because of their whole life experiences many blacks believe that they are living in a "white racist society"[1] and a significant number are determined to achieve progress toward equality. Whites occupy the seats of power; the institutional and the attitudinal patterns of our society are resistant to rapid, purposeful change and this relative inflexibility is strengthened by a polarized white resistance to black demands. Blacks feel a growing sense of outrage at their exclusion from, or unequal treatment within, various institutions. For these reasons this study focuses on the probabilities of

---

[1] The scholars whose reports were included in this study encountered considerable difficulty in identifying the various meanings of terms used by different participants. For instance, "white racist society" has quite a clear meaning for many blacks although it was used by the Kerner Commission without precision or an adequate definition and is not understandable to many whites. Many scholars writing for this study used the word "Negro" to identify a person of color who is also aligned with the establishment and reserved the word "black" to identify someone with a strong concern for black identity. Many people feel that the word "coercion" has an unfortunate connotation: it suggests that the only basis for a black challenge is pressure and ignores the "right" of blacks for "justice;" they claim that black pressures should not be labeled "coercion" if establishment pressures are labeled the "maintenance of law and order." Some use the word "compromise" as a rational step toward an accomodated agreement; others use it to mean a "sell out." In general this text seeks to adhere as closely as possible to technical and nonevaluative meanings. The particular meaning attached to each word cited will be apparent as the various concepts are developed.

overt racial conflict in some of the major American institutions and explores the potential effectiveness of negotiation as one way of meeting that conflict.

Some black leaders have expressed the conviction of many blacks that the discriminatory characteristics of what they view as a white racist society can be meaningfully changed *only* when black Americans possess sufficient coercive power to force change upon that society. This judgment is usually countered by the widely held and deeply felt conviction of many whites that adequate methods for change already exist, that progress toward equality is being made through these acceptable methods, and that no group has the right to force changes, only to operate in accordance with established rules and through established channels.

THE NEGOTIATIONS PROCESS

Throughout a wide variety of economic, political, and legal circumstances, a conflict relationship can be accommodated through negotiation strategy. This study focuses on the potentials and limitations of such a strategy when used by black protestors and the institutions whose actions and attitudes are being challenged.[2] Purposeful challenges against specific establishments enmeshed within the system are examined in the cases.[3] Black leaders believe that the specific services of blacks and the roles asssigned to them by such an establishment are unacceptable, and direct their challenges to the centers of power that control actions affecting black constituencies. The conflict that is the center of this study derives from black objections to the functioning of specific establishments, and the black actions are an effort to reach the sources of decision making to effect changes in policies and administration.

---

[2] The negotiations alternative is not the only one open to each protagonist, of course. Without attempting a full, analytical survey of all of the options, this study explores this particular approach to provide a basis for judgment on its problems and opportunities. The interrelationship of these other alternatives is developed on pages 20-27.

[3] The term "establishment" is used to refer to a single formal organization with rules, defined internal and external relationships, and recognized functions and outputs. We shall use the term "institution" or "sector" to refer to a category of establishments that are grouped together because they have common functions, structures, and outputs in American society—for example, public schools, universities, and city governments. We are not using the terms as "The Establishment" or "The White Power Structure" but think of the concept as being wider and more general than either "establishment" or "institution."

Negotiation is a process participated in by the representatives of at least two groups, each with a constituency. The institutions with which we are concerned are led by white individuals and the functioning of such institutions is accepted as being consistent with the structures and values of white-dominated American society.[4] Each participant has identified some areas of conflicting group interest and each, at least tentatively, is committed to discovering whether an accommodation can be achieved between those conflicting interests so that neither side overwhelms the other. This process involves direct communication between the spokesmen, exploration of respective positions, and consideration of alternative solutions.

Negotiators almost always have some capacity to damage or at least inconvenience the other side as part of their insistence that some compromise position be accepted. Such coercive capacity may be used, or may be threatened directly or indirectly. The model on which this study is based is drawn from the theory of negotiations in institutions, commercial transactions, union-management relations, and international affairs, in which great emphasis is placed on relative coercive power. It has been frequently said that the result, that is, the terms of a negotiated agreement, tends to approximate the relative coercive power of the two sides.

In racial negotiations the black side seeks to alter the policies or procedures of an institution that is controlled by whites. Both sides may prefer a negotiated solution. Blacks may want to obtain specific policy changes by influencing or participating in the white institution's policy making. Whites may use negotiations to seek a peaceful way to settle the conflict. Each side enters the negotiations having formulated some objectives about what they wish to get out of the process and what concessions they are willing to make.

The relative power of the two parties' coercive abilities affects the settlement area and the final distribution of the gains and losses.[5] In

[4] The challenged institution will be referred to in our shorthand as a "white institution."

[5] The word "coercion" has an emotional loading that varies with one's perspectives. These loadings became clear as the participants and scholars involved in this study discussed its general framework. The term "coercion" was used by many only when describing the actions of those who were *not* in power; when the establishment was involved in a power conflict some used the terms "exercise of authority" and "law and order." To avoid these value loadings, it would have been possible to substitute the phrase "pressure and counterpressure" for any occasion in which either side attempts to change the position of the other. Thus, such a phrase might be used to describe a situation in which university students use a strike or boycott and the administration responds with suspension or expulsion. Despite the risk of confusion, the word coercion is used in this text because it accurately summarizes the *relationships* with which the study is concerned.

racial negotiations the coercive power of the black side is affected by the degree of support of its grass roots constituency and its ability to disrupt the functioning of the white institution, to put pressure on the supportive structures of the white institution, and to manipulate the white conscience and the white side's fear of general black disruption. The coercive capacity of the white institution rests partly in its ability to outlast any threatened disruption of its functions, to mobilize penalties against black leaders and their supporters, and to rally external support for its position.

During the negotiation process the perceptions of the opposing sides will be modified with respect to the relative balance of power. Because the perceptions of the negotiators must overlap at the point of agreement, the settlement reflects the coercive potential of each.

Since the potential of a negotiating process is central to our investigation and the use of relative coercive power is prominent in that process, it may be useful to illustrate these interrelated concepts. The following step-by-step description of a racial conflict in a public high school illustrates the negotiations processs:

1. Black students present the school board with a demand: Remove the present principal because he is racist in handling discipline, curriculum policies, and extracurricular programs. The school board refuses to accede to the black demand because this action would threaten its established decision-making structures.

   The first step in an analysis of relative coercive power is the identification by each side of a conflict of interests.

2. When the school board responds with a flat "no," the black students have some capacity to hurt the board. Their leaders can call on black students who, in support of this demand, are willing to stage disruptions within the school even at the risk of severe disciplinary penalties.

   Blacks have some power to coerce the establishment, even though they risk hurting themselves in the process.

3. The school board has a considerable capacity to prevent the threat of disruption. The board can threaten to take disciplinary action against the black student leaders and their supporters. Despite the support of some parents for the students' position, the board may mobilize some black parental pressure against the students by threatening police action, and suggesting that the

educational development of their children is being blocked by continuation of the dispute.

The establishment, by using measures already built into the order-keeping aspects of the system and activating supplementary assistance, has strong resources to support its refusal to grant black demands.

4. The school board may counter by indicating that it is considering the appointment of a black counselor who could help black students work out complaints against the principal. By making this proposal, the board hopes to moderate black support for the original black student demand while maintaining the support of teachers and the white community.

    The student leaders may refuse to abandon their original demands and may reject the board's proposal because they and their parents believe that it will not deal with their complaints and that it indicates that the board is unresponsive to black needs. They may counterpropose that the white principal be suspended while they present their evidence to a board-appointed, biracial team that will have the power to discharge the principal if the charges are substantiated. In this alternative position the support of black students and parents may have been slightly diluted, although the leaders expect that the counterproposal will be acceptable to the board and its white supporters and that it will reduce their preference for an inflexible position.

    The process of proposals and counterproposals may continue. The board seeks to protect its authority position in order to maintain the support of the teachers and the white community, and to reduce student pressures by weakening the support of black students and parents for the student leaders. By their counterproposals, the students seek to weaken support for the board and to maintain or increase black support for their threats of disruption.

    Each side's change of position affects the power relationships by modifying the degree of determination and support of both constituencies.

5. As the two sides continue to interact, black students may develop their threats into actual disruptions that cause the board to lose some state appropriations and some white community support because it is "failing to educate the children." The board

may find that it is necessary to develop alternatives that are more responsive to the blacks' complaints against the principal, for example, by appointing a black assistant principal who has the authority to handle disciplinary questions.

The board may impose severe penalties on some student disruptors and some may receive court sentences. The black coercive position may be undermined and the student leaders may accept the appointment of a black assistant principal with disciplinary authority, provided that he empathizes with black student positions. The board may hope that the problem has been solved. On the other hand, the blacks would probably view the arrangement as the end of that particular incident, and would know that conflicts would recur and even expand on other issues and other occasions.

Each modification of the original positions arises from the fact that each side is being hurt by the actions of the other. Each counterproposal is designed to retain as much support and power as possible while undercutting support for the other side's position to make acceptance of its own terms more likely. Agreement on the terms of settlement becomes possible when both sides find that some proposition is more acceptable to each than is the risk of declining support and power.

6. Suppose that our illustration is enlarged by starting with two or more black student demands rather than one. For instance, blacks might also demand a Malcolm X holiday. This demand would be less threatening to the board than the demand to remove the principal and, therefore, the board might not be as resistant. The Malcolm X proposal might have strong student support since it expresses recognition of independent black identity and is a first step toward a much more general challenge to white positions by blacks. The school board's resistance to this issue might be lower and student support for it might be stronger.

The coercive position of each side differs with each issue that is included within the conflict. It may be necessary to assign relative priorities to each side's positions. Alternate patterns of positions on a number of issues can represent a "packaging" of the various issues and the development of degrees of coercive power.

7. Throughout the steps in this process the school board attempts to determine why the black students demand the removal of the

principal, what alternative proposals are likely to reduce support for the blacks' position, and whether the backing for student leaders is changing. At the same time, black leaders attempt to analyze why the board appears to be supporting the principal and what alternatives are likely to appeal to white constituencies while not diminishing the support of their own constituencies.

The process of developing and using relative coercive power is not a formula that is applied to objective reality. Rather, it is shaped by the uncertain perspectives of each side. Thus, in the negotiating process, each side seeks to develop, project, and change its own perceptions and the perspectives of the other to make the maximum use of its relative coercive power.

A contrast to the relative coercive power approach in negotiations strategy is the situation in which the two sides solve problems. The establishment sees the demands of black leaders as indicators of policies and practices that are inconsistent with its avowed purposes, accepts their help in defining the problems of the institution, and perhaps solicits their assistance in solving them. Theoretically, such an approach is a two-way street. The black leaders and their constituency may also have problems that can be reduced by changes in establishment practices. A mixture of relative coercive power and problem-solving can be used in the negotiating process to agree on an accommodation of conflicting positions.

Negotiation is therefore, an approach that can be adopted in racial conflicts. Do those who are directly involved consider it to be an appropriate method? More specifically, this study investigates the following points:

1. Whether, how, and why negotiations develop when black leaders challenge the functioning of specific establishments that are dominated by white decision makers;

2. Whether, how, and why such negotiations are carried to a mutually acceptable conclusion;

3. How much progress in the directions sought by blacks results from such negotiations; and

4. The extent to which third-party intervenors assist in the negotiating patterns.

VALUE JUDGMENTS AND NEGOTIATIONS

Behind these questions lies the uncertainty of whether the protagonists *want* to use the negotiating process. Implicit value judgments are held by those who recommend negotiations as a route to the settlement of racial confrontations. Unless these are recognized it is impossible to understand the resistance of the challenged establishment and the reluctance of many black spokesmen and leaders to become involved in a negotiations process.

Racial Peace

The labor-management analogy is particularly intriguing to many whites because it seems to suggest possibilities for racial peace,[6] just as the search for industrial peace was stimulated 25 years ago.[7] Industrial peace refers to a situation in which the parties have largely avoided overt disruptive actions, thus ensuring uninterrupted production for management and uninterrupted wages for workers. It is important to those participants and has been achieved so extensively that negotiation through collective bargaining is widely supported by labor unions, employers, and the federal government. *If* the analogy were accepted and the same results expected when the process was attempted in race relations, negotiations could be seen as a route to racial peace and might well be strongly supported by the public, the government, white-controlled establishments, and perhaps by black protestors as well. But before there can be any confidence in such an estimate it is necessary to assess the significance for each participant in racial negotiations of other values traditionally imputed to union-management negotiations.

Redistribution of Resources

A second reason that is presumed to explain the use of and support for labor negotiations is the possibility that negotiations will lead to a redistribution of resources. This criterion suggests that the judgments

---

[6] This is not to imply that the analogy can be applied to achieve an adequate understanding of racial conflict and negotiations (see our later uses). The analytical problems posed by the analogy are developed at some length in W. Ellison Chalmers and Gerald W. Cormick, "Collective Bargaining in Racial Disputes?" *Issues in Industrial Society*, Vol. 1, No. 3 (1970), 8-16 ff.

[7] "Causes of Industrial Peace under Collective Bargaining," Studies 1-14, National Planning Association (Washington, D.C., 1948-53).

of establishment and black leaders about the usefulness of negotiations will depend significantly on their expectations of possible redistribution.

In the labor situation such a redistribution of resources has been sought through wage increases and provision of fringe benefits to workers. In most racial conflicts the question is not quite as simple. Resource redistribution may require allocation of additional funds to schools in predominantly black areas; it may require preferential hiring so that more jobs are distributed to blacks than to whites; or it may involve a reordering of university priorities to put more money into black studies programs, supportive services to black students, and increasing the number of black faculty members. The underlying assumption of the challengers is that such a redistribution will represent a shift of economic and social resources.

Participation in Decision Making

By challenging managements, unions are seeking to involve workers' representatives in company decisions that immediately affect their livelihood and status. They reject the proposition that management can be trusted to look out for workers and to treat them fairly.

In racial conflicts this value is more complex. Black leaders who seek to develop black identity, black culture, and black organization and to achieve an *organized* black part of a pluralistic society may wish to use negotiations to end the segregation and separation that white America has imposed on them. White leaders of establishments, on the other hand, may not welcome organized black participation in decision making.

In summary, then, the application of the three value criteria from labor-management negotiations to racial negotiations suggests that as each group of participants in overt racial conflict considers a negotiations strategy, it will be guided by its concern for racial peace, and will also be concerned about the possible consequences for the redistribution of resources and black participation in decision making.

IDENTIFYING THE PROTAGONISTS

The confrontation-negotiations process can be categorized as one among several different kinds of black-white conflict patterns. When a black leadership uses a negotiating strategy it has selected one of several alternative responses to a white racist system. Individual blacks may internalize conflicts, choosing not to resist the system, but attempting to achieve as much personal status and self-fulfillment as possible. Other individuals may identify with fellow blacks and seek to contribute to their mutual advancement toward equality without participating in organized black conflict activity. Efforts to aid black development within the system frequently make it necessary to interpret black needs to institutions and to interpret those institutions to the black community.

There is also a range of *organized* black activities. Some leaders and their constituencies may decide that, under given circumstances, coercive negotiation is a useful process. Other leaders may believe that organized black self-help to fit into the system is the most desirable strategy. Still others may seek to mobilize black coercive power through political processes in an attempt to affect political policies and government administrative decisions. Others may choose to separate from the economic, social, and political system of the country.

This categorizing of possible black perspectives and strategies suggests the first two aspects of our problem: (1) the particular set of circumstances that can produce the confrontation-negotiation process occurs infrequently. These circumstances must be identified, not assumed; and (2) at any point in time under any set of circumstances there can be wide differences in perspectives and in preferred strategies of black leaders and constituencies. Divisions within the black community, even when the concept of community is narrowly identified and defined, are elements of our problem.

THE FRAMEWORK

There has not yet been any systematic study of racial negotiations, although it has been assumed that they follow the union-management model. However, even a first examination leads to the conclusion that the union-management framework must be substantially modified before it can be applied to racial negotiations. First, the protagonists in racial negotiations are strikingly different from those in industrial relations. Second, there are no laws or customs defining or enforcing rights to representation or duties to bargain in overt racial confrontations. Finally, the bargaining objectives of each side in most racial crises are dramatically different from those in the union-management model.

To begin our analysis, we developed a preliminary framework by selecting some variables and added some implied speculative judgments about their interrelationships. The labor-management analogy was used only to pose the dynamics of alternative, conflicting objectives that can appear in racial as well as in labor negotiations. We tried not to give priority to any one of the three values noted earlier, and assumed that all of them should be examined. General theories of social conflict and conflict resolution were taken into account. We then drew from generalized elaborations from a collective bargaining model and added relevant aspects from organization theories and black-white conflicts. We speculated that the following sets of factors are probably important in understanding the possible development of negotiations when there is a black challenge to the operation and output of white-dominated establishments:

1. The ways in which different establishments make decisions, the matters about which they decide, and the organized interest configurations within a specific establishment;

2. The objections that blacks have to establishment processes and outputs—the immediate issues on which the racial conflict focuses;

3. The ways in which black protest about such functioning is organized, including the rhetoric of protest and the rhetoric of justifying the status quo;

4. The environmental constraints operating on each of the participants that help to escalate the conflicts and also to set the limits within which any solution can be discovered;

5. The degree of relative coercive power available over time to each participant;

6. The alternative and conflicting objectives (values) of participants in racial confrontation and their differing judgments about possible results as they consider whether or not to engage in negotiations;

7. The negotiating process used to explore the possibilities of a mutually acceptable accomodation;

8. The communication processes affecting these interactions;

9. The operational choices made between zero-sum and variable-sum by the participants; and

10. The terms of possible settlement; changes in establishment outputs and procedures; changes in policies and policy administration.

As the scholars explored individual cases and as we discussed their insights with them, several more specific racial factors were added to the framework:

11. "White racism" refers to the value structure dominating much of American society and to ways in which an establishment is structured to the advantage of whites. The prejudices of white decision makers influence the welfare of blacks and the wider environment reinforces discriminatory outputs and attitudes;

12. Black identity, as it motivates the common efforts of blacks to change an establishment, affects leadership-constituent relationships and rallies larger black groupings to reinforce the actions and attitudes of the challengers;

13. Segregation as a fact, separatism as an ideology, and control as a program related to the varying values and judgments of blacks and the varying responses of whites; and

14. The interaction of white racism and black identity with institutional functions and relationships so that in any specific racial confrontation there is likely to be a mixture of racial dynamic aspects and specific demands for change addressed to a particular establishment.

The framework was further modified as work progressed. Although the study began by focusing on the negotiating process itself, it soon became apparent that the perspective must be expanded. Some understanding of why overt racial conflict developed was necessary before we could speculate about the potential for negotiations. Thus we were led to explore: (1) the ways in which American institutions function that particularly outrage blacks; (2) the relationship between generalized black anger and black demands for specific institutional changes; (3) the relative capacities and determination of black leaders to press for changes in specific establishments; and (4) the relative capacities and determination of white establishment leaders to respond to or resist such demands.

THE RESEARCH DESIGN

How can one develop answers or even hypotheses for these analytical problems? Although each of the theoretical constructs gave some clues about the possible interrelationships among the variables, we could not be sure how these pieces fitted together in the specialized and interrelated area of our particular problem. We believed that existing theories probably did not provide adequate ways to identify and explain common patterns of racial interactions. If we had been able to accept these assumptions the research tasks would have been greatly simplified; we would have been able to narrow the focus and study the interaction among only a few variables.

Perhaps an example will illustrate the research design problem: One might seek to test the hypothesis that barriers to communication would appear within a racial negotiating process because the challengers were black leaders and the establishment was headed by whites. The exploration and refinement of this specific hypothesis requires a restatement of the role of establishment representatives in decision making in terms of the particular kinds of issues that black leaders were pressing. The communication patterns would also be affected by the nature of the black leader-constituency patterns, the factor of institutional white racism, and the nature and direction of the black revolt.

Thus, our research task was not to refine existing theories of racial negotiations but to enter an unexplored area and to lay the preliminary basis for understanding. We chose to prepare a set of exploratory case studies that followed a general outline developed for the overall project. We were seeking not to describe and analyze any specific racial conflict, but to explore what each incident might suggest about recurring patterns of racial confrontation.

The total project included some 16 different case studies, each compiled by both a black and white scholar who interviewed the principal participants in a recent racial confrontation in which the experimental negotiations procedure was used. Each report sought to describe the relevant events, set them in a larger context, and search for explanations of the major moves made by each of the participants. Since the field of race relations includes the judgments and complexities discussed previously and is interdisciplinary, scholars from various pertinent disciplines were engaged to conduct these studies.

Selection of the cases was guided by such considerations as the desirability of including a variety of social institutions; the usefulness of considering each of these establishments in more than one situation;

the need to include confrontations in the North and the South, and the need for qualified and interested scholars who were familiar with the general environment within which a particular situation occurred.

CATEGORIES OF ANALYSES OF THE CASES

The research design was constructed to permit three interrelated analytical approaches: (1) idiosyncratic characteristics of each specific case; (2) common characteristics forming patterns in some sets of cases that could be contrasted to other sets; and (3) tentative overall generalizations.

The Idiosyncratic Gestalt of Each Case

The particular combination of circumstances in each of the 16 cases in this research project cannot be duplicated and will not recur spontaneously elsewhere. Each has a special meaning for the participants *and* for the observers. None of the full case study reports[8] is reproduced in this volume but a number are summarized in the following chapters. Even these short summaries suggest some of the striking differences in the facts of each case in comparison to the others. Obviously, it is a mistake to assume that one case will develop exactly like another. Indeed, a situation can change so drastically from one year to the next that, even for the same participants, neither the interactions nor the results of a later conflict can duplicate an earlier experience.

Combining Cases to Identify Patterns of Conflict

Identifying some general conflict patterns provides a basis for extending such understanding from an individual case to any other situation that appears to have similar characteristics.

Examination of data from individual case reports suggests at least four alternate ways to classify patterns of conflict: (1) time; (2) geography; (3) type of black organization; and (4) type of institutional setting. While the type of institutional setting was emphasized in selecting these cases, the case data could also have been organized under any of the first three classifications before they were analyzed by category.

---

[8] Three case reports have been published in W. Ellison Chalmers and Gerald W. Cormick, (Eds.) *Racial Conflicts and Negotiations: Perspectives and First Case Studies* (Ann Arbor: Institute of Labor and Industrial Relations, 1971).

1. *Time*: In some ways, the fundamental characteristics of race relationships in America change very slowly but, in other ways, the interactions between black and white participants change rapidly. All of the 16 cases in this project fall within a narrow time period—1968 through 1970. This may account for important similarities among these cases in contrast to characteristics of cases in earlier or later periods.

2. *Geography*: The cases are located in different sections of the country. Labels such as "South," "West," or "North" may well distinguish important sets of political and attitudinal variables.

3. *Type of black organization*: A few of the cases involve an unusual type of separate black organization—a black employee grouping within a larger union organization. By contrast, quite different types of black organizations or leader-constituency relationships appear in most of the other cases. Since the phenomenon studied began with an organization of black protest, important commonalities and/or differences might be discovered by identifying and comparing such black leader-constituency relationships. Key variables may include: characteristics of the relevant black community, such as its size and the degree of its ghetto concentrations; the number and kinds of issues that draw a group together; the degree of unity around such issues; and whether the black group is ad hoc or has a continuous organizational life.

    The characteristics of black organizations are influenced by the kinds of white establishments that are being challenged. The grouping by institutions, developed below, substantially overlaps a possible grouping by black organizations.

4. *Type of institutional settings*: We assume that, to a large degree, the nature of an institution shapes the patterns of racial conflict that arise within it. Indeed, dissatisfaction of blacks with the system frequently is generated and defined by the kinds of available jobs, the quality of their children's education, or the way they are treated by the welfare system. The structure of the institution, the relationships of the protagonists to that institution, and the interaction of the institution with society are some of the factors that determine the nature of the conflict and the way in which that conflict develops and is resolved.

Different types of institutions require different kinds of generalizations about the prospect for negotiations when racial confrontations occur. The importance of the race factor varies in the institutional response to the conflict and in the negotiations process. This variation is not surprising since these institutions have different structures, decision-making processes, outputs, and environments. Accordingly, we assumed that establishments that have common institutional characteristics can be grouped into a single category and distinguished from others placed in a different category. The factors of race and the type of institution combine to create dual interrelating roles within the racial negotiations context.

The term "sector" has been used to distinguish among the institutional patterns that are basic to the ways in which American society is structured. The cases that have been explored in this project fall into six such sectors: (1) public employment; (2) universities; (3) school systems; (4) welfare agencies; (5) the construction industry; and (6) nonprofit organizations.

General Tendencies

The third and most difficult level of analysis attempts to cut across individual cases and evaluate various institutional settings to develop overall generalizations. Since this kind of analysis draws from both the idiosyncratic and the separate sector approaches mentioned earlier, it attempts to synthesize widely different patterns of data.

Even at the end of this study, we cannot expect to develop any more than preliminary hunches. Our hypotheses suggest that the moves from overt conflict to bargaining, to negotiations, and to possible agreement are strongly affected by the institutional setting, the purposes of each side, and each side's predictions of possible results. Perhaps, at this stage, our tentative conclusions should be treated not as a prediction of the extent to which racial negotiations will develop, but as indications of the perceptions of each side as it considers whether and how to enter into negotiations.

Some of our generalizations focus on the power relationships in overt racial conflict and some are concerned with two-party racial negotiations. In addition, we also speculate on the role and possible effectiveness of third-party intervenors as they function in pursuit of their own objectives.

CHAPTER 2

The Participants

This study involves conflict situations in which one side is a specific functioning organization enmeshed in the social system. To understand the conflict patterns, it is necessary to identify the relevant characteristics of such an organization. Therefore, elements of organizational theories have been used to develop a general analytical framework. An "establishment" is viewed as an ongoing organization with a predominantly white leadership and a set of rules and expectations that guide the actions of persons within or related to the organization. The organization has a recognized internal structure and a set of interrelationships, identifiable planned outputs, numerous functional relationships to its environment, and representatives who tend to defend the status quo. On the other side of the conflict in our study are black protesting groups that object to establishment operations and try to get the establishment to change them.

What is already known of the characteristics of black leader-constituency relationships will give some clues to what is happening in the development and consequence of black challenges. What is already known about organizations will aid us in examining the characteristics that condition the ways in which establishments respond to black challenges. These two sets of characteristics, added to the general theoretical constructs of the negotiating process that has been developed, pose the questions that this study is exploring.

BLACK CHALLENGERS

In contrast to the extensive literature on formal institutions in America, there has been little research and development of theories interpreting various black protest organizations. Therefore, the following generalizations about the range and intensity of differing black attitudes as a basis for identifying leadership and organizational patterns are tentative.

Attitudes of Black Americans

All black Americans are exposed to the social phenomena of racism and most share perceptions about their position in this society because of this exposure.[1] Their shared view of the white racist character of American institutions can be summarized as follows: (1) institutions are developed and controlled by whites; (2) institutions function to the advantage of whites and the disadvantage of blacks; (3) the prejudices of the controlling group of whites affect the ways in which they perceive blacks, evaluate social change, guide establishment functions, and relate to the larger society; and (4) the prejudices of other whites in the organization result in discriminatory actions.

In spite of this common exposure to racism, not all blacks respond to it in the same manner. Blacks react with varying degrees of alienation, acceptance, denial, tension, anger, and determination to press for changes in white attitudes and behaviors. Within this wide range, responses that are relevant to the purposes of this study can be identified. Many blacks who seek to speak on behalf of a black constituency may tend toward one of two alternate thrusts: (1) Some black leaders emphasize building personal and group life-styles based on the norms of their socioeconomic white peers, although they recognize their own black characteristics. This position stresses freedom for individuals to achieve status and power through individual merit. (2) Other black leaders stress black individual and group identity and their special meanings in American society, although they recognize that blacks need to adjust to a white-dominated economic, political, and social milieu. This position emphasizes the norm of group advancement.

[1] For instance, Charles V. Hamilton found that many working-class black Americans held numerous values and judgements similar to their white class peers but also tended to share a black perspective derived from a common black experience. Charles V. Hamilton, "The Silent Black Majority," *The New York Times*, May 7, 1970.

Common patterns in black leadership program commitments deriving from these general perspectives can be identified:

1. An orientation toward the norms of white peers
   (a) Change involves group efforts to alter the unequal position of individual blacks by participating in nonracial pressure on economic or political lines while maintaining a commitment to aspirations of individual upward mobility within the existing structure of society, or
   (b) Change involves organizing a black grouping or caucus, frequently within white-dominated organizations, to ensure that avenues for upward mobility within the white-defined system are equally available to blacks

2. An emphasis on the development of black identity
   (a) Change is to be achieved by some form of individual or group withdrawal from white society to develop a separate identity, or
   (b) Change is to be achieved by redefining self-identity and by developing a sense of collective black power with a faith that this collective power can be employed increasingly to eliminate black inequality

Utilizing this scheme of classifying the attitudes of many blacks facilitates analysis of the efforts of some black leaders to promote changes in white institutional racist practices and reveals differences among blacks in their identification with their blackness. Those with a black orientation are prone to attack the psychological problem of black inferiority that white racism has created and maintained. They are unlikely to stress upward mobility, per se, as a primary goal, because this would emphasize individual self-advancement and self-interest. Instead, for those seeking to develop black power, redefinitions of self-worth are merged in a collective identity as the basis for change activities.

The group identity emphasis has become increasingly important in recent black efforts to obtain changes in this society. Since the development of the Black Power concept[2] in the mid-sixties, these black leaders have emphasized that the white system discriminates at all status levels and that there are no rites of passage for blacks into white society on a full and equal basis, regardless of their personal

[2] See Stokely Carmichael and Charles V. Hamilton, *Black Power* (New York: Vintage Books, 1967), pp. 34-56.

achievement or social standing. At the same time, these blacks have developed a positive appreciation for their cultural heritage, thereby completely contradicting the meanings that whites have assigned to this heritage. These leaders have also urged that the status distinctions among blacks be ignored and have insisted that social inequalities are common black problems.

Alternate Black Strategies for Social Changes[3]

While some black leaders identify common enemies in a white racist society, they advocate different strategies to promote change. Presented below are five alternative strategies that some black leaders seek to employ toward the nonrevolutionary attainment of social change. (We are not suggesting that black leaders or groups may be wholly committed to any one to the exclusion of the others.) Indeed, black leaders may retain flexibility among approaches to increase the probability of favorable institutional responses. Of the distinctions that follow, the fifth is the most important to the conceptualization of this study.

1. Use of the courts to secure redefinitions of rights and obligations applicable to individuals, private organizations, and public agencies. Much of such action is based on efforts to extend the operational meanings of the Bill of Rights and other constitutional provisions to different classes or situations. As indicated above, this approach is consistent with enlarging opportunities for individual blacks in a white society.

    Obviously, the successful pursuit of such programs may require dedicated black individuals and black organizations that are convinced that American commitments to justice and equality are effective in achieving changes within American society. These approaches assume white commitment to constitutional rights, acceptance of court procedures, and some feelings of guilt, as well as a degree of black political influence on legal appointment and enforcement processes.

2. Directly related to an assumed general consensus in America on the *mechanisms* of democracy are black efforts to use the political processes to achieve legislative and administrative change.

[3] Although this classification is needed to place the focus of the study in a larger perspective, it makes no attempt to explore in depth the complex organizational problems facing leaders seeking to develop black power.

Such a program can be developed either within the existing political parties or through a nonpartisan election or lobbying campaign. In cities in which the percentage of blacks is growing, this strategy requires a strong, direct appeal to white conscience or an alliance with white groups that share needs with blacks in order to combine resources to influence state and federal political units.

3. The aim of another strategy is to develop an organization with black leadership and considerable white support that is designed to interpret black needs to the white power structure. Such an organization appeals to the white conscience and acts as a mechanism to provide some services that larger social organizations may need.

4. A fourth and quite different strategy attempts to build all-black, independent units to operate *within* the larger society, although they are largely free from controls and assistance from the white community. Some of these approaches relate to the economic activities suggested by the terms "black capitalism" and "black cooperatives." Others are directed toward developing recruiting and training facilities for blacks, who then move into the economic and social structure as individuals.

5. Finally, an alternate strategy for black leaders is to press existing establishments to change the outputs, decision-making processes, and opportunities that provide for black status and roles within their organizations. This strategy, like the others, is nonrevolutionary. It does not seek to abolish or replace but only to reform existing institutions; it does not seek to violate the general social rules by which the institutions are held together, but it does attemp to modify and use those rules to achieve a better set of returns for blacks.

These five alternative strategies for reform within the American system may function in collaboration. Black leaders, black organizations, and black constituencies may participate more or less actively in several. On the other hand, the alternate strategies provide the possibilities for rivalries and disagreement partly because there are limited resources for black protest and the support for one approach may be viewed as depriving the others of the enthusiasm and power they may need.

Since each of these strategies eventually becomes interrelated with the white world and the white power structure, black judgments will differ on whether particular programmatic thrusts involve too ready and too extensive an acceptance of white dominance. Leaders of alternate programs may well become rivals for the support of constituencies and may object to the programs and the leadership claims of others for ideological and organizational purposes.[4]

Leadership—Constituency Relationships

Currently black leaders make much use of the term "black community," although black communities are made up of many different parts. Leaders use this term, however, to extend black consciousness and commitment rather than to state an existing fact of black unity.

There is a common perspective that can be evoked by black leaders. Whatever their divergent views on specific issues or strategies, there tends to be an overriding commitment to the issue of the black position in American society. This issue, while perhaps never phrased as a specific demand, appears to pervade all relationships between the black challenging group and the white organizations. In some of the case material presented later, recognition of this consideration was of prime importance to the black side, and was misunderstood or ignored by the establishment side.

Some black leaders seek to develop this shared commitment by using the generalized conceptualization of the black community and by emphasizing a set of explicit complaints about the ways that specific establishments have treated blacks. Thus, the constituency is built on a combination of two positions: an objection to white racism and a generalized need for black identity and pride, coupled with objections to certain outputs and functioning of specific organized units in the society. The merging of these two thrusts is the focus for the black challenge to one or another specific establishments and can set up the potential for a negotiation process.

The conceptualizations already developed suggest at least three major difficulties faced by a leader attempting to use race plus establishment outputs as the basis for a demand for change. Many blacks are less concerned with the development of black identity than with the

---

[4] However, public repudiation by other black leaders of the representativeness of those who speak on behalf of the black community is less frequent than this categorization might suggest. In a crisis period of institutional change even those preferring alternate strategies are unwilling to aid the white antagonists by formal challenges to black support.

opportunities for self-advancement that they believe are already available within the system. Others, although significantly concerned with black identity, have decided that struggle against the functioning of a white society is quite hopeless. Still others may be ready to press for changes but may prefer an alternative approach to the one that the leader has chosen.

Blacks seeking to function as leaders pressing for change also face other hazards. One comes from the already established leadership of black social and religious organizations. Although some of these leaders may also attempt to use their leadership to challenge white establishments and the practices, many others prefer to remain within the protected status and role positions of their own black organizations.

In addition, challenges to black leadership come from those blacks who occupy positions within existing establishments. The white executives may have assigned roles to these blacks as spokesmen for black interests. Although some of these black administrators may attempt to challenge that establishment, others are likely to insist that they can more adequately and realistically represent black interests than can outsiders. Therefore, the research design also analyzes the degree to which blacks functioning as administrators within white establishments identify with their blackness, the degree to which they seek to identify with a black constituency that is otherwise unrepresented in the usual decision-making processes of the establishment, and the reactions of outside black leaders and the constituents of black protest groups as they relate to these black administrators.

Negotiation patterns can be affected if the leaders of a white establishment assume that the perspectives of black administrators can be depended upon for accurate interpretations of the views and emotions of all blacks who are functionally related to the establishment. White executives may have further difficulties if they assume that these blacks are, in fact, the recognized leaders of black interest groups, or if the white establishment believes that it can assign the role of black leadership to any such black administrator.

Obviously, black constituencies are limited in their ability to control the behavior of these black administrators. However, the black administrator may seek to define and regulate his own behavior in a manner consistent with black values or at least similar to black definitions of basic societal values.

In summary, identifying the possible constituencies of black leaders is partly a function of general black perspectives. It is also a function of black judgments about the practicalities of getting changes in social processes and of the impact of specific establishments on blacks and the ways in which they evaluate their functioning. One might conceive of a process of developing leadership with the following possible black perspectives and attitudes:

1. Many blacks are dissatisfied and angry about outputs of specific establishments and object to the failure to assign roles to black spokesmen;
2. Among these possible adherents, only those who believe that some meaningful changes can be secured from the establishment will become constituents;
3. They must also share their leaders' belief in the need and efficacy of black power—that is, that the mobilized efforts of blacks can sufficiently coerce the specific establishment to make changes;
4. Interim steps should be taken to reduce the intensity of white racism and to lay the basis for further advances in black identity and equality;
5. Leaders may have judgments and attitudes that are reinforced because they share a perspective with many other blacks on the importance of developing black identity; and
6. These leaders may draw support from an even wider structuring of black opinion that reflects a common life experience within a white racist society.

Alternative Emphasis in Programs of Black Involvement

For each organizational effort directed toward positive black identity and toward an independent formulation of black needs there is likely to be a combination of three interrelated goals that guide the formulation of specific sets of demands addressed to particular establishments or groups of establishments. Although each of these goals may appear in each program specifically or by implication, the relative emphases and priorities will differ and probably are situationally determined:

1. *Recognition.* This goal evolves from the black concern for self-definition and psychological reorientation to a black image. The demand is for acceptance by white establishments and blacks themselves of black leaders and/or black groups as the appropriate spokesmen for the interests and needs of blacks in the functioning of the establishment and in the interpretation of the black experience in America.

Such a position does not deny acceptance of the fact that there are or may be white supporters and white interpreters of the black experience with important supplementary roles. Also, it does not require that black spokesmen be unaffiliated with a white-controlled establishment, nor does it assume that every position taken by any black is a meaningful expression of black experience and/or black needs.

Black demands for recognition from a white establishment can only be meaningful to the degree that blacks are able to reconcile conflicting perspectives and programmatic thrusts. Of particular importance to our framework is the possibility that recognition may reconcile conflicting claims to leadership.

2. *Participation.* Closely related to recognition is a need for blacks to be active in the decision-making processes affecting them, based on the conviction of the right of each group within society to be involved in such decisions. That feeling is strengthened, or even stimulated, by the judgment that establishment programs based on white decision-making assumptions and policies have been inadequate in the life experiences of blacks.

Within this general perspective there may be a range of specific positions. Some black leaders may prepare to join with nonblack groups that agree on common objectives and strategies in a coalition that seeks to achieve desired social change. In other circumstances, black leaders may attempt to become the recognized and legitimate black participants in the continuing decision-making processes of an establishment, rather than sharing such a role with representatives of other groups. At still other times, black leaders may seek black community control of those units of a larger establishment that deal with black clients.

This study seeks to analyze the degree to which these variations in the generalized objective of participation are a function of the characteristics of the situation and the particular establishment involved and the degree to which the establishment represents variations in the philosophies or perceptions of black leaders about the organizational strengths confronting them.

3. *Reallocation of resources.* Since one of the major premises in the black perspective is that white society has favored whites and systematically discriminated against blacks, any black protest program is likely to include efforts to shift the establishment's existing priorities to achieve a greater relative resource allocation to blacks. Some black programs will seek only to eliminate and

guard against discriminatory treatment that bars equal access to opportunities for individual and group advancement; other programs will attempt to correct long-standing inequities by insisting on disproportionately large reallocation to blacks of money, power, status, and opportunities to acquire all three.

Organizational Patterns

Programmatic and situational differences exist among various black leaders in their relationships to their constituencies. Because of these differences, black organizations can be classified according to type and function:

1. *Permanent or ad hoc.* Some black activists are convinced that a form of stable organization is needed to develop necessary power and the direction for protest activity. Over time, however, permanent or stable organizations may be viewed as a part of the established order, and therefore as incapable of responding to immediate needs of black people, especially poor blacks. To overcome this limitation, ad hoc groups tend to form around concrete, local issues, and to include those whose reactions to social injustice is quite immediate and specific.

2. *Single purpose/multi-issue organizations.* Leaders and their constituencies may decide that a shared single and specific concern provides the basis for more insistent pressure for change on that particular establishment. Organizations of this sort are usually ad hoc groups focused on specific issues rather than on a broad spectrum of general issues. On the other hand, a multi-issue organization is more likely to be developed by relatively permanent groups with a long-range focus.

3. *Single organization or coalition.* Some black organizations have a unified single leadership and constituency. Not infrequently, however, there may be coalitions of those with different perspectives united against a common enemy. Within that general structure, however, there are two main types of coalitions. The first is a cluster of established groups supporting similar objectives and strategies. Such a coalition tends to exclude groups or organizations that do not share the same philosophical base, and tends to have the usual leadership-spokesmen pattern that fits the white establishment definitions of those patterns.

   The second can be called a crisis coalition, put together on an ad hoc basis, composed of widely disparate groups that come together on a specific issue or set of issues. These coalitions tend to have little or no organizational structure and a series of leaders who assume the spokesman role under various circumstances.

Effectiveness as a Determinant of Black Organizational Characteristics

Judgments about the prospects for success in challenging a highly institutionalized white system affect the types of black organizations that may develop, their programs, and leadership-constituency relationships. Such judgments are based on general orientations and on past experience. They focus on the question: How successful can black organizations be when they seek change in policies or administration in a highly structured white system that by its very nature is resistant to change?

One means of getting the system to change is for a coalition of black leaders and a potentially large constituency to present a united front. However, such a unit under diverse leaders is difficult to achieve or to maintain. An alternate structure for unity may be available in an ad hoc, single-purpose organization. In such organizations the leadership often can organize a large constituency around a single concrete issue. The leadership in this type of organization can more readily enlist support from nonblack groups whose specific concerns may be similar, or at least compatible, to allow some form of a black-white coalition.

Single-purpose organizations, on the other hand, have weaknesses as well as strengths. Leaders hold their positions and receive constituency support primarily because of their stand on particular issues. Any deviation from this stand can easily result in a loss of support. Such a limitation explains part of the dilemma black leaders face when they consider changing their priorities or accepting compromises during the process of negotiations.

Another possible weakness of the single-issue, ad hoc organization is the white institution's ability to reduce black constituency support, for example, by refusing to respond immediately. The lapse of time between the articulation of demands and the response to them can reduce the blacks' constituency. Indeed, it is important for the constituency in ad hoc organizations to achieve at least a degree of success, quickly. Finally, the black ad hoc organization often projects unknown leaders or leaders not recognized by the white power structure into confrontations. Any establishment uncertainty about their leadership position poses additional serious difficulties.

Different problems in effectiveness can be noted in permanent, multi-issue black organizations. Perhaps the single most important problem is the ability to command large constituencies. Programs tend to be long-range rather than immediate and concrete because, in part, these organizations are concerned with many broad issues. The leadership in organizations of this type may elicit latent or passive constituency support because of the general nature of the organizational goals but, at the same time, it is difficult for this leadership to command a large following for specific programs because it has no immediate, concrete goals.

The very fact that an organization seeks to become permanent also contributes to leadership problems. Such black organizations also tend to be identified with the established order; their leadership tends to be recognized by the white power structure, and its efforts tend to be normatively defined, that is, the black organization's change efforts are increasingly likely to conform to some major white expectations.

Because stable black organizations maintain leadership positions that often carry status rewards, merely occupying the leadership position can become an end in itself. Leaders in such positions often experience difficulty in rallying mass support because of suspicions about their intentions. Permanency may also imply considerable rigidity and hence a limitation of the leadership to respond to varying levels of needs, particularly within different class groups.

In spite of these limitations, permanent black organizations have some advantages over ad hoc organizations in pressing for changes in establishments. Because their change efforts tend to follow normatively defined patterns, these efforts are likely to face less determined white opposition. They also tend to prefer more peaceful and more acceptable methods of change whenever they determine that their disruptive capacity may be minimal compared to the capacity of the white system to suppress disruptions, or whenever they can identify only a minimal commitment of many blacks. These black organizations may base their programs on the hope that white America can be brought to adjust its practices through reasonable and legalistic appeals to the ideals and rules for social change that presumably are built into the American social, political, and economic processes. This milder approach also may be based on a fear of the consequences of polarization. Some blacks are convinced that the general white response to black disruption will strengthen racist activities and reduce liberal or moderate efforts and that the relative power position of blacks may worsen rather than improve as a result of disruption.

These decisions do not mean that permanent as well as ad hoc groups will not seek changes. However, ad hoc groups may be more inclined to seek disruptive means to change because of the nature of mass constituency support, their leadership, and the fact that black-defined change efforts for particular issues might appear to require strategies that necessarily involve disruption.

Each of our case studies, although focused on a single confrontation and any negotiating patterns that may emerge, is also concerned with the results that may follow from a negotiated agreement for each side. One of the terms of such an agreement may be the establishment of some continuing machinery for its implementation. A permanent black organization is more likely than an ad hoc group to be capable of making such machinery work, even after the crisis situation has passed. Such a follow-through, however, will only be apparent if at least part of the group's leadership and constituency continues an active interest in the issues that caused the confrontation.

ESTABLISHMENTS

Each black challenge that we studied was concerned with a particular establishment and directed toward building black interests into the policies and practices affecting its outputs and/or the status of blacks within its operation. This suggests that the study needed to explore the structure and decision-making processes of such establishments, their outputs and relations to clients, the racial characteristics of their spokesmen, and their interaction with their environment. To understand how and why a particular establishment responds to a specific black challenge, it is necessary to identify the dynamic interrelationships between these aspects.

Establishment Outputs

In most of the cases on which this study is based, the establishment produces services intended for the public good. These are evaluated by the clients toward whom the services are directed and by the public whose generalized purposes are to be served. The establishments in our cases are presumably designed to effectively perform the services that their publics wish the clients to receive. On the other hand, the challenges of the black leaders to these establishments are likely to be based on the inadequacy of performance as measured by the criteria of their black constituency. The two sets of characteristics of black challenges and of establishment processes are the basis for the sector groupings on which the later analyses will build.

Because the framework locates some of the important but generalized controls and supports for an establishment in its publics and because these appear to function through political processes, it is important to note that the definition of outputs and the assessments of establishment performance have complex symbolic meanings for white administrators and for their publics. Black challengers may operate from the same symbols of establishment functions and performance, although they may attach quite different meanings to them.

The manipulation of these symbols, which are related to but not an exact reflection of reality, is an essential part of the dynamics of each establishment. The manipulated symbols may define the public interests affecting the performance of the establishment. Alternatively, they may be redefined by blacks as the basis for their challenge. The differences among establishments within a sector lie to a significant degree in the means and effectiveness of different interests in manipulating such symbols. These differences are of crucial importance because of the separation of actual from nominal control over establishments and because each establishment achieves acceptance and support through its own processes of communicating its evaluations to both insiders and outsiders.

These abstractions of publics, of generalized controls over the establishments, of symbols of outputs, and of the perspectives of black challengers may be clearer if the data that come from some of our studies are used to illustrate them. For example, a major symbolic function of public schools is the education of children, with criteria and controls nominally emanating from the public but largely developed by administrators and teachers. Alternative criteria and evaluation of these abstract symbols are expressed by black pupils, their parents, and the local black community. Another example is the major symbolic function formulated within the political process that the public welfare system is to provide some assistance to those who are "in need," who have not been able to "take care of themselves." But the criteria used by black welfare mothers in defining "need" and "taking care of themselves" are drastically different from those of many administrators and political leaders.

In the grouping of the cases in this study there will be three variations in the analysis of the dynamics of establishments that have been sketched so far. The first variation appears when the general model is altered in the study of the construction contractors and unions where the black challenge is not to service or product output but to the restricted opportunities for jobs within the system (Chapter 7). In such a situation, performance criteria may be formulated by a combination of public bodies but may affect the regular structure of the establishment indirectly. A second variation appears in the conflicts about city employment (Chapter 3). Here, as in construction, the black challenge relates to job status and conditions but, like the basic model, the service functions and symbols are present and public controls are involved. The third variation, which covers the nonprofit organization, concerns a service function that shapes the patterns of the establishment and in which the black challenge is based on black criteria, but the establishment's services are directed, not toward those outside the establishment, but toward the members within the organization itself (Chapter 8).

Authority Structure and Decision-Making Processes

Concepts of output and of publics that use criteria to evaluate outputs serve to identify those elements of the decision-making structures that are needed in this analysis. The public, although outside the establishment, has an important influence. The clients, the recipients of the services, are not only outside the establishment but also are without any role or authority to affect it.

Obviously, establishment processes are complex. There is likely to be a relatively small grouping of individuals which is the power elite who have roles crucial to the functioning of the establishment. They are assigned or achieve considerable authority in formulating the criteria for the performance of the establishment and in applying whatever rewards and punishments appear to be necessary. These insiders are likely to wield more power in both criteria formulation and performance evaluation than are the outside publics for whom the establishment is presumed to function. Just as a corporation is run more by its executive management than by its stockholders or its customers, a public university is run more by its administration and its faculty than by its regents, any governmental unit, or its students. The first step in locating the insiders with whom black leaders can negotiate is to find those with the authority to commit the establishment to changes in policies and practices.

Obviously, the degree of authority exercised by a central executive of an establishment varies from sector to sector. For instance, depending on the kind of outputs, there may be widely different professional roles. There may be variations in the degree of centralization or decentralization of authority in one sector or another. There may be differences in the degree to which interest groupings within an establishment are organized and able to press their particular positions in contrast to other interests either in or out of the organization.

These characteristics tend to be shared by establishments within a single sector as compared to those in other sectors. On the other hand, there are substantial contrasts among establishments within a single sector that involve differences in style and effectiveness of those in central administrations, in the decentralized parts, and in their organized functioning groups. These contrasts also appear in the responses to black challenges.

Relevant to our study, there are four essential modifications of this simplified summary of authority roles within an establishment. Within an organization, superior-subordinate relationships are reciprocal, that is, a central administration secures its most dependable and committed responses from subordinates when the subordinates accept the objectives and general strategies of established policies. In the second place, the distinction between policy formation and administration of established policies is an arbitrarily expressed dichotomy about functions that, in fact, develop both up and down the formal organizational structure in the interplay of policy formation and its application. In the third place, decision making within organizations frequently involves internal bargaining interaction between units that have their own specialized interests and achieve not unity but accommodation with other interests and responsibilities within the organization. Finally, the organization is better conceived of as a set of interrelated parts each with some constituency lines to the environment than as a monolithic structure whose interactions with the environment all flow through and are controlled by a central administration.

A conclusion based on these general concepts is that the establishment being challenged or investigated is neither monolithic nor wholly autocratic in structure. This conclusion suggests some of the problem areas that should be investigated in considering possible negotiating responses to black challenges. The first is that the challengers may find supporters as well as opponents of their demands within the establishment. Whether or not such alliances (formal or implicit) will make much difference in the negotiating patterns depends, in part, on how close the possible allies are to the centers of power for relevant establishment decisions and, in part, on how effectively the allies understand and accommodate to the black challenge.

The second problem area involves identifying (by participants as well as by scholars) the location of the seat of power. The locations within the organization where binding decisions can be made will differ depending on the issue. Some challenges, for instance, fall within the discretion of subadministrators; others may require fundamental changes by chief policy makers. Some kinds of issues may involve those performing one set of establishment functions; other kinds may involve quite different functions and, hence, other elements of the organization.

A third problem area concerns the role characteristics of anyone appearing to speak on behalf of the establishment, whether his function is to interpret its present policies and practices or to negotiate a modification or a fundamental change. Since the typical establishment is neither monolithic nor completely autocratic, it follows that no one spokesman can speak on behalf of the whole establishment except within assigned limits. If the black challenge lies wholly within the realm of that delegated responsibility, the authority of the spokesman may be quite clear. On the other hand, more frequently than not, black challengers will demand changes in policies or practices that have been determined by various groupings within the establishment. In such a situation, the spokesman can only represent the establishment to the degree that he is able to get others to modify the guidelines within which he has been operating. The interconnections between spokesman and others involved in decisions affected by the black challenges determine the degree to which the establishment agent can be thought of as a responsible participant in negotiations.

A further implication flows from the concept of an establishment agent who is considered to be authorized to negotiate with black challengers, albeit only within some limits. Typically, in the total functioning of an establishment, there are numerous delegations that assign one or another functionary to negotiate with outside groups (but always within limits) and that permit binding commitments if the negotiators are able to come to agreement within those limits. This authority also may know that an adjustment is possible even beyond those boundaries, but only if the agent can secure appropriate approval for further changes in establishment positions. In many different areas of the contact between the establishment and its environment, the establishment is represented thus during negotiating. In each such case, however, the general policy posture already has been developed and the establishment may have authorized a negotiating form of interaction with the union of its employees, suppliers, sales outlets, political spokesmen, government, administrative agencies, and even the courts. Until such a negotiating authority has been arranged, the establishment spokesman is not a negotiator, only a communicator.

Environmental Connections

The model used here conceives of an establishment structure that includes major decision-making units and processes. No direct use is made of the concept of a white power structure that is guiding policies over wide sections of the social system and making purposeful decisions based on white racist values. On the other hand, there are patterns of influence from outside the establishment unit that operate to support, guide, or constrain the policies and decisions made within the establishment.

The styles and perspectives of the chief policy makers and administrators in the establishment in all of the sectors under study are supported and reinforced by values and judgments drawn from a white middle-class culture. In most of the cases, some allocation of resources to establishments is made from outside and there is likely to be significant control over the ways the resources are to be applied. These environmental pressures operate to set limits within which internal choices can be made. In addition, those manipulating the allocation of these resources may seek to guide the internal processes of such establishments and their outputs.

In four of the six sectors that are included in this study (schools, universities, welfare systems, and government employment) the most prominent patterns of environmental influences come from some kind of governmental machinery or political process. In the construction industry case discussed in Chapter 7, there was also a strong governmental influence, although it operated less directly than in any of the other four areas.

White Racism

Our model of racial conflict incorporates two interrelated perspectives of the black challengers: objections to the outputs and procedures of establishments plus racial perspectives and drives. Similarly, the characteristics of the establishment should be examined for the nonracial patterns of controls and outputs which this section has discussed and also for the interrelated racial characteristics referred to as "white racism."

The familiar concept of the negative stereotyping of blacks by whites is useful in understanding this process. A stereotype functions to generalize data and attitudes about all members of a class of people. This stereotype is then used to guide perceptions of and interactions with each person who is identified as a member of such a group. Within the focus of this study, a stereotype can condition individual interactions; it can also be used to design establishment programs and to evaluate establishment outputs.

The stereotype of blacks held by many whites assumes that, whether due to genetic or environmental causes, by the time blacks become clients or participants in the establishment they tend to be, to some degree, inferior to whites in several ways: they probably do not meet the capacity and achievement norms of their white peers; they may not fully accept and conform to the social mores of the dominant group, and they probably are not as fully committed to the social values of the white society.

For a long time, this stereotype was openly expressed by large sections of white America. Now many whites no longer accept such overt expression. Tacit acceptance, however, is reflected in the perspectives and judgments of a great many whites. Indeed, it is striking that most white Americans do not recognize the degree to which they and their institutions hold these stereotypes and make these judgments.

Black judgments that white institutions and their leaders neither understand nor respect them fuel much of the conflict reported in this study. In contrast, white executives are likely to take the view that such stereotyping occurs not in themselves, but in other, perhaps subordinate, administrators. They see it as an individual aberration that may affect some interpersonal relations, but as not really important or influential in the behavior of their institution. Thus their remedies may be directed toward "educating" these less enlightened subordinates, instead of examining the functioning of the institution itself.

Racial prejudice may become an issue in black-white conflicts when the policies and practices of establishments cause resource allocation favorable to whites as compared to blacks, and the establishments judge that this is normal and appropriate. This issue is illustrated by the long-established contrasts in the allocation of physical resources and personnel in inner-city school systems. In higher education the issue is illustrated by public support for the disproportionate government allocations to predominantly white colleges.

The second consequence of the prevalence of negative stereotyping appears in the interpersonal contacts between whites and blacks—those contacts within the establishment and those between institutional representatives and clients. For instance, the use of the stereotype tends to produce discriminatory treatment in job status (hiring, upgrading pay scales, and responsibilities); and to lower the establishment's standards for services to black as compared to white clients.

Earlier in this chapter it was noted that there is a distinction between the needs of the clients and of the public, which may fund and more or less control the establishment. This distinction results in two additional racial issues. In general, institutions are set up and supported to meet the norms, values, and needs of the majority group within the population. Thus, the development and monitoring of establishment services is likely to be geared to white middle-class norms and experiences.

Establishment practices, therefore, are almost certain not to provide equal service to those whose backgrounds and social characteristics differ from these norms. From the point of view of the needs of many blacks, establishment policies and practices may ignore the consequences of poverty and a long history of economic, social, and political discrimination. Even when the symbolic objective may be to provide equal services, the failure to build programs related to variations in need results in unequal services.

The fact that establishments may fail to distinguish among the needs and characteristics of their clients also poses a second and even more profound challenge to the concept of equal treatment. Public policies, as reflected in public institutions, have sought to change and diversify the institution to meet the norms, values, and needs of any minority population. This approach has been developed and sustained by the historical ideology of the melting pot wherein all cultures are mixed into one homogeneous whole. Although such a process is presumed to retain some of the features of each contributor to the whole, in fact, the tendency has been to lose all but the most superficial aspects of the minority cultures. The process has been one of absorption rather than of inclusion. Where the process has been applied to those of white European origin, it has had some viability. However, where social interactions have been compounded by stereotypes about color, often neither inclusion nor absorption have occurred.

In establishing a criterion for the performance of an institution, the alternative approach is suggested by the term "cultural pluralism." More specifically, it identifies the needs of many black clients for black pride and black identity. Equal treatment within this perspective would involve identifying the needs of blacks and other minority groups and designing programs to serve those needs.

In summary, four aspects that contribute to racial conflict in establishment processes and outputs are important in an analysis of individual cases and sectors and for making speculative generalizations about using negotiations in racial disputes. The historical and current patterns of each of these aspects will be considered in order to understand their contribution to racial conflict and to appraise the degree to which confrontation and negotiations offer any likelihood of significant change: These include:

1. Disproportionate resource allocation that tends to favor whites over blacks;

2. Prejudice against blacks that affects establishment decisions about individual black participants or clients;

3. Establishment policies and practices that assume that all clients have the same needs as the majority group in the population; and

4. Establishment policies and practices that are designed to shape all participants and clients into a common mold.

CHAPTER 3

Public Employment

Job discrimination is a major cause of black frustration and anger. Conversely, blacks may find that the employment sector is the area that is the most open to change, particularly in public employment. The dominant white perspective is that employment institutions function on a nonracial basis and discriminatory acts of administrators are violations of this accepted standard. White policy makers and white government administrators tend to resist charges of discrimination as well as organized black efforts to press for the representation of separate black interests in institutional policy. Although these patterns appear in private and public employment, this chapter focuses on racial conflict in public employment, which government leaders and administrators view as undesirable and blacks regard as a potentially useful response to inequality.

If a black worker objects to treatment by a public employer but does not view it as racial discrimination, he may seek to change administrative actions as an individual. If he feels a need to force such changes, he may join with other workers in a union. If, however, he believes that his blackness contributes to the unfairness of his treatment, he may seek an organized union effort to force changes that will improve his job status as a black. As a part of this study, we explored three cases in which black workers saw their conflict in racial terms although they operated through unions that tended to minimize these racial aspects, particularly at international levels. From the case summaries, we analyzed the uses of union-management processes as a way to structure racial conflict. As black workers unite to challenge discriminatory practices and policies, the process resembles the usual collective bargaining patterns because of the employer-employee characteristics. The demands appear to be similar; the traditional coercive tactics of unions, such as striking and picketing, may be applied; and the negotiating process may be used. White administrators and white political executives become parties to this racial conflict as they resist black demands and attempt to maintain employment practices that are, in fact, racially discriminatory. When these conflicts arise in government employment, they are treated as job-related problems rather than racial issues and usual union-management patterns are followed. White power centers, both citywide and nationwide, may also become involved in supporting the status quo of the government unit. The administrative and political responses of the government, a public employer, are significantly different from those of the private employer. In the analyses that follow, the political processes affecting employment decisions are emphasized.

The three cases were: (1) a wildcat strike by a public employees' local in Cleveland, Ohio, following the disciplinary suspension and transfer of a black local union leader in 1969; (2) a strike for recognition and efforts toward a first agreement by garbage workers in Memphis, Tennessee, in 1968; and (3) the strikes by hospital workers for union recognition and a contract in two Charleston, South Carolina, hospitals in 1969. The Memphis and Cleveland case studies have been published previously in a earlier volume covering the first phase of our project.[1] Data on a variety of other public employment disputes in which race was an essential factor were also examined in this study to provide additional insights.

While all three cases are taken from the public employment sector, they represent different focuses. In Cleveland, the union was well-organized and a formal contract had been executed. The Cleveland dispute arose from a grievance and a wildcat strike that had considerable racial overtones. In Memphis and Charleston, however, the organization of these workers into unions was relatively new and the city, county, and state governments felt bound *not* to recognize or negotiate with unions of public employees. In this sense, of course, the recognition issue was one of unionism rather than of race. However, in both Memphis and Charleston, the striking workers were black, the members of their local unions were black, and a key factor was the

---

[1] F. Ray Marshall and Arvil Van Adams, "The Memphis Public Employees Strike," and James E. Blackwell and Marie R. Haug, "The Strike by Cleveland Water Works Employees," Parts 3 and 4 of *Racial Conflict and Negotiations: Perspectives and First Case Studies*, W. Ellison Chalmers and Gerald W. Cormick, eds. (Ann Arbor: Institute of Labor and Industrial Relations, 1971).

forging of a civil rights-labor coalition to attack what were seen as Southern, anti-union, anti-black establishments.

Thus, the racial factors were institutional and less overt in Cleveland than in the southern cases where they were more overt and even personal. Therefore, these cases may be more idiosyncratic than others. On the other hand, it is equally possible that moves to unionize lower-paid government employees in many cities makes these cases more representative of situations where more and more jobs are being filled by black workers.

THE MEMPHIS PUBLIC EMPLOYEES STRIKE

The Memphis strike of public employees began and ended as a labor dispute between local 1733 of the American Federation of State, County, and Municipal Employees (AFSCME) and the city of Memphis.[2] The membership of Local 1733 was predominantly black and numbered over 1,300. Most of the members were sanitation workers. Underlying the economic issues in the dispute was the issue of race. Although Memphis, unlike other southern cities of its size in the 60s, maintained relative racial tranquility, the surface changes in its public institutions obscured the perpetuation of economic and educational inequities. The support given to Local 1733 by the black community during the dispute was a sign of long-standing racial dissatisfaction far more significant than the basic trade union issues of the strike itself.

The strike and its issues, therefore, served as a rallying point for the black community, which could readily identify with the sanitation workers. The city's refusal to recognize the union was similar to the white power structure's unwillingness to recognize blacks as equals and as individuals who could decide their own destinies.

The problems facing the black community and the union did not appear overnight. From the receipt of its charter to the beginning of the strike, a period of three and one-half years, the union had sought unsuccessfully to gain recognition from the city as sole bargaining agent. Although Local 1733 of AFSCME was chartered by the international union on October 13, 1964, it operated informally because the city refused to recognize any union as sole bargaining agent for a group of employees.

---

[2] This summary was taken from a full report on this case, "The Memphis Public Employees Strike," F. Ray Marshall and Arvil Van Adams pp. 71-109 in Chalmers and Cormick, op. cit.

The Strike and Negotiations

The strike started on February 12, 1968, and, before it was settled about two months later, resulted in riots and disorder, a boycott of downtown white businesses, and the tragic assasination of Dr. Martin Luther King, Jr. Although working conditions were the immediate cause of the dispute, they cannot be separated from the larger racial issues that were raised by this strike and the events leading up to it. Indeed, the walkout itself was not carefully planned, but was almost a spontaneous reaction by black workers to what they considered to be unfair treatment by the Department of Public Works (DPW).

The incident that sparked the strike occurred on January 31, 1968, when 22 black employees of the Sewer and Drain Maintenance Division of the DPW were sent home because of rain while white employees in identical work classifications were allowed to work and received a full day's pay. The black workers complained to the DPW on payday when they discovered the discriminatory wage payment. The city responded to the black workers' complaints by unilaterally paying them two hours' call-up pay, but this was not satisfactory to the workers. Local 1733, which sought to represent all DPW workers, met and after considerable discussion, the union's president led his men out on strike on February 12. The local's all-black membership had many grievances but was particularly concerned about racial discrimination, and there was little opposition to the decision to strike.

There was no precedent in Memphis for dealing with a striking public employees' union. The mayor, the city council, and the mayor-council form of government were new. Thus, what was to develop as a negotiation procedure long known to students of collective bargaining came about through a series of haphazard events.

Initially, Mayor Henry Loeb considered the strike to be illegal. He refused to recognize the AFSCME as sole bargaining agent for the public works' employees and remained adamant throughout the strike on this and the dues checkoff issue.

Recognition, the main issue between the city and the union since Local 1733's inception in 1964, was the single most important grievance of the strike. The remaining issues (dues checkoff, a grievance procedure, merit promotion, and wages) could be resolved only after recognition of the employees' right to choose their own bargaining representative. The recognition issue was important not only because the local could not compromise on it, but also because the city took the position that it would be illegal for it to recognize any union as sole bargaining agent. The city continued to base its resistance to the union on the "right-to-work" decision regarding public employee unions handed down by the Tennessee Supreme Court. The dominance of the recognition issue highlighted the initial confrontation and the resulting negotiations. There was tremendous resistance by the white-dominated power structure to including the union in the decision-making process, especially when that union's membership and leadership were predominately black. The mayor's strong anti-union position was supported by many elements in the white community, at least at the outset of the strike, although there apparently were some shifts in white attitudes as the strike continued.

The attitude of many blacks toward the recognition issue was symbolized by a picket sign that appeared in the daily marches on City Hall, which read "I Am A Man." Its implication, which was discussed at length in the black community, was that Memphis blacks were no longer willing to let white men control their destiny. The issue was black identity. The blacks' recognition of themselves as men with certain rights was the first step in the process of change that was to follow. The second step was the exercise of these rights by gaining a role for the union in decision making.

AFSCME sought recognition of the employee's right to determine who would represent him in any bilateral policy-making process. Thus, the issue of black identity caused the recognition question to become a racial issue. Collective bargaining meant replacing the unilateralism of Old South politics with the bilateralism of the New South. The union, however, was only the vehicle of change. The real force toward change came from the black community itself. In his efforts to defeat the union, it is questionable whether the mayor understood the significance of this force.

The mayor's adamant refusal to recognize the union and the use of mace by the police to break up a demonstration united the black community in support of the strikers. Extensive organization of the black community occurred and the dispute was more clearly defined along racial lines. Coercive pressures used by the union included an economic boycott, mass demonstrations, and protest marches. Pressures used by the city included an injunction against marches, police power, and the hiring of scabs to perform the functions of the striking workers. The fight for recognition was supported by national labor union leaders and local unions across the country, which sent money for the strikers as well as people to walk on the picket lines. A march of nearly 500 white union members on March 4 was organized by the Memphis AFL-CIO Labor Council. The presence of white support lifted the morale of the strikers and reinforced the position of those seeking to restructure existing white institutions. It de-emphasized racial aspects of the strike and underscored for the mayor the fact that he was dealing with trade union issues affecting both black and whites. The case has been labeled as being the first in which there was a coalition of blacks, the poor, and organized labor.

The Use of a Mediator and Third-Party Intervention

By resolution of the city council, Frank Miles, a local business leader and a former member of the Federal Mediation and Conciliation Service, was asked to serve as mediator between the union and the mayor in the dispute. This was the first direct effort by the council to resolve the conflict, and it came after Mayor Loeb's opposition to third-party intervention was overcome. Mediation took the dispute from the public media and returned it to the bargaining table. It replaced the growing emphasis on racial issues with renewed emphasis on the economic issues. In view of the absence of a precedent for recognition of public employee unions and the newness of the city administration, the use of mediation took on special significance. It provided an arena for orderly discussion where the union could negotiate as an equal with city government. This level of participation was significant when considering black identity as an issue.

One scheduled protest march brought Dr. Martin Luther King, Jr. to Memphis, where he was assassinated on April 4. This focused national attention to the city. Following the assassination, President Lyndon Johnson sent Undersecretary of Labor James Reynolds to Memphis. Reynolds told Mayor Loeb that he wasn't "here to impose a solution or to circumvent his position, but . . . was here to try to bring the parties to some form of agreement they could live with." Mayor Loeb agreed to Reynold's entry into the case after the undersecretary explained that "this thing *had* to be settled." After the mayor agreed to his mediation efforts, Reynolds and Frank Miles called a meeting of city and union representatives for April 6. The two sides met with the mediators until early the next morning, and adjourned until later in the day. The second meeting continued into early Monday morning, at which time the mayor and Jerry Wurf, president of AFSCME, were called in. "Enough progress had been made in the language of the agreement, including the issues of recognition and dues checkoff," said Miles, "so that the issues were narrowed down to one: wages."

The sessions were adjourned April 8, for the King Memorial March and April 9 for Dr. King's funeral. The parties met again on April 10 and each day thereafter until agreement on the wage issue was reached on April 16. According to the settlement, the union members received a wage increase of ten cents an hour, effective May 1, and another increase of five cents an hour to become effective September

1. The key to the solution was to find a means for the city to pay for a wage increase until June 30, the end of the fiscal year. (The city had already indicated that a wage increase could be written into the budget for the new fiscal year beginning July 1.) The compromise finally reached on this issue was the result of behind-the-scenes work by Frank Miles and other interested third parties. "An anonymous benefactor and longtime friend of this city provided our solution," said Miles. This individual contacted Miles, offering to supply $60,000 of his own money to finance the wage increase for the remaining months of May and June in the current fiscal year. The city agreed to accept the offer.

A merit promotion plan, a no-strike clause, a no-discrimination clause, and a grievance procedure were added to the agreement, which also included a dues checkoff through an employees' credit union. The grievance procedure provided for nonbinding arbitration by a panel of three persons. The city and the union would select one member of the panel, and the third member, who would be chairman, would be jointly selected by the appointees of the union and the city. The final power to resolve a grievance remained with the mayor. "It would be unlikely," said Miles, "that the mayor could justify rejecting any decision reached by an impartial arbitrator."

The final memorandum of understanding was presented by the city council and passed by a 12-1 margin on April 16, 1968, after the strike of 64 days. It provided a working agreement between the union and the city through June 30, 1969. The union voted unanimously to accept the agreement. Factors that led to the settlement were unifed black support to the strike, articulate black union and community leaders, coercive pressures from the black community, support from organized labor and national civil rights leaders, communication through neutral third parties, the presence of skilled labor mediators who could communicate with both sides and remove obstacles to agreement, growing pressure on the city for settlement by a white community concerned with adverse economic effects, and pressure from the White House following Dr. King's assassination. The organization of the black community, led by the black clergy, continued. In June 1969, an agreement was renewed through negotiations accompanied by extensive maneuvering but requiring no overt action by the black union or black community.

This case is of particular interest for many reasons. First, it occurred in the employment area and thus is directly analogous to the labor-management model of dispute settlement. Second, the black workers were organized into a union and had a stable organizational base from which to challenge the establishment. Third, the escalation of the dispute from one that could be interpreted in relatively narrow labor-management terms to one that involved the entire community is of importance in understanding the dynamics of the racial overtones present in different types of disputes. Fourth, the strength of the race issue underlying the dispute is demonstrated by the fact that the black community interpreted the issues so that the garbage workers became symbols of a general desire for black identity and recognition. Fifth, the coalition of black demands and organized labor set a pattern that was repeated in other locations such as Charleston, South Carolina and Baltimore, Maryland. Sixth, the apparent need for the black community to undertake a variety of coercive activities before the white establishment was able or willing to bargain is of key importance, particularly in light of the fact that settlement was reached the following year without such coercive activities. Seventh, the local was affiliated with AFSCME, a national union of public employees. Since there is reason to believe that public employee unions will include increasingly large segments of blacks and that disputes between them and governmental bodies will continue to include racial factors—if not coalitions—this case offers opportunities for generalizations. Finally, the strike was resolved through the use of a third-party intervenor after earlier mediational efforts had failed, permitting an examination of the role of the third party and the process of intervention.

CLEVELAND WATERWORKS EMPLOYEES' STRIKE

The second of the case studies presented here also concerns a dispute between public employees and city officials.[3] Like the Memphis case, the workers were organized (indeed, the same international union was involved), the membership was predominantly black, and the racial factors appeared to be of considerable importance. Thus, this case has a degree of comparability to the Memphis situation. In contrast, however, are its northern location, the incumbency of a black mayor seeking reelection, and the fact that the strike was concerned with a grievance rather than with a wage demand. Also, the case study in Cleveland was handled by a black-white team of sociologists, in contrast to Memphis, where information was compiled by a pair of white economists.

[3] This summary was taken from a full report on this case, "The Strike by Cleveland Water Works Employees," James E. Blackwell and Marie R. Haug, pp. 109-50, in Chalmers and Cormick, op. cit.

More importantly, this case was selected because it afforded an opportunity to study the mediation process in racial dispute. The mediation process, which was so crucial to the final settlement, was carried out by Willoughby Abner, director of the National Center for Dispute Settlement of the American Arbitration Association. Thus, we were provided with an unusual opportunity to examine a dispute in which the protesters were black, the establishment included blacks and whites, and the successful mediation was effected by a black. The racial context of the intra-union and inter-union relationships is also interesting.

Union Organization and the City of Cleveland

Employees of the city of Cleveland were represented at the time of this study by 14 unions, three of which were of major importance because of their size. Local 244 of the teamsters covered municipal and county drivers, chiefly of garbage trucks. Local 1099 of the laborers union, AFL-CIO, included municipal and county laborers, some of whom worked with the garbage drivers. Local 100 of AFSCME, AFL-CIO, had a wider jurisdiction, covering not only waterworks personnel, both blue collar and white collar, but also employees in a number of other city departments. The major blue collar segment of the union was the waterworks; these workers comprised about half the membership. In each of these unions, the membership was largely or substantially black, while the paid leadership was white. This was, in part, a reflection of the changing racial composition of the city workers.

Until the administration of Mayor Carl B. Stokes, none of these 14 unions had written labor contracts with the city. There was a hodgepodge of gentlemen's agreements, under-the-table deals, and past practices. Business agents would meet over dinner and drinks with the commissioners to settle grievances or to do each other favors. Problems were dealt with on a political basis, and Local 100 functioned in some ways like a political club rather than as a labor union.

Particularly during the last few years, however, this situation had been changing. Frequent stoppages were staged by the militant blacks in the water department and a number of written memoranda of settlement were negotiated. Because some local members were growing weary of the continual loss of earnings involved in these confrontation techniques and also because there was a general national movement toward written labor contracts with government bodies, Local 100 made a formal demand for a negotiated contract in 1967. There is some indication that the new city administration wished to move in the same direction because of the stabilization of relationships that it would ensure. Shortly thereafter, the mayor announced in a press conference that contract talks with all 14 city unions would begin.

In the early summer of 1968, 25-month agreements were drawn up for 13 unions in the joint council of public employee unions and signed for the city by Mayor Stokes. Each contract provided a wage increase, grievance procedure, no-strike clause, revisions in the progression schedule, and other benefits. However, on the whole, these contracts were management-oriented, with a strong management-rights clause. Furthermore, the legal status of the contracts was somewhat cloudy. Some persons in the city law department theorized that the entire contract would never stand up in court because its provisions were contrary to civil service rules and because there was no charter authorization for the mayor to act on behalf of the city in labor negotiations.

Local 100 refused to accept the same contract terms as the other unions, and held out for more. The negotiating committee at the time included Clarence King, steward in the waterworks and a union militant who consistently refused to compromise on contract issues. The first tentative settlement was rejected by a vote of the local, and even after the city made a few more concessions, it was rejected again with King leading the opposition. Neither side wanted a strike at this juncture, and it was agreed to submit the unresolved issues to arbitration, a procedure that King was instrumental in persuading the membership to accept on the basis that any settlement would be retroactive. The arbitration produced additional individual adjustments, specifically for white collar workers in the water department.

The Local 100 signing did not bring labor peace. Grievances began to mount, some involving continuation of past practices and others concerning disciplinary actions. The union was demanding full compliance with the terms of the agreement. Lower level city management, on the other hand, which had no part in the negotiations and did not understand or perhaps had never even bothered to read the contract, insisted on continuing in the old way. Furthermore, the old ways of winning concessions at the waterworks also continued. There was a series of confrontations and disputes and grievances and arbitrations, with the city frequently taking an inflexible stand, twice getting an injunction against the union. The union called wildcat strikes and threatened to strike. King, who had been suspended during the negotiations for heading a stoppage but then reinstated, was active in attempts to enforce the agreement. The parties were on a collision course, as hostility built toward a power struggle.

The Strike and Negotiations

The conflict culminated in a dispute between the waterworks employees of Local 100 and the waterworks department. The original incident precipitating the dispute occurred on August 14, 1969, with a wildcat strike following almost immediately thereafter. Agreement was reached on August 29, 1969. The strike started because of a relatively minor jurisdictional dispute regarding the reassignment of a job on a truck from Local 100 to Teamster Local 244. The contract was a relatively new one, having been drawn up in the early summer of 1968 to cover a 24-month period. Under the contract a procedure was specified whereby advance information regarding reassignments was to be supplied to the unions in question. King, shop steward of Local 100, alleged that this procedure had not been followed. He therefore took steps to prevent the truck from leaving the Harvard Yards. It was this latter action that was the real basis for the dispute since the jurisdictional question was quickly resolved on the spot by the business agents for the two unions and the appropriate city administrator.

The city administration insisted on the dismissal of King, the shop steward involved in the incident, and this insistence precipitated a wildcat strike to demand his reinstatement. The waterworks employees were predominantly black; the administrators and members of other city unions were predominantly white; Mayor Stokes was black and was seeking renomination, thus introducing an additional political factor; the formalization of contracts with unions of city employees was relatively new, and many city administrative personnel were new and untrained in the area of labor relations.

All of these items compounded a dispute that escalated more rapidly than the specific issues seemed to warrant. Indeed, the reassignment was settled on the first day; all further negotiations dealt with the degree to which the shop steward should be penalized for his actions. Some of the difficulties of the case could have arisen in any public employment situation where the administration was determined to exert its right to manage, where experience with labor contracts was limited, and where competing unions approached contractual relationships with the city in different ways. However, it seems clear that unconscious and inadvertent racist ideas were expressed by some of the white administrators—or inferred by the blacks involved—and that this perception, added to previously held ideas of discriminatory tactics, produced an even more intransigent and militant stance by the black shop steward. In addition, the local and the black shop steward were determined to use the mechanism of the union to achieve not only economic justice but status, dignity, and recognition for black workers in competition with other ethnic groups living in Cleveland.

At this stage in the development, the union's position was that Clarence King should not be discharged and that the city's dictatorial methods of dealing with union matters had to be curtailed. On the other hand, the city remained adamant in its stance that King was to remain suspended, that the authority of the city had to be respected, and that the matter would come before the civil service. The union questioned the necessity of taking the issue to the civil service for a number of reasons. The letter of suspension presented to Clarence King did not specify the limits of the suspension. However, under the terms of the Agreement of Understanding (also called the Contract of 1968), any decision to suspend a member of the union for a period of 30 days or more would be a civil service matter. If the suspension was for less than 30 days, the union could take the matter directly to arbitration as a grievance. A very basic and fundamental factor operating at this juncture was the union's distrust of the civil service. This distrust was based upon the widespread belief that the civil service was no more than an instrument of the city administration and did not perform useful services for city employees. The civil service commissioners were appointed by the mayor and had been accused of being discriminatory, especially in the appointment of black people in high positions. The union claimed that the civil service often had used its prerogative of selecting one of the three top candidates who scored the highest on a competitive examination to discriminate against black Americans. It claimed that even when a black person scored the highest on objective tests, the civil service passed over him for qualitative reasons. The apprehension over allowing King's fate to be left in the hands of the civil service must be viewed in this context. Union members picketed the Harvard Yards throughout the weekend in support of King and a limited strike began on August 16, 1969. Although the pickets continued throughout the week, efforts were being made to settle the basic problems. However, these efforts were complicated by a series of events and crises that forced each side into a more militant position. For example, union members and officials charged policemen with "invading Harvard Yards like the Gestapo" on August 18 and with acts deliberately designed to provoke union members into incidents that would result in mass arrests. On the same day the city charged that union representatives were harassing supervisory personnel at the Harvard Yards.

The city charged the union with additional threatening acts and intimidation of city employees as a result of incidents that occurred at various buildings and plants where members of Local 100 worked. It was claimed that these incidents were intended to coerce reluctant union members to walk out or to refuse to cross the picket line. Because of the reported violence and threats to physically abuse workers who wished to cross the picket lines on August 19, Clarence King was arrested and charged with violating the State Riot Control Act, and the mayor appeared on the three city television networks to denounce the violence and intimidation allegedly perpetrated by members of Local 100 with outside assistance.

The Mediation

On August 20, management and union representatives realized the necessity of third-party intervention in order to reach an acceptable solution to the strike. Willoughby Abner of the National Center for Dispute Settlement of the American Arbitration Association was brought in as the mediator. Mr. Abner, a black, was acceptable to both sides largely because of his reputation for objectivity and fairness in the mediation process. He was particularly acceptable to the union because he was known for his past militancy.

On August 23, the local took a formal strike vote of its 1,300 members and issued an ultimatum that if the dispute were not settled within two days, the city would face an officially sanctioned strike on August 26. Mediation sessions continued from August 21 thru August 25. Since the city had already backed away from its position of firing King, the mediator's major effort was to focus negotiations on the number of days that King would be suspended. The local-wide strike began officially on Tuesday, August 26, when more than 1,000 members of Local 100 remained off their jobs and/or participated in the picket lines where they worked throughout the city. The expansion of the strike exacerbated an already tense situation between the union and the city.

The final settlement was reached through Abner's efforts to arrange a meeting between Mayor Stokes and Jerry Wurf, the international president of AFSCME, a meeting that Abner insisted was the only remaining recourse. The lengthy meeting resulted in a final settlement that ordered King to be suspended for 30 days to date from the beginning of the stoppage and included a reaffirmation of the no-work stoppage clause in the original agreement complete with a union guarantee, and a public statement by the international union president.

Although this case remained at the local-union level, did not include community involvement or coalitions, and involved relatively minor issues, nonetheless it contains many elements that are of considerable interest. Once again there was a stable union organization and a situation that is directly analagous to the traditional labor-management model of dispute settlement. The fact that the same union was involved in both Cleveland and Memphis made the case particularly valuable for this project. Its greatest importance, however, rests on the opportunity to study the significance of race and racism in a situation where, although representatives of management rejected white racism at the surface level, the internalization of racist ideas resulted in behavior on the part of some management personnel that was perceived in racist terms by the black shop steward and workers. The largely unconscious racism—real or perceived—was a factor in making the issue difficult to solve. This subtle racism is in contrast to the more overt type exhibited in Memphis. It may, however, be more pervasive then is generally realized by whites and may be more difficult to handle since it involves unconscious behavior and differing perceptions.

A final item that made this case of considerable importance to the project was the fact that the mediation, which was so crucial to the final settlement, was carried out by a black mediator who understood the feelings and perceptions of the black shop steward, gained his confidence, and interpreted his reactions and perceptions to the white administrators.

CHARLESTON, SOUTH CAROLINA HOSPITAL STRIKES

This study focuses on separate but closely interrelated strikes by black service and maintenance personnel against two hospitals in Charleston, South Carolina.[4] The strike against the South Carolina Medical College Hospital began in March 1969, and was not settled until June, 100 days later. Workers in the Charleston County Hospital also began their strike in March and did not obtain a settlement until July, 113 days later. Coming after the civil rights-labor movement coalition in the strike of Memphis garbage workers in 1968, these strikes represented a further extension of that kind of an alliance, specifically with New York-based Local 1199 of drug and hospital local union members.

---

[4] This summary is taken from a case study prepared by Charles Grigg with the collaboration of Charles U. Smith and with the assistance of Robert Hall and Jeffrey Jaques.

Background

Charleston, South Carolina, is a traditional southern community, which included approximately 78,000 blacks in a population of about 215,000 at the time of the strike. Median income for the black population was $927 per year in 1959 ($1,684 for males and $605 for females), lower than the income for nonwhites in the other two major cities of South Carolina, Columbia and Greenville. Only a small fraction of the employed black females was classified as professional or technical, and the bulk of the female work force was comprised of private household workers.

The civil rights movement of the 50s and 60s had left Charleston largely untouched. Dr. Martin Luther King, Jr. had led a sit-in in 1963, which resulted in the formation of a biracial committee, but in most ways Charleston remained largely unaffected by the large civil rights demonstrations that had occurred elsewhere in the South. The voluntary desegregation of public facilities in the early 1960s apparently defused the general unrest among the black community. Some of the black community, however, felt that most of the desegregation was of a token nature and they had gone to the courts to seek action on de facto segregated schools. At the time of the strike the city council included no black members and the biracial committee was not functioning actively.

Important whites in the community perceived race relations in Charleston to be "the best in the United States." White community decision makers judged that the establishment of a biracial committee and the voluntary desegregation of public facilities—however token in actuality—had established a truce and racial harmony. Since there were no major, overt challenges to the status quo, it was assumed that race relations were under control. Apparently the black community of Charleston had accepted the limited objectives symbolized by the actions noted above and had had very little experience in organizing and in uniting behind a common cause.

The Union in Charleston

Hostility to unionism was widespread in South Carolina and government officials considered it illegal for governmental units to recognize and bargain with unions of public employees since anti-union right-to-work laws existed in the state. Some hospital workers in Charleston had expressed interest in a union before 1968, but their position was weak and their knowledge of organizing was minimal.

Local 1199, the drug and hospital workers local of the Retail, Wholesale, and Department Store Workers Union (RWDSO), had actively organized hospital workers in New York City since 1959, and because so many of its unskilled and semi-skilled members were black, Dr. Martin Luther King, Jr. had long been involved with that organization. Thus, the ties between Local 1199 and the Southern Christian Leadership Conference (SCLS) pre-dated the Charleston strike although the local had not been active in the South before that time.

The union in Charleston gained strength through an incident that occurred in February 1968. Five black licensed practical nurses (LPNs) were fired from the medical college hospital after a dispute with a white supervisor. The supervisor had ordered the LPNs to ignore a regulation requiring them to check a patient's chart upon reporting to work. The five black women saw this as undercutting their ability to perform their duties adequately and as a denigration of their status as semiprofessionals. They refused to work without reviewing the charts and were discharged. A complaint was forwarded to the U.S. Department of Health, Education, and Welfare, which sent an investigating team to the hospital; the five LPNs were re-hired.

However, as a consequence of this action, organizational meetings were held every week in the black community. Starting in February 1968, growing numbers attended these sessions and some signed up as members of a union. In September, a representative of this newly formed union sent a letter to the administrator of the medical college hospital claiming that the union represented a majority of the hospital employees. The administrator sent a letter to all employees stating, "We do not want a union here at the Medical College," and enclosed two cartoons depicting the exploitation of union members by union "bosses."

The Background of the Strikes

Action centered around the South Carolina Medical College Hospital, the teaching hospital of the University of South Carolina, and the Charleston County Hospital, which served the area's poor people. Dr. William H. McCord, the president of the medical college, and Dr. Vernon W. H. Campbell, medical director of the county hospital, were the chief figures in the negotiations. Since the hospital was a part of the University of South Carolina, the regents were also involved, as were various state officials including Governor Robert McNair. Because some funds were provided by the federal government, the U.S. Department of Health, Education, and Welfare, headed at that time by

Secretary Robert H. Finch, was also a part of the situation. Dr. Campbell was joined by a committee of the county council in major negotiations, although the county council refused to meet with union representatives during most of the strike.

Following the firing and reinstatement of the five black LPNs at the medical college hospital, union membership had grown substantially. The union pressed Dr. McCord for a meeting but was unsuccessful. It was alleged that he said that he was willing to meet with individual workers about individual grievances but that he would not meet with groups or with union representatives. In February 1969, a group of 40 unionists went to the state capitol at Columbia to see the Charleston county legislative delegation. They made an abortive attempt to see the governor as well. On March 14, a union representative and ten union members met with Charleston's Mayor J. Palmer Gaillard to ask him to use his offices to arrange a meeting with Dr. McCord. Thus the situation was broadened to include the city of Charleston, with the mayor playing the role of a third party.

As a result of his intercession, a meeting was arranged for a group of union members to discuss grievances with Dr. McCord at the hospital on March 18. When the unionists arrived they found that Dr. McCord had selected eight additional black workers to be present. The union members felt that they had been tricked. Approximately 90 hospital workers gathered in the auditorium as they heard about the events. When one of his assistants announced that Dr. McCord refused to talk to such a large group, the assembled workers moved on to Dr. McCord's office. Officials of the medical college called the workers disruptive and repeated that McCord would only meet with groups of 15 workers. Police were called, and a vice-president of the medical college announced that the meeting was over and ordered the workers to return to their jobs which they did, after consulting with a union representative from Local 1199.

Following this incident, the hospital administrators fired 12 workers whom they perceived to be ring leaders of this gathering, although an additional 80 workers who had left their jobs were not disciplined in any way. This firing triggered the 100-day strike that followed at the medical college hospital.

The Issues

Underlying all other issues was Dr. McCord's refusal to meet with union representatives to discuss grievances. The workers were seeking job security, adequate grievance procedures, and an end to racial discrimination in pay, promotion policies, and job assignments. They were also dissatisfied about wages but this was not a major issue since there was a state plan to raise the current hourly minimum wage at the medical college hospital from $1.35 to $1.45 on July 1 and to $1.60 by the end of July. Also projected at the state level was an appeal board for any state employee who felt that he had been unjustly fired.

There had been little communication between the workers and Dr. McCord and a backlog of grievances had accumulated. A major one was a matter of pride and dignity. In the tradition of the Old South, these black semiskilled and unskilled workers had been called by their first or last names while at work. The workers were predominantly women who viewed jobs in the hospital as a way of improving their lives, and the insult to their dignity was enormous. Their slogan, "I *Am* Somebody," became an important symbol of their need for black identity and personal recognition, which was added to their thrust for union recognition.

The Strikes

The coalition of civil rights and labor union organizations was manifest on the first day of the strike when it was announced that the union local had received the support of the Southern Christian Leadership Conference (SCLC) and that Mrs. Coretta King, the widow of Dr. Martin Luther King, Jr., was honorary Chairman of the National Organizing Committee of Hospital and Nursing Home Employees. The day after the strike began, a group of clergymen attended a meeting with elected local union officials and Local 1199 representatives. They requested a meeting with the mayor and set up a three-man committee to make arrangements. On the following day, the mayor expanded the clergy group, answered questions about the role of the city in the dispute, and set up a six-man committee to meet with himself, the attorney general, medical college executives, and some worker representatives. Additional meetings between concerned clergy and hospital executives were arranged.

By March 25, the hospital executives had gone into court to get injunctions regulating the pickets. This delayed a meeting between the clergymen and hospital executives. When held, that meeting did not yield any substantive negotiating results although the clergy did establish a fund to aid the strikers. On March 23, 57 persons were arrested for violating the injunction on picketing. On the following day the federal court ordered the workers to honor the injunction and instructed the U.S. marshall to assist local and state police in its enforcement. By March 27, a proposal called "Peace with Justice Proposal" was made by the clergymen's committee to the union and hospital officials. Among other things it called for dropping the charges made against the pickets. The hospital rejected this, saying that lawlessness could not be sanctioned.

Paralleling union activities at the medical college, workers at the county hospital, organized into the same union, struck on March 28. The demands of these black hospital workers included recognition of their organization and other union-oriented issues such as grievance procedures, dues check-off, and a pay increase. The black community organized extensively in support of the 500 striking hospital workers, identifying the presence of a common racial issue. There were mass demonstrations, a boycott of downtown merchants, and a sympathy boycott of classes by black high school students. There were mass arrests, resulting from an injunction against demonstrations, and a city-wide curfew. Dr. Ralph Abernathy of the SCLC was arrested and jailed during one of the demonstrations. The strikers received national support from a civil rights-union alliance, which helped raise money for the strikers and their families. UAW President Walter Reuther visited Charleston to walk with the striking hospital workers on their picket line.

To a large extent, the hospital administrations were backed by the governor of the state. The dispute at the medical college hospital was settled after three and one-half months following a threat by the International Longshoreman's Association to close the Port of Charleston in support of the strike and intervention from Washington when some congressmen appealed to President Nixon to take action in the dispute. The agreement included a grievance procedure, de facto union recognition, a wage increase, and a credit union, which was established for purposes of a dues check-off. The county hospital did not settle its strike until three weeks later, and the settlement was not as favorable to the workers as was the agreement reached with the medical college hospital. The grievance procedure at the county hospital was subject to further negotiations and apparently there was not even de facto recognition of a union. Further, workers at the county hospital did not receive the same assurances of the rehire of strikers as did their medical college hospital counterparts.

Summary of the Hospital Strikes

To many observers these two strikes represented the highest degree of cooperative action between the civil rights groups and the labor movement. Like the other two cases studied here, the issues were trade-union oriented and involved the right of public employees to organize in states hostile to union efforts. Formal union recognition was not won, but in the county hospital situation, the county council moved from absolute refusal to talk with union officials to at least an informal recognition of their status.

The race issues were again intertwined with the trade union questions. The issues of dignity, self-respect, and the right to representatives of their own choosing were strongly tied to job-related grievances. The strikers were black and most support came from the local black community and from trade unions across the county. The strike served to unite that black community in a way that had not been done previously.

While there were almost no formal negotiations in the medical college strike, there was substantial informal and behind-the-scenes bargaining. In that case, it appears that, ultimately, pressure from the White House in the form of a group of presidentially appointed observers, brought a settlement. In the county hospital case there were more formal and overt negotiations, which even included some acknowledgement after many weeks that the union was a party to the dispute.

GENERAL ANALYSIS

The Structure of Public Employment

In many jurisdictions, strikes by government employees are prohibited either by legislative or court action. Frequently, neither union recognition nor collective bargaining is accepted by law or by administrators who head government units. However, these anti-union and anti-bargaining perspectives, regulations and laws are changing. To some degree, this process is reflected in each of the cases we studied.

In Cleveland, under the pioneering leadership of the new black mayor, unions of city employees were operating for the first time under formal written contracts. Until Stokes' election in 1968 de facto recognition and informal arrangements had been used in lieu of written contracts. Some officials were not convinced that contracts between the city and unions were legal and, consequently, the city had had little experience with such formal agreements. In Memphis and Charleston, officials believed that it was illegal for any union to be recognized as a sole bargaining agent for a group of employees in states that had right-to-work laws. Both cities had a long tradition of refusing to bargain, and government and hospital officials of Charleston discussed grievances only with individual workers.

The civil service system, which provides stability but considerable inflexibility in the personnel policies of most governmental units, has established job classifications and salary relationships, a pattern of rights on the job for employees, and criteria that control or circumscribe their hiring, promotion, and discharge. Restrictions on the right to strike, unwillingness to engage in collective bargaining, refusal to recognize a union as sole bargaining agent, and the alternative formulation of a civil service system that is assumed to provide protection and equities for government workers are all based on a concept of the unchallengeable sovereignty of a government unit. It is presumed that the political processes of decision making represent an acceptable expression of the public interest. Institutional support for this set of arrangements is frequently available to governmental administrators through the courts.

Two of these case studies deal with city governments, one with agencies related primarily to the county and state. In Memphis and Charleston there was also federal involvement. Each government unit has relationships with others, of course, and it is these interconnections that may provide clues for the most important influences constraining or causing actions by political and administrative policy makers.

A key aspect of an analysis of the policies and actions of a government unit involved in conflict with its black employees is the identification of the varying levels of authority. The immediate supervisor is likely to be responsible for work assignments, work rules, and salary adjustments but not for the policy formulation governing such rules and assignments. As one moves up the hierarchy in a complex city government there are also changes in the perspectives and influences affecting administrative decisions. The application of general policies may vary widely. Higher up in the organization political judgments are likely to be influenced by the pressures affecting the top of the government unit.

Four different kinds of perspectives and pressures, therefore, affect the various government decision-making levels: the need to provide adequate services to citizens, the need to maintain a personnel system that is well established, the personal prejudices of administrators, and the specialized political pressures that dominate elected officials and reach into the organizational hierarchy.

The Parties

The Black Workers and Their Union

Black city employees in these cases were convinced that they had not been given fair treatment and that they could not expect that these injustices would be corrected within the civil service structure by the decisions of major political figures or the pressures of citizen groups. Like all workers, blacks expresss their demands for justice in the work place in job-related terms. They share common employment experiences with other workers whose response has been through unionism. They also believe that the city administration and its constituents, on the one hand, and their own supporters, on the other, are likely to be more responsive to union-management demands and familiar procedures than to racially-oriented issues. This is, of course, more complex in the southern states that still hold strong anti-union views.

The black workers involved in our three case studies were close to the bottom of the economic, skill, and status scales for city employees. In each of the disputes, they were developing or changing their relationship to the government unit that was their employer, to each other, to the black community, to white union members, and to the political structure of the respective international unions.

In Cleveland, they were significantly redefining relations to their paid local union leaders, with the predominantly white members of other city employee unions, and with the AFL-CIO city council. In Memphis, an emerging black leadership was working out new patterns with other local unions and with the international union, AFSCME. In Charleston, black employees were developing their own strengths through the medium of organization, aided by a New York local whose efforts among low-paid hospital workers had accelerated in recent years. The dispute remained essentially on a union-management level in Cleveland and did not involve the black community, coalitions of any sort, or government above the city level, although the international union did become directly involved. The case had considerable racial overtones since the grievance revolved around the actions of a militant black shop steward. The challengers were the shop steward, who had already gained recognition from the city, and local and international union officials.

In Memphis and in Charleston, the organized union base was supplemented by active support from the black community and civil rights groups. In Memphis, black community members gained representation on the bargaining team along with local and international union representatives. In Charleston, the striking workers at the medical college hospital gained support from the workers at the county hospital who also went on strike. The Charleston workers specifically invited the SCLC to join them and representatives of that organization and other civil rights groups played important roles in the negotiating process. Thus, the challengers in these two cities were the union members, their representatives, the black community, and civil rights organizations.

The widespread support given to the workers by the black communities during these disputes was a sign of racial dissatisfaction that was rooted far deeper than the economic issues of the strikes. As black workers with black interpretations of job experiences and job discriminations, the workers shared with the community a racial identity that contributed to the conviction that determined efforts were needed to change job conditions. This shared black view led to a structuring of black interests that extended beyond the union movement, and tended to define even job issues in racial terms. In both Memphis and Charleston, therefore, upper-class blacks and black leaders who were not within the union movement responded to a need to support the strike as a symbol of the generally felt oppression of blacks.

National civil rights leaders who took part in the Memphis and Charleston disputes broadened the issues and addressed the larger sets of forces that were judged to be blocking immediate job and local union demands. Dr. Martin Luther King, Jr., who was assassinated in Memphis, and the Reverend Ralph Abernathy, who went to jail in Charleston for defying the court injunctions against large-scale demonstrations, rallied the local black community and national black and white support. In both cases the union movement provided financial support and the physical presence of labor leaders like Walter Reuther on the line of march.

In these two southern cities, therefore, the organization of black public employees received support from the whole union movement. Most of the direct bargaining and negotiating included local and international union figures in addition to representatives of the black community and civil rights groups. This was a coalition of sorts, although in both Memphis and Charleston the international union and the civil rights groups were generally careful to act to strengthen the local leadership.

The Establishment Side

As has already been noted, the challlengers in a public employees dispute face a hierarchy of administrative personnel to whom their grievances must be taken. In addition to the appointed professional staff there are the elected city officials who may also be influenced by state functionaries, including the governor and members of the state legislatures. Thus, the positions taken by the establishment representatives, who must be responsive to a variety of constituencies, tend to have a strong political element.

Also, appointed or elected federal officials may involve themselves in the conflict either through political party machinery or through rules and regulations governing federal financial assistance. Within this complex structure, a wide range of judgments and approaches to disputes may arise. Theoretically, where there is a civil service system, workers are protected against such outside political influences, but this is not always so simple. In Cleveland, cases only went to the civil service commission if the penalty exceeded 30 days. Moreover, the unionized black workers tended to distrust the civil service system, which they perceived as discriminatory, and were unwilling to abandon their own union-arranged grievance system for that of the civil service.

In Memphis and Charleston, no such system existed. In Memphis, the wage rates were set by the city, not by the state. In the Charleston Medical College Hospital dispute, monies were received from the state and federal governments. In the county hospital dispute in that city, the county provided funds. These were subject to minima set by the state of South Carolina.

The Cleveland case was complex since the mayor had been professionalizing departmental leadership by new apppointments. The department head involved in the dispute was inexperienced in labor relations and most of the negotiating was carried out by a city lawyer. In the final stages the negotiation was taken over by the president of the international union and the mayor.

In Memphis, the precipitating incident occurred as the result of a decision made by a Department of Public Works supervisor. The mayor had already set an anti-union tone, and refused as a matter of law and principle to negotiate with representatives of a group of union members. Since the city had just moved from an aldermanic to a city commission form, city councilmen were unsure of their responsibilities and they apparently considered it the function of the mayor to handle such administrative conflicts. Although a city council committee was formed later, the mayor was once again the major establishment representative in the final stages of mediation.

In the Charleston Medical College Hospital negotiations, the hospital director represented the establishment throughout the dispute, and, like the mayor of Memphis, refused to negotiate with the union. The mayor intervened to arrange meetings, the governor appeared on several occasions, and throughout the entire conflict the hospital director was subject to many other influences, including that of the U.S. Department of Health, Education, and Welfare, which had been investigating charges of discrimination. In the Charleston County Hospital dispute, negotiations were carried out largely by members of the county council who were charged with this responsibility and although the executive officer of the hospital was involved, he was not the major establishment representative.

Even this brief summary indicates the complex nature of the establishment side. In Cleveland, Memphis, and the Charleston Medical College Hospital cases, third-party intervention was necessary before settlement was reached.

The Issues

Each of the cases was triggered by job-related administrative action. In each case affected workers defined the action as at least partial racial discrimination: the discharge of the black LPN's who objected to the omission of a function that they considered to be a mark of their semiprofessional status; the assignment of a limited work schedule to white workers while excluding blacks from performing the same job on that particular day; the disciplinary action against a shop steward who was a black militant. Each incident became the call to united action by many other black workers who had long been aware of the same patterns of discrimination by white administrators and who supported the protest. Other unresolved job-related grievances included wage levels, working conditions, and grievance procedures. Black workers sought to find a power base through collective action to remedy those discriminations just as many other workers have used the device of unionism and collective bargaining to correct unfair treatment.

Although the *form* of the demands of the black union members may be identical to those of other public employee unionists, the substantive demands, and particularly the demands for recognition, are likely to have specialized meanings. While the international union representatives tended to define the conflict issues in economic rather than racial terms, this did not appear to be true of the local black workers. In Cleveland, the union had won recognition, but the major issue was the degree of the penalty that management had lodged against a black shop steward who initiated a wildcat strike and the union's commitment to its no-strike pledge. At no point did the issues broaden beyond this level.

In Memphis, the call-up of whites rather than blacks for the limited work available triggered a strike, but the issues were broadened to include wage levels, grievance procedures, and most importantly, recognition of the union and its chosen representatives. Essentially the same issues were at stake in the Charleston hospital cases: union recognition and recognition of black identity and black dignity. Thus, in Memphis and Charleston, the slogans "I *Am* a Man" and "I *Am* Somebody" became symbols of the black workers' determination to have a voice in their own destinies. In both of these cities the form that the agreement was to take and the demand for a dues check-off system were also major issues. In Charleston, the rehiring of strikers became an additional problem before settlement was reached.

The coalition of black workers and the black community tended to broaden the issues at least temporarily in Memphis and Charleston. Thus, demands for improved police-community relations arose, in part, out of police actions taken against the demonstrators in the course of the strikes. Other issues involved schools, housing, and public services. To a large extent, these appear to have served primarily to legitimize the participation of the wider black community and not as a basis upon which the dispute was predicated or settlement was reached.

Black workers believe that patterns of discrimination on the job have racial as well as economic motivations. They seek solutions that, although job-related, are seen as steps toward racial equality and racial justice. By demanding that the administration negotiate agreements with their black unions, they seek to improve working conditions, raise their economic standing, and acquire a status with the government unit and dignity for themselves.

In each of the cases, the administration responded to the charge of discrimination by denying it and, in two of the cases, by moving to penalize those who had raised the issue. It was assumed that appropriate policies were already being adequately administered and that blacks should accept these available procedures as satisfactory. The administration also rebuffed demands for changes in wages and working conditions. With the union's additional demand for recognition, management hardened its determination to maintain existing policies and procedures.

Coercive Pressures

The Challengers

Since these incidents involve black government workers who pressed their demands through union organization, it is useful to summarize the usual devices available to public employee unions to understand the ways in which the members' blackness affects these patterns.

A local union of governmental workers has a number of resources for pressing a reluctant political administration for concessions. First, the professional administrators find that the workers are disaffected and unwilling to function under unsatisfactory conditions. Considerable pressure for change occurs if the union leadership can convincingly demonstrate that the administrators can function effectively only after an understanding is reached to correct the workers' complaints. For efficient performance those within the total bureaucratic structure must accept the judgment that they are being reasonably treated in relation to one another. This may not be a very strong pressure, of course, because administrators and complainants may differ drastically in their perceptions of what is fair.

A second source of coercive presssure for a complaining union is the support of others who urge corrective action by the administration. Other local unions of government employees may share judgments of unfairness, and may hope that changes won by the particular group will then be available to them. They may feel that their own ability to progress is limited until those at the bottom are advanced.

The political administration of government services is also subject to pressures from its constituencies. If the union can persuade politically powerful outsiders that its grievances are legitimate, it may induce them to press for, or at least support, corrective administrative action. Complaints against administrative action and appeals for support are likely to have a much greater impact if the complaining union has forced the issues to their attention by such devices as oral and written appeals, including appearances before other organizations and public bodies. Strike threats activate possible latent support. Obviously an active strike is an even more potent way to demand attention and to enlist aid and interest.

If the union is able to suspend vital services by a strike, there will be considerable pressure on the administration to offer a set of concessions to the union if no alternate way to develop the needed services is available. The more the loss of services affects those for whom they are provided, the more the constituencies will press the political leaders of the administration to find an adjustment. Pressure on the administration will be much greater, of course, if, along with losing needed services, constituencies judge that the complaints are justified and that the administration is being unfair.

A third supporting pressure on behalf of the unionized workers may be provided by the labor movement, primarily by the international union with which the local union is affiliated. Services can include expertise in advocating for the grievances of the workers, assistance in uniting the local union membership behind the strategies that are adopted, and aid in speaking for the local's cause with the administration and with possible supporters.

Finally, an important resource available to the complaining union is the judgment that collective bargaining is an appropriate mechanism for accommodating workers' grievances. Such a set of normative expectations is strongest in workers who have observed that others achieve gains through this socially accepted procedure. Considerable acceptance of collective bargaining comes also from segments of the community who, even though their services are affected, judge that the city administration is obligated to accommodate to worker interests. Such a conviction may even be present within a political administration, particularly if there are satisfactory precedents in dealing with other union groupings of its employees.

Considerable resources are therefore available to black workers to operate through the usual patterns of unionism. Indeed, there is a record of substantial success for government employees in using these pressures to achieve meaningful improvements in their conditions and recognition of their separate interests to which a political administration must accommodate.

These resources, however, may be quite inadequate to achieve the desired changes from an administration. Contrary judgments of administrators and counterpressures on them from their constituencies, particularly from their political superiors, may overwhelm the union pressures summarized above. Thus, although public employee unionism has made great strides in the last few years, it is far from the status that many unions have achieved in private industry.

Each of the dimensions summarized above, however, has different characteristics when the issues are black, the union organization is black, and the coercive resources are structured in terms of race. In the first place, the black worker may become an active union member because he has been aroused by the hope that something can be done about the discriminatory characteristics of the administration of his job and workplace. Further, he may find a common cause with other black workers if it appears that united actions rather than individual efforts address their racial complaints more effectively. For blacks equal opportunities on the job include equal treatment, wages, and working conditions and the assurance that, through a recognition of their blackness, they will achieve the status of equality denied in their life experience.

Other parts of the black community will also feel that black government employees are getting second-class treatment since this is their common perspective, drawn from their black experience. The effectiveness of black community response, however, will depend on the degree to which it can be enlisted in coercive actions against the administration. Local black community support can take several forms. It can be mobilized into direct political pressure on the administration and can be effective if the political administration is dependent on the support of the black community. Where the black community enjoys such political power, it may move to press white political supporters of the administration to bring their influence to bear on the government decision makers.

A second coercive device available to the black community is the threat of violence. This threat may be implicit in the situation, rather than explicitly enunciated by black leaders. It may influence whites who fear social instability and who see potential violence as endangering the city's attractiveness to new businesses and industrial expansion. During the period when riots were prevalent in major American cities, the desire to avoid or reduce the danger of continuing violence effectively influenced the behavior of the establishment. It is important to note, however, that the degree of violence in Memphis was minimal, even following the assassination of Dr. King, although the fear of such violence proved to be a viable coercive tool for the black challengers. On the other side, the use of mace by the police against some nonmilitant black ministers in Memphis served as a catalyst in uniting a divided black community in support of the black workers. It is probable that the arrests of key figures like Reverend Ralph Abernathy in Charleston served the same purpose.

In Memphis and Charleston, considerable use was made of nonviolent demonstrations, rallies, and marches. The large groups attending these expressions of solidarity aroused fear in the white community that violence would occur. Repressive court and police actions against these demonstrations apparently served only to swell the numbers attending.

The most demanding form of black pressure against the white power structure is the device of the boycott. Since neither 1,400 garbage workers in Memphis nor 500 hospital workers in Charleston could effectively boycott the mayor or the hospital administrations, the boycott had to be applied against some other group. That group was the white business community. Since the white business community was perceived as having political power vis-à-vis the public authorities, it was expected that the business community would pressure the public authority to make concessions to settle the dispute and stop its economic losses. The limited constituency of the striking workers, however, could not mount a successful boycott and wider support was needed. The Memphis and Charleston black communities were involved in the generally successful use of the boycott as a coercive measure. In these cities, black community support also attracted leaders whose presence gave national publicity to the strikes and pressured the public authorities to change their positions.

The Administration

The response of the white administration can best be understood by examining the resistance to any worker and union demands and by exploring the specialized meaning of such resistance when the race-related demands come from black workers. For some time after collective bargaining had been accepted in private employment in this country, political administrations assumed that it was inappropriate in the public sector since the authority structure for employment policies rested in an administration that was responsible to the general electorate. To do otherwise, it was held, would be to compromise the sovereignty residing in the people and the execution of that sovereignty by the political agents of the people and their appointed professional administrators. It was also assumed that political administrators and their subordinates needed guidelines and checks to asssure the public that they were, in fact, operating to carry out public interest. Two forms of such checks were added. First, political administrators were subject to general rules about employment conditions that were determined by the political processes. Also, civil service procedures were developed to assure fairness in administrative decisions and to develop criteria for maximum efficiency and equity in the operation of governmental services for the public.

A second source of pressures against concessions to the demands of public employee unions was the political control of funds and resource allocation. Since the government unit secured its resources from taxes, there was a strong tendency to restrict the funds available to administrators. Employee demands for equity with the private sector confronted taxpayers reluctant to expand the finances available to administrators.

A political administration, however, is constantly adjusting to specialized forces that are insisting on services important to them. Within the complicated structuring of the administration of services, more powerful employees and governmental units gain advantages over others. Equity as a guiding principle in employment administration, as in other aspects of government operations, is only the vaguest kind of guide and advantageous positions for some are accepted as normal. Thus, the equity demands of some workers may meet the response that inequality is normal and that any rearrangement of the equities in response to the demands of some segment of the work force will be viewed as threatening to others.

Race modifies each of the above characteristics for the government administration and for the black workers. In developing and executing general employment policies, white professional administrators may condition their judgments and reactions by their stereotypes of black workers. The policies adopted may be based on built-in institutional racism that retains previously held assumptions that black workers can, and indeed should, be treated differently from whites. Thus, there will be civil service patterns that have built-in discriminatory consequences in hiring, upgrading, and setting salary scales. A second important racial element in the structuring of conflict arises from the differential support given to black and white employees by power groups within the community. It may seem appropriate to political constituencies of the administration to treat blacks differently from whites in determining the kinds of jobs they should occupy, in their work requirements, and in their compensation. Discriminatory patterns in the larger community and in private industry make differential treatment for public employees seem natural, as though it were equitable to have similar discrepancies in the treatment of white and black workers inside as well as outside of government employ.

Finally there is the phenomenon of polarization. When blacks define their job and other needs in terms of discrimination, other forces in the administration and in the larger groupings of constituencies consider it urgent to suppress such a tendency. They fear that black power responses will extend from the particular job-related incident to a rallying by blacks to change social alignments in the larger society. They are determined that advantages enjoyed by whites must not be lost. Police, prosecutors, and even courts are available to support the concept of sovereignty and maintain the status quo within the structure of public employment. They are even more available if the conflict is judged to challenge prevailing white patterns.

In Memphis and Charleston, injunctions were obtained against marches and mass demonstrations and, particularly in Charleston, restrictions were placed on the number and arrangement of pickets allowed. The overwhelming costs of these court actions were supported by the local black community, the international unions, and the national civil rights movement. Legal assistance was available through these sources, bail money was found, and the injunctions were defied. Without such support, the injunctions would probably have coerced the workers into returning to their jobs and dropping their demands.

The economic losses to these low-paid workers, frequently the sole wage earners in a family unit, would also have been a strong coercive measure except for the assistance that came from outside sources. International unions, in particular, provided the funds that enabled the striking black workers to survive the long period without wages. Financial help from unionists in other parts of the country bolstered the morale of the black workers and reinforced their determination to achieve that same union strength for themselves. The most effective coercive weapon of the public authority was the replacement of the striking workers with other workers. This was most prominent in Charleston and the resolution of the rehiring question was the most difficult issue in the negotiations.

The Negotiation Process

The procedures in the Cleveland case were substantially different from those in either Memphis or Charleston because the union had gained recognition, was operating under a contract, and the issue was a grievance involving a single worker. While the department heads were relatively inexperienced in labor negotiations, the city attorney was not. Similarly, local and national union leadership had considerable expertise. A careful reading of that case, however, reveals that institutional and personal racism, perhaps unconscious, were crucial factors in the process of arriving at a solution.

All three of these cases suggest a progression from the civil service approach, which employs policies that are unilaterally decided by the political authority and unilaterally applied by their administrative subordinates, toward a collective bargaining demand of the black union. The unilateral position meant that white administrators considered and rejected the complaints of workers who were black. In each of the cases, all of the further steps followed only because the black workers rejected this approach and used the collective pressures of the union to force additional gains.

In Memphis and Charleston, the second step was a readiness to consult with black complainants. At this stage it was assumed that, after hearing and considering the black complaints, the administrative and political authorities would make and announce unilateral decisions. In Memphis, the administration did accept the spokesmen for the black complaints as the freely chosen union representatives. At this stage in Charleston, however, negotiating with union representatives as spokesmen for the union and for the common black interests of the affected workers was refused. Such recognition had already been established in Cleveland.

The third stage of true negotiations was reached in each case only after the black union and its allies put greater pressures on the administrators and the government unit accepted the necessity of an agreement. It followed that concessions would have to be made by each side to secure the consent of the other. In reaching this stage the black unions in Memphis and Charleston achieved the substance of the recognition that was so important to the organizational units and especially to their black membership.

The second consultative stage and the third stage of negotiations can be carried on in a variety of ways. All three cases included use of a go-between to convey the perspectives and positions of each side to the other. In Cleveland and Memphis, this device supplemented face-to-face discussions as the way in which negotiations were conducted. Charleston, on the other hand, was well into the third stage before face-to-face negotiations occurred. In each case, as indicated above, parties eventually agreed upon some terms, although the public authorities initially opposed these procedures.

The form and the announcement of the agreement was handled somewhat differently in the three cities. In Cleveland, the city and the union signed a joint formal agreement and the two chief spokesmen announced it together. In Memphis, a recommendation was jointly drawn up, signed, and referred to the city council, which formally, and in this sense unilaterally, announced it. In Charleston, there were unilateral announcements of terms that had been informally accepted by the union and its black supporters.

Where pressures have been developed strongly and used strategically, it has been possible for the black spokesmen to achieve a form of negotiations. Through intermediaries and in face-to-face discussions there can be an exploration of the reasons for various demands and administrative responses, an interchange of judgments on the consequences of various alterations in policies and practices, a revision of judgments by each side as to the merit and strength of each priority, and a testing of terms that might be used in conflict settlement.

Each side must decide what concessions it is prepared to make as a price for concluding the conflict. In these cases the black spokesmen tended to give first priority to the recognition of their black union organization as a symbol and as a promise of continued recognition of steps toward equality. In the bitter Charleston conflicts, second priority was given to the protection of those who had led the coercive pressures for, if they were subject to severe penalties, the prospect of continued unity and recognition appeared dim. In Memphis and Charleston, a third set of priorities involved the substantive changes in administrative policies around which the disputes had originally developed. Finally, there was an expressed need for grievance machinery, particularly by the union spokesmen who used as their model the patterns of the union-management machinery developed and recognized elsewhere.

Administrative decisions reversed the strikers' order of priority because they tended to give assurances of the consideration of future complaints and the modification of policies that appeared to be inequitable. In all cases, however, the administrators strongly insisted on the punishment of the troublemakers whose actions had precipitated the conflict. Finally, they were reluctant to concede that changes were being made by a collective bargaining process that depended on joint rather than unilateral decisions.

Results of the Negotiations

The case data permit some general speculations on the possible results of conflicts between black workers and public authorities dominated by white administrators and white power constituencies. These data, however, only summarize the immediate conclusions in each of the cases. Thus, our later speculations will be tentative when we determine whether this approach provides meaningful change in directions sought by blacks for jobs and in their relations to public employers who control the jobs.

In the short run, it seems reasonable to apply a union-management model and to suggest that, whatever the issues and priorities of each side, the immediate conflict is concluded on terms that approximate the relative coercive position that each side has been able to develop. This proposition appears to be supported by the results in the Memphis case where the massed power of the black community and an expressed national concern produced an agreement in which the black workers achieved many of their original demands. In Cleveland, the political needs of the mayor and assistance from the national union were instrumental in saving the local black militant leader's status and reducing his penalties, although a promise was elicited that wildcat strike action would not be used again. In Charleston, support from the local black community and from a national union intensely concerned with the outcome of the dispute saved the jobs of the original protestors, and led to a minimal form of union recognition.

The black focus on recognition, the changed conditions, and the outside protections apparently provided the local union with sufficient bargaining power to make progress, although the results seemed to be only a small step toward full equality to some blacks. Some political supporters of the public authorities believed that blacks had indeed been discriminated against, and feared an even more violent black posture if they remained completely frustrated. The data also suggest a polarized white opposition to the black focus, so that the positions of the white administration were somewhat confused and ambivalent.

Viewed from the perspective of peaceful and stable industrial relations rather than from the need to make substantive changes for blacks in America, these cases suggest that it is possible for public authorities to establish a working relationship with black unionists that includes a degree of recognition and a degree of negotiations. This appears to be more likely if the conflict is defined within union-management parameters rather than in racial terms. It is also possible to operate a system that maintains the appearance of undivided sovereignty while proceeding to reach an accommodated agreement with the interests of blacks as well as other workers. Indeed, applying another value pattern to the above conclusions, the data of these cases suggest that it is possible for political administrations to conclude a racial conflict with black workers in such a way as to extend their acceptance of and involvement in the system to which the administration is committed.

The longer-run consequences of racial conflict within a union-management structure are more difficult to predict. It is not clear from the cases whether black workers who hold low-status government jobs develop a meaningful power base within the union movement or in relation to the political government machinery as a result of individual, ad hoc incidents. Although the black community played an important role in these cases, it is also possible that the use of the union-management pattern may lead black workers to less rather than greater black community identification. It appears that these particular disputes did not create any ongoing machinery for the interaction of the black community and black public workers. In addition, it is not clear whether a coalition between black civil rights organizations and labor organizations has any continued life and meaning beyond the period of the individual disputes.

The questions raised by our case studies include the following: Are the opportunities for blacks to extend their influence within specific international unions and the union movement generally enhanced by success in an ad hoc case of bargaining with a public authority and reduced by failure in negotiations? Is the likelihood of wider black coalitions on other issues that affect larger groupings of the black community increased by successful negotiations and reduced by failure? Do the relatively successful conclusions of such racial negotiations result in an increased black acceptance of the prevailing economic, social, and political system, even though it remains largely dominated by whites?

CHAPTER 4

Universities

The analyses in this chapter are drawn from confrontations at The University of Michigan, San Francisco State College, and Duke University. They involved a large black grouping at Michigan (Black Action Movement) and a smaller group at Duke (Afro-American Students); at San Francisco State, the Black Student Union was the largest unit in a coalition that included Chicanos and Asians as a Third-World Liberation Front Movement.

Despite the different characteristics of the institutions and the black challengers, striking similarities in all three cases derive, in part, from the protestors' shared views of university goals, organizational structures for decision making, and characteristics of predominantly white universities.

The 1970 confrontation-negotiation at The University of Michigan was the most successful based on the greatest change in university policies, the minimum of violence, and the adjustments made through negotiations. Using the criterion of the need to enforce a disciplinary refusal to negotiate an accommodation of black pressures, the San Francisco State case might be considered the most successful, although it included considerable violence by students and police. The Duke University case represents the least focused of the three in terms of black pressures on the university and the process of formal negotiations between protagonists.

This chapter includes summaries of the three cases and focuses on their commonalities. However, specialized characteristics made each case unique in important ways. In addition, the research design developed data that suggested a more precise articulation of positions than in fact occurred and implied a greater capacity of each participant to predict the possible consequences of any choices. Finally the project design forced the data into a relatively restricted focus. The Duke University incident, for example, was played out by a variety of individuals and organizations, involved many issues more or less related to the specific challenges of black students to the university, and included a range of outcomes.

The research design and the model for analysis of campus conflict bring into focus some of the developments and patterns, but by no means all of the interrelated motivations and actions.

THE BLACK ACTION MOVEMENT AND THE UNIVERSITY OF MICHIGAN

This dispute took place in 1970, after the other studies in this sector had already been commissioned. Since it occurred at the home site of the project and appeared to have many elements of general interest, however, it was undertaken by the project director and a black assistant.[1]

As in most of the cases, the roots of the dispute lay in the past. The specific confrontation under study, however, started in February 1970, and continued until April 1, when agreement was reached. In the intervening period there were meetings between Black Action Movement (BAM) representatives and various members of the university administration, student marches, disruptions of library facilities, faculty involvements, and a student strike, which culminated in three days of intensive negotiations and a settlement.

The University of Michigan is a state university with a student body of approximately 35,000. At the time of the demands, the number of black students was approximately 3 percent of the total. Michi-

---

[1] This summary has been taken from a case study prepared for this project by W. Ellison Chalmers and Chessie P. Jeffries of The University of Michigan.

gan is generally considered the "elite" institution of the state university system and has a heavy concentration of graduate students. Its president, Robben Fleming, is generally considered to be a liberal with a considerable reputation for handling disputes in both the labor-management area and in universities.

In early February BAM presented a list of seven demands to the university. These essentially fell into three related areas: (1) an increase in black enrollment to reach a goal of 10 percent by fall 1973; (2) a change in policy for admissions and financial aid in order to reach that enrollment; and (3) university support for the establishment of a center to link with the local black community and provide relevance to black studies programs. The first administration move was to delegate responsibility for discussion with the students to a special assistant to the president. An interview with this official was printed in the student newspaper before the demands reached the board of regents, eliciting a warning from at least one regent that the university must not yield to coercion by black students. This confusion in the locus of decision making and the complex relationships among the regents, the administration, and the BAM students existed throughout the confrontation, and tends to be usual in university cases.

The university first offered a series of unilateral proposals only partly responsive to the BAM demands, emphasizing programs already formulated and progress already made. These were couched in general terms as programs for the disadvantaged, and seemed to ignore the legitimacy of the BAM demands as specifically related to black students' interests and needs. It also appeared that the university was responding to BAM, not as a special group with legitimate grievances, but as another student group making demands of the institution. These approaches tended to play down the racial nature of the situation.

Although informal support from the predominantly white student body and from some faculty had already been evidenced, in early March the official student government body joined the BAM protest. The most important addition to the BAM ranks came when black faculty and staff joined BAM and helped in redefining specific goals. Black student representatives and faculty members spoke at a mid-March meeting of the board of regents urging serious consideration of the BAM demands, called that day for a student strike, and asked for white student support. The regents met in closed session on March 19, passed a resolution committing the university to doubling the number of black students to 7 percent of the student body with a general goal of 10 percent, and responded to some of the funding items as well. These offers were considered to be inadequate by BAM and the student strike proceeded.

Within the next week the strike gained considerable support from students, teaching fellows, and some faculty. Some university departments and offices closed in support of the BAM students. On March 24, over 1,000 persons participated in a BAM march. Strike support from the unionized nonacademic service workers (AFSCME) was enlisted, particularly those serving meals in the residence halls, with the BAM students providing coffee and doughnut breakfasts and sandwich lunches to the students in the dorms.

By March 26, 75 percent of the students in the Literature, Science, and Arts School were not attending classes and daily rallies and marches through several selected buildings disrupted classes. Faculty members were severely divided by the issues and tactics; a majority seemed to be sympathetic to the issues but were concerned about standards of admissions and performance. The disturbances in halls, which made it difficult to conduct classes, were seen by many teachers as a violation of student and faculty rights, as well as unbecoming to a university community.

The strike was under the direction and control of BAM leaders and black faculty. At each noontime rally white students were told that the tactics were to be nonviolent and were to be determined by BAM. It is significant that this direction was accepted by the large numbers of white students who were striking in support of BAM demands and that there was little destructive activity throughout the nine days of the strike.

The university president met at various times with the regents and academic deans and indicated his willingness to meet with BAM leaders to discuss their demands. BAM's insistence on a *mea culpa* statement from the president and his repudiation of the regents' position prevented direct negotiations for a period.

Finally, a meeting between BAM and the president occurred on March 26 and two days later, seven hours of negotiations between BAM and university administrators led to an announcement by the president that each department had pledged itself to a funding for a 10 percent black enrollment by 1973-74. On the first of April, after several more negotiating sessions, the agreement with the regents was announced and accepted by BAM at a meeting at which only BAM students were permitted a vote.

In large part the agreement met the major demands of BAM for an increase in enrollment of black students and provision of necessary funding for recruitment and supportive services. BAM demands for a black studies center in the black community and for free tuition were rejected by the university as not feasible under its rules.

This confrontation was notable for a variety of factors. In common with many university situations, it involved the complete institutional structure of a university in which limited powers were available to the president. On one hand, program implementation, control of some funds, and the allocation of priorities rests with individual faculties. On the other, broad changes in policy and shifting of extra funds rest with the board of regents. The president of The University of Michigan views his role as that of a "mediator among conflicting and varied pressure groups." The role of the faculty was ambiguous. There were occasional attempts by individual influential faculty members to act as mediators, but on the whole, there was no real third-party involvement in the usual sense of the term. Some faculty provided technical services and even office space to the strikers. Others were so incensed at what they considered to be coercive tactics that they took disciplinary action against some of the protesting students. The faculty senate eventually played a role in persuading departments to allocate the necessary funds for an expanded black enrollment.

The fact that the university was part of a state system introduced a political factor, with various legislators threatening reprisals against the university administration if it yielded to "coercion." The protesting students found themselves carrying on "discussions" rather than "negotiations" with a variety of university administrators who were essentially not empowered to "settle."

The Michigan students were well-organized and had stable, accepted leadership and support from black faculty and staff. BAM showed a great deal of skill in maintaining control of strike activities and cooperating with the predominantly white student body. Occasional "trashing" actions by a small group of radical white students were repudiated and somehow contained. Police involvement was minimal, although the university schedule was seriously disrupted. Both sides thus "played it cool" and no real violence occurred.

The case is also of interest because the demands centered around issues that were of no immediate academic value to the members of BAM: opening up the university to *other black students*. Indeed, many of the BAM students ran real risks with their own academic careers. BAM members and some of their white supporters showed considerable imagination in bringing their views before the total academic community and relieving the level of sacrifice required from the protesting students.

CONFRONTATION AND CRISIS AT SAN FRANCISCO STATE COLLEGE

The story of the crisis at San Francisco State College is too long and complicated to be fully summarized here.[2] What is presented is an abbreviated chronology to provide some background for the interpretations and illustrations that are particularly relevant to the racial characteristics of the conflict.[3]

The crisis had been building up since 1967, a time when faculty and administration had begun to experiment with an enlargement of the roll of that urban college within the statewide master plan for higher education, and to develop a greater minority enrollment and a greater community role for the college. An early incident that illustrated the tensions building on campus occurred when black students invaded and disrupted the offices of the student newspaper, charging it with racist statements in a recent issue.

Tensions accelerated to such a degree that President John Summerskill closed the campus in December 1967 as he sought an accomodation with the increasingly militant stand of black students and a few black faculty. However, this effort was not sufficiently firm for the board of trustees; in February 1968, he submitted his resignation to take effect in September.

Conflict continued on campus and in May 1968, the trustees fired Summerskill and replaced him with Robert Smith. However, the conflict continued to grow to crisis proportions during Smith's administration. Increasingly insistent criticisms of the slow pace of change came from black students and faculty. From the point of view of the trustees, the militant rhetoric of instructor George Murray and other black faculty and students crystallized their discontent. In late September the board of trustees recommended that President Smith remove Murray from the classroom. Smith refused, judging that, "The polarization that we had attempted to avoid was now well underway: on one side the governor, Rafferty, the chancellor, and the more conservative trustees; on the other, the college administration and most major faculty organizations, with the activist students certain to join in, along with the minority groups both on and off campus."[4]

---

[2] For a full account of the confrontation, see Robert Smith, Richard Axen and De Vere Pentony, *By Any Means Necessary* (San Francisco, Jossey-Bass, Inc., 1970).

[3] This summary has been drawn from a case study prepared for this project by Curtis C. Aller of San Francisco State College with the assistance of Jack Alexis.

[4] Smith, Axen, and Pentony, op cit. p. 109.

On October 30, the Black Students Union (BSU) called a campus-wide one-day strike for November 6, 1968, to protest delays in the implementation of a black studies program. The next day Chancellor Glenn Dumke ordered President Smith to suspend Murray. Smith delayed in taking action until November 1, but then complied.

The demonstration-strike brought out many black and white students and closed many of the classes. President Smith responded by summoning the police and closing the whole campus for the rest of the day. That night the BSU extended the strike until ten specific demands were met. They centered on the rapid expansion of the black studies program, black control of its curriculum and operation, and the reinstatement of Murray. The BSU was later joined by other minority groups that were part of a loose coalition, the Third-World Liberation Front (TWLF), and five additional demands were presented to express their concerns as well.

Increasing violence on the campus culminated in a clash between students and police on November 13, a day that became known as "Bloody Wednesday" as students and police engaged in a riot and President Smith ordered the campus shut down.

On Monday, November 18, the board of trustees met in an emergency session and ordered Smith to reopen the campus immediately. At this stage, blacks were determined to force their demands on the trustees and the trustees were determined to defeat the blacks. On Tuesday, the faculty voted not to teach but to hold a convocation to discuss the strike, a meeting that may have polarized rather than clarified the issues. On November 27, President Smith announced his resignation following a 15-hour meeting with the trustees in which they had indicated that they were not prepared to support his efforts to conciliate the positions. Chancellor Dumke immediately appointed S. I. Hayakawa, long associated with the college, as acting president. On Monday, December 2, following a brief respite offered by the Thanksgiving weekend, Hayakawa moved to commandeer the strike's sound truck and suspend student strike leaders. Immediately a new round of clashes between students and police began and large contingents of police were used to keep the campus open.

The student strike lasted over four months and was accompanied, starting in January 1969, by a strike of college faculty and graduate teaching assistants. A new local of the teachers' union sought to press the college administration to meet student demands. The faculty strike occurred, however, after the failure of initial attempts to reach agreement assisted by the services of an outside mediator. The mediator, plus a local mediational panel, continued to work with the college administration and particularly with the trustees. An understanding was finally achieved with the teachers' union and was unilaterally announced by the trustees who insisted that the image of their sovereignty be undisturbed. The teachers' union by a narrow margin voted to return to the classrooms on March 5.

The teachers' strike was essentially tangential to the student strike but must be considered as a factor. For a time it strengthened the position of the students, providing both moral and financial support. Ultimately, however, the teachers accepted a settlement that did not include any of the student demands.

Mediational efforts to resolve the student strike had also taken place in December. The black outside mediator translated the rhetoric of nonnegotiable demands and of unilateral university decision-making authority into more academically relevant terms. But neither the trustees nor the militant BSU leadership considered the terms acceptable. Apparently, the intransigent positions of both sides made a solution impossible, although numerous groups of faculty attempted to work toward a solution.

The resolution of the conflict was difficult because of many factors, including the inflexible position taken by the state officials, trustees, and college president; the extended use of police; and student insistence on the nonnegotiable nature of their demands. By January, an even more inflexible student leadership had taken over the strike. A month later when it became apparent to the BSU that the positions of Murray and the dismissed chairman of the black studies program could not be saved and that amnesty would not be guaranteed either on campus or in the police courts, a more moderate BSU leadership worked out a final settlement.

Thus, throughout much of February, an ad hoc committee of the college senate unsuccessfully attempted to mediate the student dispute. But, on February 21, a select committee of faculty members and administrators, nominated by the academic deans, was appointed by President Hayakawa "with authority." After extended negotiations, and with the substantial assistance of the chairman of the mediational committee that had sought to assist both the faculty and the student strikers, the select committee and the BSU came to an agreement by March 18.

Although both groups had assumed that the select committee could count on the approval of their terms by the president, he at first evaded a response, and then finally, on April 12 in a news conference, responded to a question by saying: "I accept the substance of the agreement."

BLACK-WHITE AT DUKE UNIVERSITY

This case covers a specific confrontation between a small group (75 students out of a total enrollment of 8,000) of organized black students, Afro-American Students (AAS), and university officials at Duke University in Durham, North Carolina, a private coeducational institution.[5] The major confrontation occurred on February 13, 1969, when the black students occupied part of the main administration building and presented a list of 11 demands. The university administration insisted upon student evacuation of the building before talks could take place. The students withdrew that evening just before police forced entry into the building and clashed with some white students outside the premises. A long series of subsequent negotiations resulted in a very tentative resolution in June of that year.

While this incident is a single one, the case itself traces a long series of unresolved discussions and confrontations that developed over several years. The manifesto that black students issued upon entering the administration building ended with these words:

We seized the building because we have been negotiating with Duke administration and faculty concerning different issues that affect black students for two and one-half years and we have no meaningful results. We have exhausted the so-called 'proper' channels.

The central issue was the establishment of a black studies program, although there were other demands that included the percentage of black students enrolled at Duke, supportive services, the number of black faculty and administrators on campus, the establishment of separate black dorms, and the kind of education being offered. At various times the issues also included the treatment of black students by Durham police; the use of segregated facilities for social functions by administration, faculty, and student groups; the affiliation of the university president with a segregated club; and the right of nonacademic employees to a voice in changing their working conditions.

The demand for participation, if not control, in determining the kind of educational functions relating to black students was made in various forms throughout the conflict. These demands tended to increase as time went on. Issues such as police treatment of black stu-

---

[5] This summary has been taken from a case study prepared for this project by Jack J. Preiss of Duke University.

dents and black student support for the unionization efforts of black nonacademic employees helped to unite the black community of Durham in support of the black students' demands. The assassination of Dr. Martin Luther King, Jr. moved some white students to support the issues raised by the black students. The refusal of the black students to form a coalition with this segment of sympathetic whites is of real interest as a signal of their insistence on black identity and black control.

Pressures on the administration from the board of trustees, some political figures, and the alumni appear to have been a determining factor in the stance of the university president, who resigned in March just six weeks after the sit-in. In addition to the constraints on the president's behavior noted above, students and administration had widely differing perceptions of what constituted negotiations. The administration tended to be willing to *discuss issues* with students, but considered it inappropriate to *negotiate demands* with them.

This general attitude prevailed among the faculty in discussions with students about the black studies programs. Faculty members were willing to discuss the content of such programs, while the black students were more concerned with the structure and the degree of involvement and/or control that they would exercise over the programs. The ambiguous position of the faculty, its lack of power, and its reluctance to share the control of programs with students were further factors that appeared to make communication difficult and real negotiations almost impossible.

Complicating the picture was the establishment of a free black university, Malcolm X University, in the community. This was first seen as a move to coerce the established institution into more serious concern with a black studies program that would be responsive to the needs of the black students as they perceived them. The university did open and a number of the black students did register for at least part-time work. However members of AAS announced that they would also return to Duke and that three AAS representatives would participate on a faculty committee on Afro-American studies.

From that time until the end of the confrontation, black student-university tension declined. A summer remedial program for current and incoming black students was begun. The administration requested, and six months later received, a foundation grant to finance an Afro-American Studies Program. A faculty search committee with some student help finally chose an acceptable black program director. Malcolm X University continued and appeared to be developing, but it moved from Durham and black students at Duke had less involvement with it. White students interests tended to turn to Vietnam and national politics.

This brief summary fails to convey the degree of turmoil that developed on the Duke campus in the course of these events. Torchlight parades, picket lines, abortive class boycotts, angry charges and countercharges through the media, and the threatened use of police power were all a part of the scene.

The changing nature of the black student organization; the lag in understanding between administration, faculty, and students; the sense of isolation and alienation of a small number of black students in an ocean of campus whiteness; their disenchantment with efforts to change the institution; the growing demand for a separation; and the difficulties faced by faculties in determining their role in campus disputes were factors in this case. The relationship between the AAS and the nonacademic employees, including the students' efforts on behalf of the attempts of the employees to unionize, was somewhat unusual. It apparently served as a mechanism for organizing the black students, and provided strong linkages to the local black community.

The complexities encountered by an educational establishment that is attempting to respond to black student demands without giving up any of its assumed prerogatives are particularly well-illustrated by this case in which it is possible to analyze a specific event within a larger context.

ANALYSIS OF CAMPUS RACIAL CONFLICT

The Black Challengers

Many black students and black faculty members on university campuses feel a need for black identity. They deeply resent discriminations and feel a concern to eliminate them. Some students judge that much of their college experience is irrelevant to such concerns and that their university is falling short of its responsibilities for changes in black status. Thus, the black students at Duke sought to develop black identity through the promotion of Afro-American history and culture. They wanted power to determine their educational environment, to evolve an educational program that would "sustain the culture of black people and at the same time ... develop skills which will satisfy the needs of our people in a racist society."

There are important differences, however, among black students and black faculty members within a single campus and among the various universities. The concept of black identity is vague and there may be differences in the objectives, degree of urgency, and judgments of appropriate means to use in the commonly felt push for change. For example, the community-based black (and other TWLF) students at San Francisco State College felt more urgency and developed a much more sweeping set of demands than those at Michigan and at Duke.

The stimuli for black student objections to the outputs of the predominantly white university system frequently originate off-campus in the increasing black community search for individual and group identity, the concern of some black university students about their obligations to the black community, the inadequate elementary and secondary educational systems, and the uncertain prospects for satisfying economic and social experiences for black university graduates. Ultimately, black students object to the discriminatory patterns that they encounter in their interpersonal and organizational relations with white students, white faculty, and white administrators, and many prefer a group life together.

In each of our cases black students' objections focused on the university function of educating students. Specific demands related to the number of black faculty, the absence of relevant courses for blacks, and the need for a black studies program. A second set of demands was for supportive services such as adequate financial assistance; supplementary educational, social, and psychological help; and an opportunity for social interactions that were limited to black students. A third set of demands concerned the numbers of black students on a campus. Target enrollments that are substantially higher than those currently prevailing are established by numbers or percentages. When this type of goal is implemented, demands frequently are made for more realistic admission standards, more financial assistance, and more extensive recruiting efforts in which the university's new attitude toward matriculation is emphasized.

By contrast, in our cases there were almost no black student demands that focused *directly* on research outputs of the university (sometimes a major emphasis of white students). The emphasis appeared indirectly, however, in the demand for more black faculty and for black studies programs. In both cases, black students judged that research outputs are needed to make courses and curriculums relevant to blacks. They challenged university priorities and the failure to allocate adequate funds for black needs, but this implication was neither specific nor limited to research programs.

In these studies, black students emphasized campus-related and community-related activities more than research outputs. They demanded that the university channel a greater amount of its service resources to the black community and that it assist black students in *their* service functions for the black community. Frequently this thrust was relatively specific, and appeared in the demands of black students in social work, business administration, and psychology.

So far, we have been considering the general characteristics of black student perspectives and demands in relation to each of the three major functions of the university: teaching, research, and community service. In this, as in other sectors, black demands were articulated through an additional thrust, the demand for accepting the *separate* interests of black students and incorporating their spokesmen into the decision-making processes on issues that affect them. In each of our cases, no role for black students concerning university policies and administration had been organized or even contemplated until their challenges began to appear.

In each of these disputes there was an identifiable grouping of black students whose leaders presented their demands to the university. These individuals may be functioning as leaders because they proposed to their fellows a set of grievances or demands, even though they may not be officers to an established black organization. In such a case, of course, their constituency will at first be fluid and disparate and neither they, nor the university, may know how extensive or committed is their following. Their leadership role may have developed from an established black organization and their current actions may be a logical outgrowth of its perspectives, positions, and organizational relationships. A third alternative may be that several black student organizations form a coalition for the specific purpose of the confrontation. In any of these three alternatives, of course, there are varying constituency responses as the crisis develops and more black students and faculty are caught up in the dispute.

When black students and faculty seek additional support for their pressures against the university, they usually attempt to cooperate with white allies rather than forming a black-white coalition. The Third-World group was a coalition, not with whites, but of three minority groups: blacks, Chicanos, and Asians.

Alliances or coalitions of black students with one or more of these other groups may break apart and, therefore, the university may be pressed to deal with more than a single protesting group. The university may attempt to manipulate divergencies within such alliances or coalitions to weaken black pressures and to encourage alternate black leadership.

It appears from the data that these variations of allegiances and leadership can be understood as permutations of a model that identifies a single black position and that provides the strongest protest when a unified leadership has been achieved and maintained over a period of time.

The University

Obviously, the white university members are likely to see the institution and their roles from a different perspective than that of the blacks. It is, after all, "their" institution. An understanding of university responses to black demands should be approached from the self-perceptions of faculties, administrators, trustees, and white students and the statuses and decision-making processes that appear normal and acceptable to them.

The black students will probably have accepted the general symbols of the functions of a university—education, research, and public service. The bases for racial conflict, however, arise when these abstractions are translated into specific programs and in the black students' interpretations and evaluations of the institution's performance. The black students' perspective predisposes them to develop criticisms of the decision-making process of the university.

Each of these abstractions has great symbolic meaning in producing accommodated agreements within a university about its purposes, directions, and off-campus support. Consequently these differential meanings become bases for white support and for conflict between blacks and whites.

Education of students. As generally used, this refers to the intellectual maturation of the student, his development of intellectual skills, (including those that serve vocational ends), and his social adjustment as he prepares for an individually and socially productive life. These intellectual and social achievements are to be developed in an entering student whose earlier education and training is presumed to have had the same objectives. All of these projected individual and social attributes are intended, still symbolically, to prepare for consensus society.

Apparent agreement on this syndrome of goals, summarized by the symbolic phrase, "education of the student," masks significant differences of emphases and, indeed, conflicting values among the present participants in and supporters of the university. Each of these goals may be defined differently and assigned different priorities. But even the values and perspectives to which they are usually related are subsumed under a consensus that can be labeled as "white and middle class." Differences among these values and perceptions of education condition the racial confrontations between universities and their black students and align groupings within the university into different positions on the conflict.

Research. Even within the university establishment there is little consensus on desirable patterns of university research output and on its relative priority as compared to the education of students. Research, or at least writing, holds first priority for many faculty. This emphasis varies among departments and schools, depending on a discipline-wide set of status-determining criteria, but its strength also comes from the university "publish or perish" process of rewarding or penalizing, faculty members. A second set of different meanings of the research symbol arises from the distinction between basic and applied research and many faculty put the desirable emphasis on the former.

Conflicts and uncertainties about priorities and kinds of research permeate the whole university system. Of course, the importance of these output symbols and conflicts is much wider than the specific focus of our study. They appear in our model not so much because black students challenge research directions, but because research pressures strongly affect university priorities and especially the whole structure of faculty power.

Community services. Within the typical university system, community service is given the lowest priority of the three university functions. The symbolic, organizational, and financial support that it commands are largely committed to the status quo within institutions and society as a whole. University services improve the efficiency of ongoing organizations, and stress activities within a nonconflict consensus. With rare exceptions the life-styles of the individuals and the organizations aided by university community services fall within the white, middle-class standards.

Three curious consequences of these symbolic evaluations are relevant to our problem of campus racial conflicts: (1) the evaluative symbols are subject to substantial manipulation in whatever direction is desired; (2) they may continue to be applied even though the reality substantially shifts; and (3) the effort to retain any accepted symbolic evaluation may have urgent emotional connotations whether or not the reality has changed.

Some groupings of faculty, administrators, regents, alumni, and even influential outsiders give the teaching function the highest priority, and urge that the quality of that teaching be as high as possible. This position was a central focus at The University of Michigan in the early days of the reported conflict. But, although the symbolic importance of high educational output may be great, the reality of the educational development of the students at a specific university is a function of many things: the capacity and dedication of a large number of individual faculty members; an important set of curriculum decisions made by faculty groupings competing for scarce resources; a vague policing function performed by faculty and, incidentally, by administrators; predictions about the quality expected of new faculty members and those retained and rewarded for their teaching; and the resource allocations of deans, central administrators, regents, and legislators. Students and student organizations, not usually directly involved in the decision-making processes, have immense importance in the reality of the quality of student education. It is usually assumed, but largely unverified, that student quality, too, is under the control of faculty and administrators who adopt and apply admission, retention, and financial aid policies. As we have indicated above, black students in our cases challenged these educational criteria.

While the symbolic emphasis on the educational function of the university is great, in practice there has been a tendency to reward research functions and to assume that an emphasis on research leads directly to a successful teaching program. Student challenges were first made in this area, primarily by white students, at institutions such as the University of California at Berkeley.

State universities and public urban colleges are under considerable pressure to give high priority to community service. Not only may this appear to some within the university as a conflict of priorities, but the differing elaborations of this symbol can be considerable. At San Francisco State College, black student efforts to redefine and drastically elaborate its community function clashed with an alternate emphasis on the more traditional educational and research functions.

Despite the differences in university decisions and actions that have been developed above, there is sufficient consensus about the functions of a university and the way in which it should operate that it is organizationally unified when it faces a black student challenge. This leads us from the symbols and values that hold a university together to consideration of the university's structure and decision-making processes. Exploring the process of racial conflict requires identification of the spokesmen for a university response to black challenges.

Who speaks for the university and what are the wellsprings of his authority and responsibility? The formal authority patterns in the performance of each of the three major functions of the university flow in two directions, from the trustees down and from the faculty up.[6] The downward flow is usually spelled out in incorporation and/or legislative and internal rules, and is applicable to the major decisions in resource allocation. For instance, in each of our cases, the final enunciation of university policy was made by a unilateral trustees' resolution. In areas of academic personnel, policies, and performance, the authority role of the trustees is present but is shared significantly by organized groupings of the faculty, although the authority and organizational structures are formally the product of policy decisions of the trustees.

The faculty role in decision making in academic areas derives from two interrelated sets of factors: the tradition of faculty autonomy, which has a long and honored history and which is expressed as academic freedom; and the practical impossibility of administrative officers and trustees specifically directing the teaching, research, and public service activities of individual faculty members or of closely supervising the quality of the performance of any of these three functions.

Thus, there are two general sources of power and authority and two general roles structured into decision-making processes: the authority roles of the trustees, delegated through the university president to the deans, department heads, and individual faculty members; and the considerable initiative and flexibility exercised by the individual faculty members, their selection of representatives to the executive committee of departments and schools, and the formal structure of general faculty interests in a senate or other such body. Within these formal structures the lines of authority for policy and its administration tend to coverge in the role of the university president. His office reconciles divergent interests within and between each of these groups of trustees, administrators, and faculty. In this role, and in accord with his personality and that of the whole university as an institution, his style may also include substantial leadership in reconciling conflicting interests and in shaping policies that are congruent with his own values.

Each of our three cases varies from this general description. At The University of Michigan, the president not only had great talent as an administrator-mediator, but also had a commitment toward greater opportunity for blacks that affected the way in which he handled his

---

[6] As every study of organizations, and particularly of university organizations, shows, the actual authority flows and decision-making processes are much more complex than the outline sketched here. Differences appear within individual universities and among universities both as a function of time, of issue, and of personality, as well as of specific environmental contexts.

task. The role of the president of Duke University was much less elaborate and clear-cut. It appears likely that he called the police to the campus because he was expected to do so by the trustees. He never worked out an accommodation with the black students and he finally stepped aside before the confrontation was over. At San Francisco State College there was an even greater shifting of roles, both because the first two presidents were unacceptable to the trustees and because the trustees and the governor played important roles in supporting a repressive response to black students.

This model of university decision making does not include students, who have been the clients but not the participants within the system. Sooner or later the model must include student interests that have been incorporated into the formal structure of the university. But this is not yet generally true and the degree of student power to affect institutional decisions was—and still is—too sketchy to be significant in the analysis of campus confrontations.

This analysis, therefore, has used a two-party model: a set of university interests represented by the role of the university president which is challenged in these cases by black students. Although the university is neither fully unified nor dominated by a single interest, the responses, negotiations, and any possible agreement with black students are seen as having two sides. Three important implications can be explored by the use of such a bipartite model.

First, a negotiated agreement between black leaders and the president is likely only if he is judged to be able and willing to get the decisions implemented within the university. From this follows a corollary: before the president agrees (and applies) any provision essentially affecting others within the university, he may need to secure their agreement so that he is able to produce actions from them that conform to the positions he is taking.

Second, the coercive pressures by the blacks may have some leverage when they are applied to any part of the university. If they do not focus directly on those whose functions are specifically affected, there still is likely to be a transfer of these pressures within the system, usually by way of the president in his intermediary role. This, for instance, was a tactic attempt by BAM when they tried to develop a sympathetic strike of nonacademic dormitory employees. It was most dramatically apparent at San Francisco State College in the temporary mingling of faculty and student pressures on the administration and the trustees.

Finally, there may be extreme contrasts between the abstract announcement of symbolic objectives by the trustees or the university president and the specific application of these by the colleges and departments. Thus, although the authority and the decision-making structure of the university are centered in the board of trustees, in each of our cases the relations between trustees and faculty purposely are limited by both sides and operate largely through the chief executive officer. It also appears that the abstract and general policies with which the trustees deal do not encompass many specific aspects of the blacks' demands in the various cases.

Within the cases there are at least two modifications of our general model. In the San Francisco State College dispute, the TWLF group apparently intended to influence fundamental policy of the entire California college system and sought to obtain action by the statewide regents on individual campuses only as a part of a statewide policy for which the regents, and not the local president, were responsible. As it turned out, the final solution was limited to positions within the San Francisco campus, and did, in fact, involve the acting president as the focus of a campus-wide set of decisions.

The second modification occurred at Duke where the role of university spokesman was shifted by the regents from the president to a chancellor, apparently because of a disagreement with the president's policies. At San Francisco State College, the trustees caused two different presidents to resign and selected a third who could be expected to act as firmly as they and the governor insisted. Although this variation appears to have occurred at Duke University and San Francisco State College, it can be more easily handled as a modification of a two-party model than by the adoption of a different model.

Perhaps a more difficult problem is construction of a model that considers the semi-independent faculty role in decision making within a university and the relations between faculty and president. One may think of the faculty as a third force, that is, a set of organized interests interrelated with, but different from, either the administration or students, including black students. Under this formulation one could seek to identify the ways in which black students exerted pressures on an organized and predominantly white faculty, administration, and board of regents, and sought accommodated solutions in cross-coalitions. The San Francisco State College data can be analyzed within such a formulation, but greater insights are provided by treating the faculty select committee as an agent of the president.

Still another alternate perspective is gained if one conceives of the faculty as playing a mediational role between the conflicting interests of the university, represented by the president and the regents, and the protesting black students. For this approach it would appear to be necessary to distinguish between the formally organized and structured faculty and the involvement of individual faculty members. The role of the individual faculty member could well differ from that of either of the two conflicting parties. This intervenor role will be explored below.

TO NEGOTIATE OR NOT TO NEGOTIATE

The University

In an organized campus conflict, a university spokesman must first evaluate the necessity or desirability of negotiating with the protesting group. If a challenge can be ignored or suppressed, the decision whether or not to negotiate can be made on other grounds. But when the costs of ignoring or suppressing the opposition are high enough, the objections to and the difficulties of negotiation may be accepted. In this formulation it is not whether the university *wants* to negotiate, but whether it *has* to negotiate.

In all three of our university cases, the first response of the administration was to treat the black demands as recommendations that should be considered, just as other suggestions from students should be considered by university decision makers. The president at Duke University found the black student concerns meaningful and their demands inappropriate. At The University of Michigan, first the president and then the regents went through a process of unilaterally modifying programs and policies on the basis of the proposals advanced by the black students. Only when BAM, surprising the president, rejected the modifications of policy and successfully shut down the university did real negotiations begin. Even then, the regents and the administration were careful to phrase the outcomes as a set of decisions adopted by the regents, and as administrative rulings made by the president, rather than as a joint agreement between contesting parties.

Readiness or reluctance of the university president and his team to negotiate is also a function of the difficulties involved in the process. The president may be uncertain about the leadership roles of those demanding change. He also may doubt that they will focus their demands and alternate positions realistically and that they are sincerely committed to an effort to reach agreement rather than enhancing their personal and organizational positions as blacks.

Our cases suggest that the most important single impediment to a decision to negotiate with the protesting black students is the unwillingness to enlarge the structured and interrelated processes of decision making within universities. To admit an additional group into the decision-making process is to reduce the authority of each participant. In accepting the need to reach an agreement with the protestors, the regents, the president, and others must acknowledge that decisions can be made only with the concurrence of black students and their leaders. Similarly, the independent authority of individual faculty members and the organized faculty decision-making processes must be modified so that, on at least some of the academic affairs of the university, black student agreement is necessary.

The most probable university position is to insist that university procedures and policies are nonnegotiable, since negotiations would admit students into the decision-making process, and undermine the sole authority position of the faculty and administration. The conception is of a process of consultation in which discussions with recognized black spokesmen would be used by the university authorities to gain perspective and information to aid them in *their* functions of program development and policy formation. If the programs thus developed seem to have some relevance to the proposals that have been made, the university may enlist enough support from black students and others to weaken the coercive position of the black leaders. Indeed, such a strategy may hope to persuade some black leaders that, for themselves and for their cause, such a response is preferred to continued confrontation and conflict.

The Black Spokesmen

A first question for the black student leaders parallels that facing the university administration: Is it likely that they will secure agreement on acceptable terms, considering the preliminary university judgments of the coercive capacities of the black students and their allies? This question, realistically, is how much change can be hoped for through agreement now as compared to that which might come from the development of further pressure? That judgment, of course, involves the prediction of available pressures and their likely effects.

Another uncertainty facing black leaders who are considering whether or not to negotiate with university representatives is their relative skill in this form of interaction. Although it is one of the major, full-time roles for the president and other administrators, black student leaders may lack appropriate experience. One aspect of this problem is the relationship among the black leaders. For instance, at various stages four different individuals functioned as chief BAM spokesman at The University of Michigan and only in the last stages of the negotiations was it clear to the university spokesmen exactly who would conclude and accept an agreement. At San Francisco State College, neither agreement nor negotiation was possible until there had been a shift in leadership. This point is illustrated differently at Duke University where the AAS was effectively guided by an off-campus black activist who was their recognized negotiating spokesman in meeting with the president.

The next consideration is the relationship between leaders and constituencies including the other black students, black faculty, and perhaps their allies. Typically, campus confrontations appear without a formal, stable organization of blacks whose goals have included such confrontations and negotiations. There is a constant need to dramatize conflict to enlist and extend support. But almost always negotiations are carried on in private and it is assumed that they will result, at best, in agreements that represent less than the original demands. The secrecy attached to negotiations may weaken the support of the constituencies and a compromise agreement may be greeted unenthusiastically. Thus, an uncertain leadership may receive more continued support by assuming a posture of intransigence against what they have defined as the university's white racist positions than by undertaking the leadership risks of negotiations.

Finally, there is a complex problem of whether or not the black leadership wishes to insist that a position is nonnegotiable. Our analyses should distinguish among the various meanings and implications of such a symbolic statement. The possible meanings include the following:

1. To accept a compromise position is demeaning since it acquiesces to the white racist designation of blackness as second class. Such an uncompromising position is more likely to be adopted on the whole question of recognition rather than in regard to specific demands. The recognition question can refer to the "right" of blacks to define black interests without the manipulation of whites, to freely select and follow their own black leaders, and to manage their own affairs.

2. In some cases the term may be used to refer to minimum positions beyond which no compromise is acceptable.[7] Within the racial context this expression of a nonnegotiable demand has a deeper meaning than in labor negotiations. This aspect can be understood by recognizing that many black students are convinced that the white society is unfair and discriminatory. These students feel that only modest changes toward equality are possible in a university at any one time. Even the original black student demands may express the minimum changes toward the goal of equality that ought to be expected.

3. Finally, the term nonnegotiable may be used as a ploy to conceal an unwillingness to meet with university representatives. This tactic may be based on the conviction that a "revolutionary"

---

[7] This process of taking a particular position and then sticking to it without yielding at all is a familiar alternative pattern in other forms of bargaining (in some labor parlance, for instance, it is called the G.E. Formula).

black movement (in contrast to a relationship of accommodation) should be developed and that a pattern of negotiation and possible agreement weakens revolutionary development. The leadership group may have too little support to negotiate meaningfully so a gesture of defiance has more importance for the leaders and their black constituents than the meager substantive changes that might be secured through negotiations.

At San Francisco State College, the black leaders were unwilling to negotiate until the final stages of the confrontation when they judged that it was impossible to influence and perhaps negotiate with spokesmen for the regents. They also felt that community-based support would not remain sufficiently strong to affect the outcome, that they were unable to affect the course of court cases or the activities of the police, and that they were losing the coalition support of the teachers. On the other hand, the BAM leadership insisted on pressing The University of Michigan to a negotiations stance with their recognized spokesmen and on issues and priorities they themselves had defined. In a narrower context, the AAS sought to negotiate with the president of Duke University before they would leave the building that they had occupied. At Duke University, the blacks' off-campus advisor functioned as their negotiator to reach interim tactical agreements.

Negotiating Positions on the Issues[8]

Assuming that a negotiating stance has been developed between the black students and the university spokesmen, the cases provide some clues about the specific issues that are likely to be pressed, the general directions of university responses, and the priorities of each.

Black Negotiating Positions

The original set of demands may be similar across campuses because general trends have affected black students at many different universities. Additionally, these common tendencies occur because the original demands are formulated without consideration of priorities. Our case material, however, suggests that this demand pattern is likely to change during the conflict. Shifts may occur because the original posi-

---

[8] In the research design used in this study, negotiating is a mechanism by which conflicting parties test and modify their own priorities and refine their respective positions while they are assessing their respective coercive positions on each issue.

tions may have been established as rallying points for black protest rather than as bases for actual university changes. Also, such shifts may be the consequence of a greater participation in the process by additional black supporters including, perhaps, black faculty and/or administrators. Finally demand patterns are likely to change as the black leaders reassess their coercive capacity and their demands if their strength appears to be greater than they had anticipated, or, more likely, reduce them if the reverse is true.

The first formulation of black demands is likely to stress various aspects of the campus educational process: the demand for more black students and professors, more courses focused on the black experience, and a black studies curriculum. If and when negotiations proceed, the emphases on one or another of these demands depends on local campus circumstances. At The University of Michigan, the original emphasis on the number of blacks enrolled retained its high priority. At San Francisco State College, there was a strong effort to develop, and then to protect, a black studies program and its faculty. At Duke University, the focus tended to emphasize a need for black participation in setting up a black studies program.

Early in the confrontations reported in our cases, black spokesmen tended to adopt the demand that the black studies program be controlled by black students. Although such a demand did not appear at Michigan, it was expressed at Duke and strongly pressed at San Francisco State College. As the negotiators faced up to the characteristics of the campus and to the strength of the support for the academic tradition, black spokesmen tended to withdraw from such a flat position. In the case of Duke University, they ended with the position that an effective, relevant black program would have to be established outside the university—in that case, at Malcolm X University. At San Francisco State College, the substantial degree of black direction of the program was weakened when the students finally settled for terms that failed to protect two black professors who had played a role in its development. At Duke University and at The University of Michigan, the issue was not treated in the final agreement but there was, in fact, an expanded use of black faculty and administrators on such programs.

The demand of supportive services was less clearly enunciated by blacks and less well understood by university spokesmen. One element of this demand at Duke and at Michigan was pressure for separate social activities and a separate center. Faced with university ideology of integration and a hostility to separateness, this idea has been largely conceded, at least in the past, as negotiations have progressed.

Black students also demanded assistance for students who were having difficulty in meeting the academic standards of the campus.

This demand does not suggest a belief that black students are incapable of academic achievement. Rather, it speaks to the failures of the secondary schools to provide either an adequate preparatory education and/or adequate experience in a predominantly white environment. Since these distinctions are hard to handle publicly, there is less pressure on this point than on some of the other demands and the settlements in all three of our cases put little emphasis on this issue.

Increased black enrollment was included in the first list of demands presented by blacks in all of the cases. The degree to which this demand survived the stresses of negotiating varied widely. It retained its importance for Michigan's black students but dropped to a low priority in the other two cases.

Although each original list of demands is likely to include community-related issues, the meaning of these and the degree to which they are pressed are clearly a function of the type of university and its location. This issue was never given prime importance at Duke University or at The University of Michigan, but was of great importance in the San Francisco State College dispute.

The Responses Formulated by the University

The universities' responses to these black demands were affected by university judgments on the degree to which the demands were consistent with, or violated, the symbols of its functions. These judgments were developed and formulated by the predominantly white forces that currently affect university policies and practices. On every campus there was likely to be support for some affirmative responses to black demands.

As each of the specific issues became articulated and modified on the various campuses, some general trends appeared as the consequences of the relative coercive pressures in individual situations and of the campus attachment to general academic symbols. For instance, there might be a reluctant admission that blacks should be added to the faculty, coupled with an insistence that scholarship should not be dependent on color and that competent black faculty candidates are hard to find. Despite the admission that it would be appropriate to expand course offerings, there is considerable worry about the "propagandistic" rather than scholarly nature of black courses, and strong insistence that a black studies program should be available to and meaningful for the whole student body and not primarily for blacks.

If more black students are recruited, most university personnel take the position that additional academic help will be necessary for them. Indeed the area of supportive services is one in which black student pressures could make the most gains, *if* they were prepared to accept the terms on which university responses were predicated. On the other hand, separatist thrusts that have been noted as a part of the supportive services demands are likely to be widely opposed within the university, just as, at The University of Michigan, the demand for a black center was adamantly refused as its exclusively black character became clear.

Finally, except in quite unusual circumstances, little community service is presently directed to the poor and blacks in inner cities or defined as an urgent function of universities. Present service functions of the university reach quite a different segment of the society, that is, business, labor, and government interests. It is unlikely that universities will yield any significant degree of their resources to demands for reallocation and redirection.

Coercive Patterns

In the minds of black leaders the question of coercion becomes that of judging the capacity of the black challengers to hurt the university. In response the university judges its capacity to resist the pressures and to assess the degree to which it can hurt. This problem of coercion needs to be defined in perceptual, rather than in real terms. Except for important slippages, the perceptual position of each protagonist is relative to the other and they will be identified separately. A general black perspective may be suggested by the judgments of the black students at Duke University when they said: "The white people at Duke have not been educated ... [that] further rational discourse would not produce desired changes and that direct action was necessary ... Power concedes nothing without a struggle; it never did and it never will."

Coercive Patterns Available to Blacks

In the confrontations analyzed here, black student leaders commanded substantial black student support, which can generate social pressures toward a united front of blacks against the white establishment. Accumulated angers against all kinds of white practices that have affected students, their relatives, and their community reinforced a demand for unity and strengthened an allegiance to the leaders who seemed to be pressing a common black position. Such constituency support becomes a basis for substantial coercive pressures if black students perceive a serious discrepancy between university responses to black demands and their judgment of what the university should do.

Black rejection of a minimal university response can attract considerable nonblack support. If adequate support comes from whites and other ethnic minority groups, it can provide a "critical mass" as occurred at San Francisco State College. Some of these supporters may be organized whites whose previous disillusionment with the system produced a search for allies, but unorganized whites who have been alienated by the system and/or attracted by the issue of white injustice to blacks may also add their support. These white supporters need not be concerned specifically with the immediate demands formulated by the black leaders, although it is not clear how much sacrifice such allies will absorb before their support begins to wane.

Support from nonblack groupings has some coercive effect aside from the threat of campus disruption. Its existence may influence faculty members and administrators to modify university practices in the direction of black interests, particularly if black spokesmen relate to the abstract output symbols accepted by powerful university groups and translate their meaning to blacks.

Further coercive devices available to the black students include disruptions that interfere with normal university functioning; intimidation of white faculty, nonacademic staff, and perhaps white students; substantial reduction of the effectiveness of the teaching and research outputs of the university; physical interference with the normal procedures of the university, including massed picket lines, disruption of classes, and acts of sabotage; and destruction of property and personal injury.

Each of these patterns of coercive resources triggers reactions inside and outside the university. Although some of these university reactions affirm and support the student position, other reactions are hostile and reduce the degree to which coercive methods affect university policies and practices.

Coercive Patterns Available to The University

Some of the university's determination to resist black student demands arises from its objection to the methods employed or threatened and the judgment that the decision-making processes of the university are, or at least ought to be, rational rather than subject to coercion. Further, the university fears that any concession to such tactics will set a precedent.

There are also strong objections to demands that arise from substantive as well as procedural grounds. Large and powerful segments of the university judge that they have no involvement in the issues raised by black students, and are resistant to any university responses that might weaken their own positions, resources, and image of the university. In general, many faculty members in engineering, the hard sciences, and other fields perceive their teaching and/or research interests as remote from the current social science scene. These positions are reflected in the departmental and college-wide postures of deans and executive committees and in the decision-making processes of university-wide faculty organizations. Whatever their personal judgments, those in administrative roles are responsible to these interests.

Supporters of this nonblack focus, who may take an anti-black position when faced with black demands for reorientation of university functions or priorities are found throughout the larger community that influences university decisions. These negative pressures flow primarily through the trustees, whether they are elected or appointed and whether the institution is public or private. Trustees and public legislative and executive bodies may react to coercion on financial and racial grounds and can be unwilling to approve added expenditures for black-related programs or reallocation of resources if they appear to detract from their image of university outputs. If black students use disruption as a coercive device, the negative responses in the university and the community are likely to be more elaborately mobilized and more vigorous.

We do not suggest that all of the reactions, both inside and outside the university, are negative. On the contrary, black students have significant, if not overwhelming, support within the establishment, and need only to find an effective way to mobilize it. Many white professors, administrators, and regents are convinced that American society owes an enormous debt to blacks. If they judge that any part of this debt could be paid without the loss of university standards or reallocation of resources already committed within the university, many would accept and applaud. Even when some modest sacrifice of standards or resources is involved, there tends to be considerable acceptance.

These sentiments can be mobilized by using university symbols to challenge the adequacy of the university's policies and practices for blacks. Are the admisssion and retention criteria adequate to find and keep the best students? Do the courses deal satisfactorily with black characteristics, black roles within America, and white racism? Are the services for community development and adult extension courses really directed toward and meaningful to blacks? If these and similar questions are answered negatively by whites within the university and if the negative responses have an emotional as well as a rational base, the coercive power of the black students is advanced. If the black demands are viewed as calling for substantial changes in university procedures and functions, however, the affirmative support tends to be overwhelmed by strong faculty and administrative resistance.

Black leaders and students can evoke threats or actual suppresssive responses. Individual faculty members can fail or downgrade students, a device that is very difficult for any student to contest. Departments and colleges can use the devices of suspension and expulsion, which are somewhat more subject to review. Finally the central administration can use injunctions, or call in the police. All of these procedures are very costly to the student and some academics view them as too costly to the university as well. The more the university perceives the black student action as threatening, the stronger the pressure to counter with more severe penalties.

Just as students should calculate the negative responses likely to be stimulated by their coercion, the university is faced with restraints on its countermeasures. Some within the university may oppose penalizing the disruptive actions of black students and their supporters because they may consider them to be creative ways to achieve approved ends by unfortunate, but necessary, means. In addition, the faculty and administration may have difficulty judging how far to carry repressive responses without overreacting. The distinction between peaceful demonstrations and disruptive activities can become clouded and the university's capacity to influence police action is limited once it has appealed for police help.

University decision makers also must consider the degree to which student and community support for the strikers is increased in reaction to the use of police and the establishment of repressive relations between the university and its dissenters.

The police alternative response was used at Duke University and at San Francisco State College. Within a few hours after the AAS began occupying a building at Duke University, the president reported to the faculty that he had issued an ultimatum and that the responsibility for any possible use of force rested with the students. The faculty passed a resolution supporting the ultimatum, and pledged efforts to provide "justice and equal opportunity for all students." Shortly thereafter the police were summoned to "clear and secure" the building. Despite the fact that the black students left before the arrival of the police, the police moved against the crowds gathered outside the building and five white students were arrested.

In his study of this case, Preiss concludes: "The administration clearly viewed itself as caught between the campus community, and various 'outside groups,' including its own alumni . . . It took virtually no responsibility for the course of events, attributing these to such factors as 'coincidence' and the actions of others—students, police, the governor, etc." Preiss summarizes these pressures: "The more vocal alumni who labeled student dissenters as troublemakers and as threats to law and order . . . now found it possible to combine all fear and dislike of hippies, drug-takers, long-haired intellectuals, and black militants into one image." To a large section of the public, these groups merged into a stereotype of "deviant." It is not surprising that an administrative regulation was issued at this time that prohibited "disruptive picketing, protesting, and demonstrating" and "unauthorized occupancy of university facilities or buildings." Thus, when a rally of students from several campuses was held in downtown Durham, the Durham police, in riot gear, moved in and arrested 81 persons.

At San Francisco State College there were frequent clashes with police, some damage, and numerous arrests. The college's president, the governor, and the police force had resolved to suppress violence and the students and members of the local black community were equally determined to resist the police.

At The University of Michigan, the university and BAM were concerned about police involvement. BAM insisted that their supporters adhere to their tactical decision to avoid violence. The university president was also reluctant to bring the police on campus despite the urgings of individual regents and some faculty members. In fact, the probability that police might be used was an important factor in bringing both sides to an accommodating posture.

Changing Perceptions of Coercive Patterns

When black students initiate a confrontation with the university, their leaders will have a number of important uncertainties about support for their position. In addition, the original leaders may be supplemented or replaced by persons who may redefine the total situation, modify the emphasis within the general goals, or move the group toward different tactics. Finally, the original responses from the university side may be either stronger or weaker than originally anticipated. Thus, an alert black leadership can be expected to modify its positions on the negotiating process, substantive isssues, and coercive tactics.

Some black student leaders may hope that the university can be counted on to respond affirmatively to their demands, especially if they see the demands as being reasonable and as a step toward real equality. They surmise that the informal exploratory posture suggested by the administration will produce a university response that is approximately adequate to the immediate expectations of the black group. When the black leaders subscribe to this approach, the issue is not so much whether blacks are participating in the decision-making process as whether satisfactory results can be expected.

When these first perceptions appear to have been seriously inaccurate, a second stage develops; the leaders decide that more aggressive pressures on the university are needed to produce even an approximation of the black demands. At that point other perceptual problems arise in the interactions. For the blacks, the problem is determining the intentions of the university and locating the authority bases that will be responsible for reconciling their demands.

Black leaders' judgments of the intentions of their adversaries are affected by their whole life experience. For many black militants, the black experience has demonstrated that whites lack an understanding of black positions, are unwilling to negotiate, and adopt a superior status position. Others find wider differences among whites, and may hope for more affirmative white responses.

Also, it may be difficult for black leaders to locate the power bases within the university. They may face contradictory rhetoric about the authority of the trustees and the independence of the faculty, and be led to believe that all of the relevant power is in one place or the other. Or they may assume that the university president has an unlimited ability to influence trustees and faculty.

University positions also will change during the confrontations. There is likely to be experimental effort to respond within already established patterns and policies and to treat black demands like any other student demands—as inputs to be considered within the established, complicated process of university decision making. In this state the university position may anticipate modifying university policies and practices in ways that are consistent with the general functions of the university and its power alignments, and may assume that black leaders will not press further. Only when such an approach fails does the university consider more elaborate responses.

It may be very difficult for the administration to judge the support and commitment that the black leaders can muster. No past experience with the responses of other students on other issues is likely to be much of a guide. The administration may also inaccurately evaluate the position of various segments of the white faculty. It may well be that an approximation of black coercive capacities can come only after the process has moved from threat to action. Even at a later stage, however, it is difficult for the administration and its related groups to project increases or declines in the black position because each side is using a combination of subtle communication, understanding, and bluff.

The second major perceptual difficulty facing the university administrators relates to the drives of the black students. Administrators usually have had contact with black students who have wanted to be assimilated into a white-dominated culture, or with black students who expressed their alienation from white society in challenging and disturbing rhetoric whose real meaning is hard to understand. There is danger that the rhetoric will be accepted and the real meaning lost.

A third perceptual difficulty concerns administration judgments about the personalities of black student leaders and their constituency relationships. In loosely knit organizations there will be shifts among the apparent spokesmen for the group. It is difficult for an outsider, or for those within the black leadership group, to identify the relative roles of each leader or to assess their combined or rival constituencies.

Misperceptions serious enough to distort the judgments of each side were apparent in each of the cases studied, and complicated the negotiation process. For instance, strategically placed whites had difficulty understanding black strivings and commitments and, on the other hand, black student perspectives of university organization and processes were far too simplistic.

Arriving at an Agreement

The conclusions to the negotiating process in the three university cases we studied were quite different. At The University of Michigan, the resulting agreement included a substantial university movement toward BAM objectives. At San Francisco State College, the agreement that was reached with a faculty committee contained little of the major thrust of the TWLF demands and the acting president never fully implemented it. At Duke University, there was no formal conclusion at all, although the university adopted some directions urged by AAS.

One can explain these alternate outcomes as follows: At The University of Michigan, the two sides eventually appraised their coercive capacities, matched their relative priorities, maintained their constituencies, and shared the judgment that agreement was to be preferred to the alternative of violence. At San Francisco State College, the TWLF group seriously misjudged its coercive capacities. The president, trustees, and governor put a higher priority on the defeat of the student position than on reaching an accommodation with it. Students and the faculty committee preferred an agreement only at the last stages, although the president did not concur even then. At Duke University, the black students never had enough capacity to hurt the university and to force the minimum responses for which they were ready to settle. The university, moreover, was not ready to accept an organized black involvement in campus decisions.

From these outcomes, abstractions can be developed for any serious campus racial conflict. The prospects and the terms for a settlement through negotiations depend on how coercive positions and priorities are matched, the relative interest of each party in achieving an accommodated solution, the capacity of each to understand the position of the other, and the ability of each to carry along its own constituency in a compromise agreement.

For each side, there are problems in announcing agreement. For the university the problem is primarily symbolic, as the administration and trustees seek to retain the image of undivided authority and accept terms that have been decided only by joint action. For the black students the announcement problem involves the need to relate to their constituencies and possibly to their allies, and to preserve their leadership positions. The University of Michigan handled this problem most elaborately. The regents made an announcement that assumed their continued unilateral authority; the faculty announced policy changes that it had long supported; the president spelled out substantial administrative changes; the black leaders announced a negotiated victory!

Third-Party Intervention

The contrasts among our three cases provide some clues about the potential for useful third-party intervention. At The University of Michigan, no off-campus or faculty person played a significant mediational role in a conflict that ended in agreement. At San Francisco State College, a preliminary effort by an important out-of-town black to aid in the resolution of the bitter conflict was finally abandoned. Later, with the help of a local bishop, a duly constituted faculty committee reached an understanding with TWLF spokesmen on terms. At Duke University, an off-campus black leader interpreted black positions to the university administration and advised black students as they sought to press their demands. There, also, a formally organized faculty committee played a major role in developing programs of changes, but could not get agreement on them from either the administration or the black students.

The first general proposition that appears to emerge from these cases is that an off-campus third party may be of limited usefulness. Neither side is receptive, each for its own reasons. University spokesmen may feel that they have the necessary skills, that they know their own positions, and that an outsider can contribute nothing to the situation. Further, they may believe that the process of developing each stance of the president involves many internal moves that the intervenor cannot undertake.

Black leaders may be suspicious of anyone who fails to support their general perspectives completely, and may reject an off-campus person who is acceptable to the university. Or they may think that no outsider could understand their positions as well as they do. Their inexperience with negotiations may promote a distrust of the whole process and of the complicated role of the third party.

The second general problem of the acceptability of a possible third-party intervenor involves his stance in relation to the parties. In making their demands, the students are insisting on a separate role within the decision-making process. If the university is not prepared to accept black leaders as the spokesmen for black student interests, the original deadlock may turn on the issue of recognition. Built into that position is the question of university acceptance of *negotiations* rather than *consultations* with the black protestors. It may be that a successful intervenor must believe that the university has a need to recognize *and* negotiate with the challengers. To some degree, then, a third-party intervenor who is more likely to be helpful to the two parties will have to be *non*-neutral on the question of recognition.

These stumbling blocks do not rule out the possibility that an intervenor might be able to help the parties reach an agreement, if he understands their relevance to the specific case and if the parties wish his assistance. There are a variety of ways in which misperceptions may interfere with agreement, and result in misunderstandings of the internal dynamics of each side's respective positions, relative power potentials, and relative priorities. If the intervenor could improve the accuracy of the perceptions of each party, he could be of service to both and he could also aid those who have little experience or skill with negotiations. In addition, he might perform a number of other functions: the mediator could provide the mechanisms for negotiations and some imaginative new approaches toward agreement; he could even assume the responsibility for a settlement, and thus save leadership prestige for those on one or both sides. Fundamentally, in order to deal with the position of the two sides, the potential intervenor must recognize the black leaders as spokesmen for interests that the blacks insist should be built into university decisions.

Faculty Members as Intervenors

Finally, faculty members could serve as intervenors. There were striking differences in faculty roles among our three cases. At Michigan, the organized faculty finally accepted an obligation to modify departmental and school budgets, and cleared the way for a larger financial commitment by the university to support expanded black enrollment. BAM effectively used black faculty members to help guide and assist the black effort. This supportive action was also joined by a small white "radical faculty" group.

The Duke case shows that faculty roles can vary with circumstances. At different times the faculty committee was the principle university group dealing with the AAS, the mediator in a disciplinary action situation, and the developer of a black studies program.

At San Francisco State College, faculty roles also changed with the situation. Under the earlier presidents the organized faculty participated in the development of black studies programs. Subsequently, the independently organized faculty union used its bargaining weight for changes demanded by the TWLF coalition, as well as for their own salary and other faculty issues. This effort was finally abandoned as the teachers' union reached a bargaining agreement with the administration on their own issues without including a settlement of the issues posed by the TWLF group. Finally, a faculty committee, formally appointed by the regular faculty machinery, secured the authorization of the acting president and negotiated a set of terms with the TWLF group, which were more or less put into effect by the president, even though he never acknowledged that his decisions were a result of a negotiated bargain.

Faculty members played a number of alternative roles in these racial conflicts. The BAM case suggests the supportive role that individual faculty members can take. Significant numbers of the white faculty dismissed classes in support of the BAM strike, and offered off-campus sessions or tutoring services to decrease the cost of the strike to the student participants. Black faculty members can also become advisors to the student leaders and even spokesmen for a black position. Obviously, other individual faculty members can play similar roles on the administration side of the conflict.

A different role can be played by an organized faculty, independent of the administration, to support the black position. The experience at San Francisco State College suggests that an organized faculty can cooperate with, but not be subservient to, black positions, and that an organized faculty, independent of the administration, can participate in what could become three-way bargaining. On the other hand, The University of Michigan case illustrates how organized faculty can participate in university decisions and thus be represented at the bargaining table by the president who, at the same time, is also representing the trustees.

RESULTS

Within recent years, various predominantly white universities have expanded their efforts to attract black faculty and students and have initiated black studies programs. In many cases, these efforts were not preceded by either elaborate confrontations or formal negotiations with black students. However, it is probable that our cases indicate that widespread black student dissatisfaction contributed to this redirection and change in university policies and practices. Such a speculative conclusion suggests the directions, and perhaps the limits, within which trustees, administrators, and faculties have been responsive to black positions even when little pressure was applied.

The campus changes that developed from the confrontations in each of our cases were moderate. The limited character of those advances underlines the limited coercive power of black students and the strength of university resistance to more extensive change. But our data do suggest that some changes can occur when black students mount substantial pressure if they are also able and willing to translate such pressure into negotiating positions for moderate change and if the university is flexible and accommodating.

At The University of Michigan, for instance, the combination of black coercive power and the flexible responses of administrators and faculty changed the preliminary university decision to reach a target enrollment of about 5 percent disadvantaged students in four years to an announced target of 7 percent black enrollment and, finally, to a commitment to a black enrollment of 10 percent within four years. It was also recognized that this program was established while the university was in a bargaining relationship with representatives who were speaking on behalf of black students and faculty.

Whether such results of confrontations and negotiations are viewed favorably or unfavorably by the university depends on one's viewpoint, of course. Our data also reveal that a university can make only minimum modifications and no important changes if the black challenge is not well-organized and pressed. The cases show that forces within the university that prefer violence to accommodation achieve only a very modest change in its programs, and that they can also create a climate that does not tolerate vigorous dissent. Data show that a university that is flexible and willing to recognize black interests and independent black spokesmen can achieve an accommodation, perhaps with some disruption, but without significant violence by either police or students. A negotiating process, if well used, can eliminate violence even while motivations for settlement can be affected by the prospect of violence.

As a result of conflict, exclusively black social activities tend to be recognized and supported on campus. Perhaps most significantly, recognition of black identity and its distinct and important meanings for black students and faculty has increased substantially.

Although few ongoing procedures for racial conflict resolution have been established, consultative devices are beginning to appear within smaller units of the total university. Apparently, neither the universities nor the black students are ready to build a continuing negotiations relationship in which independent black student organizations would participate in campus-wide decisions about policy and administration.

Even universities that have modified their policies to meet black demands have indicated no willingness to accept black students into the administrative processes. At the same time, black student organizations have demonstrated neither sufficient determination nor sufficient stability to make such an arrangement viable even if the university were to accept it.

Even the moderate successes for the black students and the concession to change from the universities produced subsequent problems. If change came, it came only after an insistent black definition of black needs and it is not clear whether such changes will continue to develop if organized black efforts do not continue. It may be significant for future prospects that, in each of our cases, the ad hoc coalition that pressed demands initially did not develop into a continuing organization. Indeed, the incidents analyzed here are not necessarily predictive of future black student moods. At Duke University, Preiss found that, by the end of 1970, "many of the previously activist students have decided, either individually or collectively, to pursue rather 'straight' academic careers. . . ." The trend was noted by the off-campus leader of the Duke black students who was concerned that blacks were not pursuing their independence but were "moving back into the mainstream of white America." He deplored "beating a few verbal drums and then going 'back to business as usual.'"

Black Administrative Officers

An alternative pattern that may develop following racial conflict and subsequent campus negotiations, affects the role of black administrators. We can only speculate about its significance since it was not directly in the focus of our studies.

Even before the time of the incidents under study, there were black administrators and black faculty members at The University of Michigan and at San Francisco State College. Their roles had already been expanded following earlier confrontations. At San Francisco State College, the fate of some administrators of the black studies program and some faculty members was a major element of the long deadlock. The TWLF Coalition failed in its effort to protect them. At The University of Michigan, by contrast, the agreement specified that additional black staff be hired for recruiting and counseling. Although not stipulated in the agreement with BAM, more were added later in other administrative posts. At Duke University, black administrators have been added even though there was no agreement on this point during the conflict.

Our speculation concerns two aspects of such developments: the role of black administrators when conflict develops and the degree to which black administrators can build on an earlier conflict and play a black role in changing policies and practices within a campus. During periods of social conflict, the white administrators who appointed the black administrator may consider that he understands the perspectives of black students and is able to communicate with them. He, himself, may also feel that he is committed to blackness and is able to understand and communicate with black students. However, there is the question of whether black students perceive him as black since they have not selected him and he is not organizationally responsible to them for his actions.

In each of the three cases, some university administrators and faculty inaccurately perceived the roles of the black administrators. They appear to have assumed that black university professionals could and would define black student positions accurately, could develop programs that were acceptable to blacks, and could communicate to black students about the organizational complexities that hindered actions toward the resolution of demands. Yet, at none of the three campuses could blacks already within the establishment play such an extensive role. At Duke University, the single black faculty member had less contact with the black students and less opportunity to reshape university programs than was necessary to anticipate the conflict. At The University of Michigan, black faculty and administrators were not producing results that were satisfactory to students, nor were they in a position to convince them that the institution was really responsive to black needs. However, the active involvement of the black faculty in the strategy sessions of black students and in chairing and speaking at the daily information meetings gave the black student challenge a high degree of legitimacy. In the earlier stages of the conflict at San Francisco State College, black staff members played important roles in developing black programs within the institution. Before the confrontation was concluded, however, only those whose activities allied them with the students against the college position retained unqualified student confidence.

These data suggest that, if and when racial tension on a campus builds toward a confrontation, black administrators are unlikely to head it off and may not even serve as a communications link between students and the central administration. However, in more stable times on campuses, black administrators can perform a variety of important functions. They can play a role in the administration of any new, black-related policies; they can explore the possibilities of new, expanded black programs and can participate in their administration; they can expand the perspectives of white administrators and faculty about black needs; they can build relationships between the campus and the black communities to which the campus might relate; they can attempt to moderate white racist tendencies in the administration, faculty, and student body; they can contribute to the building of black identity.

We did not collect data concerning the black administrator's dual role in relating to blackness and to administrative policies. Obviously, the problem is not peculiar to this particular campus situation. But duality of loyalties and roles poses questions about the eventual consequences of conflicts that bring about an expansion of the number and responsibilities of individual black administrators and faculty without the backing or the control of an ongoing black student organization. The spectre of co-optation looms here as it does in other areas where blacks are added to the staff and where the institution remains predominantly white.

In summary, the development and the resolution of a racial crisis on a university campus appears to be shaped largely by the strength and the determination of the black students and the effectiveness of the president in adjusting many conflicting educational pressures. The students may be so weak or so divided that they fail to make any impact, or they may be strong enough and have enough allies to achieve at least modest gains. The president may be too weak to achieve common university positions or so authoritarian that he imposes his own answers to the challenges. Alternatively, he may be sufficiently committed and skilled to bring about a resolution toward desired ends. In some cases, he may welcome the appearance of such black challenges because they demonstrate to other segments of the university and to the community the need for change.

CHAPTER 5

Public Schools

Confrontations involving public school systems display the widest variety of potentially conflicting relationships of any institution included in this study. In a typical multiunit public school system, parties to the conflict may include state boards of education and their administrators; local school boards; system-wide school administrators; local administrators (and their unions and/or professional associations); teachers (and their unions and/or professional associations); parents; and students. In some large cities, teacher aides or teaching assistants are also emerging as a force. Private organizations such as the American Civil Liberties Union (ACLU) or public education associations may also be involved. Finally, in some situations, a set of federal administrators deals primarily with finances and/or matters of desegregation or integration. This broad spectrum is also true of the issues, which may range from the food or service provided in a school cafeteria to the kind of education that is provided for the students.

Confrontations within the public school system have been numerous, particularly at the high school level. Many studies of these problems have been concerned with the degree to which the schools are performing or failing to perform their professed function of educating students. Other analyses focus on professional standards and criteria, internal structures, financing, and integration goals of one or another group or political unit. We considered these studies and issues as we

114 *Racial Negotiations*

interpreted the specialized meanings of the racial characteristics of some confrontations in public schools.

The cases included in this study were limited to the role of black pupils and/or black parents and community as they challenged elements of the educational establishment. Our study examines the nature of their protests and the efforts they mounted to get changes. But even before we examine the data presented by the case summaries that follow, it will be helpful to describe the general characteristics of school systems.

BACKGROUND

The essential structure of public school systems is hierarchical and authoritarian and pressures to keep it this way are exceedingly strong. The curriculum is established by state boards of education and is implemented at the local community level by administrators and teachers in accordance with those requirements. Although there may be considerable flexibility for the city boards, their guidelines are laid down by the state.

Many of these requirements were established in the general push for professionalization of education. Additionally, various teacher organizations, including unions, have worked to set rules that protect the teachers' tenure from the vagaries of local community feelings. It is assumed that such controls will operate to ensure that each child will be afforded essentially the same educational opportunities anywhere in the state and that the basic decisions about the educational process are best made by those who are professionally trained. State laws and a state educational administration are developed for and by the professional educational establishment: the schools of education, and educational administrators, and the teachers. Lay involvement is channeled through the activities of the local school boards, usually elective, which operate for an entire city rather than for specific parts of the community. These city boards have been conditioned to permit the professional administrators and teachers to perform the educational function and to shield them from the pressures of laymen who may be pressing for either specialized forms of education or for the development and application of different evaluative criteria on the educational performance of the schools.

In general, students and their parents have little or no involvement in the decisions that are made about the process of education. Thus, educational organizations are essentially service units that do not select their clients, yet whose clients cannot refuse to participate. Until recently, it was more or less assumed that the schools were performing the service for which they were established and that individual failures within the system were caused by students who were not adequate to the tasks set before them. These inadequacies were assumed to be either inherent within the student or the result of home environments. Accountability for failure by the school, the professionals, and the educational process is only beginning to be seriously entertained. However, there is much disagreement about the desirable educational goals for which schools can be held accountable and how performance in relation to these goals can be assessed.

Thus, professional educators share a common perspective that the system needs substantial controls from the state, the city school board, the administrators, and teachers in their functioning with the pupil. Many teachers exercise constant vigilance to maintain their authority over students in the classroom and to resist inroads on their authority in the school from the pupils, parents, and administrators. Challenges to this view have come from various community organizations, parents, and students. These challenges are found in schools that are all white, all black, and integrated. They may arise from an objection to the authority structure of the school; they may be sparked by challenges to the educational criteria or methods being used by the professionals; they may derive from different generational perspectives. Our particular concern has been with those situations in which the racial factors have been strong.

The data for the speculative generalizations of this chapter were gathered by studying seven different cases in large northern cities. Each set of cases covers a different segment of the public education system. One includes a group of four cases in junior and senior high schools in Detroit. Another summarizes a special vocational center administered by that same school system. A third involves a confrontation between the black community of a New York City district and the central city school board concerning an intermediate school. The last of the four sets describes a confrontation between one of the black communities in a large urban center and the higher education authority of that city.

The Detroit secondary school cases include confrontations between students and administration, with some parent involvement, over a wide range of issues: quality of facilities, quality of education, allegations of white racism against the administration and faculty, and student participation in some areas of decision making. The vocational center confrontation also was a student-administration dispute, largely over the issues of alleged racist attitudes of personnel, kinds of curriculum, and student participation in decision making. The students involved were older than those in the secondary schools. The New York City intermediate school case did not directly include student involvement except as parents in the community threatened to keep their children out of school until their demands were met. The community was concerned with the selection of a principal and the establishment of a community committee for policy determination. The higher education case also did not include students. It was concerned with the attempts of one of the black communities of a large city to obtain a city-financed college in its district and to participate in the planning, staffing, and running of that institution.

In one of the four sets, mediational efforts were instrumental in obtaining an agreement. All of the cases include some facet of the demand for community control and were confrontations between black clients of the public educational system and the white system representatives. The complexity of the public educational system, the overlapping authorities involved, the issues of professionalism versus community control, and the difficulties of making meaningful changes within such a hierarchical system are illustrated in various ways in all of the cases studied. Two of the cases illustrate the difficulties of unifying the black community and the reluctance of the establishment to accept and legitimize representatives selected by the black community.

DETROIT SECONDARY SCHOOLS

Because of the range of issues, participants, and institutional structures involved, this summary synthesizes reports on a series of case studies of four junior and senior high schools in Detroit.[1] In-depth analysis was sacrificed to get a sample of the confrontations that are occurring within the public school system. The confrontations selected for inclusion in our study took place in either of two kinds of schools: (1) schools serving areas that have been predominantly black over a long period of time, or (2) schools serving areas that have undergone radical changes in racial composition within a relatively short time period.

---

[1] This summary has been taken from a case study prepared for this project by Arthur E. Antisdel of Wayne State University and Donald J. Roberts of the Neighborhood Service Organization, Detroit.

A series of confrontations and limited kinds of negotiations occurred as students and/or community groups attempted to force administrative attention to a set of grievances within each of the specific schools. The range of grievances was wide, including such things as the physical plants available to black schools, the quality of food in cafeterias, the kind of curriculum, the quality of teaching, the characteristics of administrative and teaching personnel, and disciplinary procedures. Specific grievances also appeared to relate to the right of the students, parents, and/or community to have a voice in the affairs of the school. In general, these issues seemed to stem from the feeling of the schools' clienteles that the educational institutions were serving them badly, whether it be in the quality of the food served in the cafeteria or in the quality of the education offered in the classroom.

By late 1967, the composition of the student body of "Detroit HS" (the composite case) had become about 80 percent black, reflecting the changing residential pattern of the neighborhood. The principal and assistant principal were both white; there was one black counselor and a handful of black teachers; the school plant was relatively old and badly in need of repair. Relationships between white and black students had been deteriorating and reflected the kinds of relationships found in changing urban areas. The school had been the scene of frequent episodes between black and white students and between students (primarily black) and faculty and administration for several years. On several occasions, it had been necessary to obtain police protection at Detroit HS.

The school administration, through its Department of Intergroup Relations, apparently recognized the existence of the ongoing racial conflict at the school since one of their staff developed and planned a series of faculty-community awareness workshops. It was recommended three times between late 1968 and early 1970, that these workshops be held, but they did not ever take place.

During the fall and winter of 1968-69 tensions between white and black students began to mount and included an episode of hair snipping attacks on three white girls by a group of black girls in early February 1969. Several of these episodes brought two youth officers from the Detroit Police Department to the school on a relatively permanent assignment.

The black students formed an association and prepared a set of demands for the school administration. These can be divided into three general groupings:

1. Issues dealing with the physical facilities: cleaning and fumigating, cleaning the exterior of the school, and similar demands.

2. Issues dealing with student activities and curriculum: a program based on Malcolm X; relevant material dealing with the problems of the black communities; stopping the procedure of putting black students in nonacademic, noncollegebound programs without regard for their wishes or capabilities; black studies programs and assemblies.

3. Issues dealing with administrative and teaching personnel: more black teachers and counselors; a black principal or assistant principal; charges of racism against the white principal and some of the white counselors and teachers.

The black students met and drew up a list of demands that they tried to present to the principal. He refused to hear them; the assistant principal allegedly responded to the students by words and tones that sounded to them like "niggers" and "black bastards." Some of the demands were supported by white students but groups of white students and parents protested any more programs dealing with blacks, particularly blacks like Malcolm X. The school officially refused to consider the student demands.

A black student boycott lasting several hours was followed by confrontations between black and white students. In accordance with what one informant labeled "standard school system policy," the police were called to the school. Black students reported that the police behaved in a "racist" manner, using clubs and making arrests, primarily of blacks. Members of the central administration, black parents, and the white officers of the parents club took partisan positions and some community organizations also became active in the confrontation. Sporadic incidents of "trashing" were followed by suspension, transfer, and/or expulsion of some of the students considered by the administration to be troublemakers. When negotiations finally took place, the atmosphere was hostile. The negotiators for the establishment came from the district or central administrative level, rather than from the school itself. The students found their positions taken over by community organizations and/or parents, which was not always satisfactory to the students. The administration promised to look into complaints about the physical plant and indicated that some changes might be made in this area. Curriculum changes were not fully discussed, although there was some talk about special assemblies commemorating events such as the assassination of Dr. Martin Luther King, Jr. The students and their spokesmen found the matter of racist behavior and statements by administrators, teachers, and counselors more difficult to handle. There was little real discussion of these issues but investigations were promised and some changes were made. The principal and assistant principal were removed and a new principal was appointed but without consultation with the black parents or the students.

For a variety of reasons, there was opposition to the new principal and, in the middle of the next school year, he was transferred and another principal was appointed. The report notes that the third principal (although white and also selected without the involvement of the parents) did "what other principals have avoided for several years: He met all of the students in a series of eight assemblies ... Not only did he introduce himself and explain briefly his ideas on how the high school could be a success for all concerned; he asked for suggestions and answered questions."

The principal held "plain talk" sessions with faculty groups, and the local committee of the Detroit Federation of Teachers, and met, for the first time, with the school community council, which was a group of parents, community leaders, students, teachers, and clergymen formed to act in an advisory capacity to his school administration.

The 1969-70 and the 1970-71 school years were marked with ongoing confrontations. The difficulties of meeting various kinds of pressure in schools where there are black militancy and white racism are highlighted in these incidents. A number of questions are inherent in such school confrontations, including decentralization of authority within the administrative structure; the degree of community involvement in questions of personnel selection, curriculum development, and disciplinary policies; the faculty-student and faculty-administration relationships; and the development of procedures for handling student grievances against administration, faculty, and other students. In general when the parties tried to negotiate, they tended to engage more in cease-fire actions than in lasting conflict resolutions. Alleged manifestations of prejudice of whites against blacks appear to be central to all such cases, as is also the generational problem of student versus faculty and administration. The introduction of police into the schools in an attempt to keep order seems to escalate rather than reduce the conflict.

In general, the failures of the school system to respond quickly and affirmatively to grievances and the demands for recognition and participation has a snowballing effect that seems to lead to frustration and additional conflict. Perhaps more than in any other sector, cases in the educational establishment appear, even where negotiations are successful, to yield only minimal results. The institution itself seems to be particularly resistant to effective change when each level of the hierarchy is able to ignore, water down, or fail to implement agreements made at a school level. The broad questions of resource allocation, community control, and accountability are central to this difficulty.

DETROIT SKILLS CENTER

In some important ways this case differs from those centered in the Detroit junior and senior high schools.[2] The skills center is operated by the Detroit Board of Education but is not an integrated part of the regular public school system. The skills center is a job-training facility designed to operate programs in occupational skills. It has operated since 1964 and is administered by the Detroit public schools in funds from the federal government through the Manpower Development and Training Act of 1962. The Michigan Employment Security Commission (MESC) is integrally involved in its operation and the Michigan Department of Education, through its vocational education unit, also plays a role. Thus there is an administrative pattern of differential involvement of state-level employment security and vocational education staff with key operating responsibilities lodged in the local school system.

In fall 1968, a confrontation occurred between the trainees, represented by the executive board of the student council, and the administration at the McNamara Skills Center. The training program had been funded by the federal government and was administered by the Detroit Board of Education. That responsibility was shared, however, with the MESC, which was expected not only to provide the data on what training programs were needed but also to assist the graduating trainees in finding jobs.

At the time of the confrontation, the trainee body was more than 90 percent black. All members of the executive board of the student council were black and quite militant. The administrative and instructional staff was predominantly white and, in the higher administration positions, totally white. Although not all the demands presented to the administration by the trainees were based on charges of alleged racist attitudes or actions by faculty and/or administration, some were. Another demand was for the hiring of more black faculty and administrators.

Background

The few months prior to the onset of the confrontation were times of growing unrest among the trainees. Two years before, a citizens' advisory council had been formed to study the skills center and make rec-

---

[2] This summary has been taken from a case study prepared for this project by Joe A. Miller of The University of Michigan (currently at Pennsylvania State University).

ommendations for the improvement of its training programs and general administration. The council was a response to complaints by some trainees that parts of the training program were being poorly administered and that no good channels existed for trainees to voice complaints to the administration. Prior to the council's formation, a walkout by some trainees had occurred, but it was brief, apparently poorly organized, and failed to gain general support.

The result of the council's efforts was a report containing recommendations about most of the skills center's operations. These recommendations were so vague and nonspecific that no effective changes were made in the center's program or its administration. The report recommended a grievance process whereby trainee complaints could be heard by a representative of the MESC, but this procedure was not well-publicized to the trainees and did not become a meaningful addition to the center's administration. In effect, the report was soon shelved and forgotten.

By early 1967, the skills center administration encouraged the development of a student council modeled after the traditional student councils in public high schools and viewed in part by the administration as a leadership training ground. It was hoped that a student advisor working closely with the student council could bring trainee concerns to the attention of the administration and help resolve them quickly.

During its first year of operation, the student council functioned largely as the administration intended. Two factors seem to have contributed greatly to its success during this time. First, the council and its executive board were composed largely of older trainees, most of whom were black but not militant. Second, the student advisor during this period was a black male counselor who took great interest in seeing that trainee concerns voiced in the council were brought to the administration's attention and responded to quickly and decisively.

In early 1968, the skills center lost this counselor and from January to approximately mid-August of that year no new appointment was made. During the interim, this advisory function was covered by one of the regular trainee counselors who apparently lacked commitment to the task and decisiveness in dealing with trainee concerns. A breakdown in communication between the administration and the trainees occurred, leading to a backlog of trainee concerns that were not brought to the administration's attention. A general malaise developed among the older trainees in leadership positions who felt that they were largely being ignored by the administration.

Into this breach, created by an apparent decline of administration interest in the student council, stepped a number of younger black militants. A distinct shift in the leadership orientation of the student council and its executive board was the result. In the spring and summer of 1968, definite changes in the leadership style of the student council members were occurring and by the summer the council and the executive board was dominated by younger black militants who were determined to be heard.

In August 1968, a black male who had formerly been a counselor at the skills center was appointed as student advisor. He was strongly committed to the advocacy of trainee concerns before the administration, a position that did not endear him to most of the teaching and supervisory staff. The leadership changes in the student council and the orientation of the new student advisor combined to set the stage for the confrontation that began in September 1968.

Issues and Parties Involved in the Negotiations

By late summer of 1968, a sizable backlog of trainee complaints had not been handled by the administration or had not been handled to the satisfaction of the executive board of the student council. In September, the executive board presented the administration with a list of demands. The original list was lengthy, containing a number of specific items gathered by the executive board from individual trainees. This first presentation was coupled with a rumored strike threat if action was not forthcoming. Trainee demands fell into three major categories:

1. Revising the skills center handbook with respect to existing rules for training allowance deduction and docking for absences, tardiness, and visits to personal physicians; further, that the handbook incorporate clearly stated grievance procedures for trainees and substantially revise staffing procedures (that is, procedures whereby trainees could be disciplined or terminated for rules infractions) to permit due process treatment of trainees in disciplinary matters.

2. Redesigning the job training curriculum to provide better job opportunities for trainees upon completion of their program at the center; and involving trainees in decisions about the selection of new training programs instituted at the center.

3. Appointing more black administrators and instructional staff and removing five members of the existing all-white administrative

and instructional staff because of their racist attitudes and/or incompetence in dealing with trainees.

In the early stages of the confrontation, there is evidence that the skills center administration and the central school system administration did not take these demands very seriously. However, the principal grew more concerned with the trainees' unrest and more frustrated at his lack of success in impressing the seriousness of the situation on other representatives of the school system.

Through October 7, three meetings had been held between the executive board of the student council and representatives of the school system. None of these meetings contributed much, if anything, to the resolution of trainee demands but did serve to consolidate the trainees' determination to be heard and dealt with. The trainees were particularly angered by the fact that the school system representative was different in each of these meetings so that there was no continuity in the deliberations. In addition, the trainees soon became aware that the school representatives had come only to discuss, not to decide. The last of these sessions, on October 7, ended with a student council walkout and the subsequent announcement of a strike to begin October 14.

A considerable amount of behind-the-scenes activity involved third parties in both advocacy and mediational roles. A black congressman, influential in the Detroit community, was approached by the trainees with a request for assistance in getting their demands heard and seriously considered. The congressman, acting mostly through a key assistant, was instrumental in impressing upon the central school administration the seriousness of the trainees' complaints and their determination to see action taken. In addition, the congressman's assistant attended some of the negotiations sessions subsequent to the October 7 meeting, serving primarily in an advocacy role for the trainees. Another third party was a white member of the Skills Center Manpower Advisory Council, well known as a skilled mediator, who went directly to the school system superintendent to convey his impressions of the seriousness of the situation at the skills center. Working largely off-stage, he also began to move between the administration, the congressman, and the trainees, attempting to forge communications links that would lead to meaningful negotiation of trainee demands.

On October 10, the black deputy school superintendent in charge of staff relations was dispatched by the school superintendent to meet with the trainees' executive board and, if possible, to reach a settlement through negotiations. Sessions were held on October 10 and 11.

During these sessions the announced strike was called off and general agreement was reached on all three of the major demands presented by the trainees.

The Settlement

The negotiated settlement between trainees and the administration touched upon each of the demands:

1. The docking procedures for absences and tardiness were substantially revised in the handbook during a series of meetings between the skills center administration and trainee representatives. In addition, a grievance procedure for trainees was clearly spelled out in the handbook, with the final point in the procedure being the submission of an unresolved issue to a three-person arbitration panel composed of one representative appointed by the school system, one appointed by the student council, and one from the community who was to be mutually agreed upon by the school system and the student council.

   The white mediator referred to earlier was instrumental in bringing to the skills center a representative of the National Center for Dispute Settlement, an arm of the American Arbitration Association. The individual effectively explained the potential of such a panel for the skills center and encouraged its adoption by the parties involved. Subsequently, his organization also contributed to the settlement of the dispute by agreeing to supply funds to offset the expense of the panel's member-at-large from the general community.

2. An advisory committee on training programs and curricula was established, with representation from the student council, the center administration, and the MESC. This committee was to evaluate and recommend current training efforts and the installation of future programs at the skills center.

3. It was agreed that the school system would make all possible efforts to respond to the trainee demand for more black administrators and faculty, with the immediate appointment of two black assistant principals at the center. No specific actions were agreed upon with respect to specific individuals whom the trainees wished to see removed.

Although these are the major details of the agreement reached, it is important to note that only two components of the agreement were placed in written form. The revised handbook containing the negotiated revisions and grievance procedures was printed and a letter was signed by the deputy school superintendent and the executive board president in which they agreed to the selection of a particular individual as the community representative on the arbitration panel.

The racial character of this case is clear. Most of the student body and all of the members of the executive board of the student council were black and they used and responded to militant black rhetoric. On the other hand, the administration and faculty of the center were predominantly white and had difficulty understanding a black perspective. Many of the demands had a racial basis: the demand for more black faculty and administration, the charges of racism, and even the insistence that the curriculum do more than train blacks for low-paying, dead-end jobs.

The existence of an ongoing organization to formalize complaints and undertake negotiations with the administration was important. However, the failure of the administration to regard those demands as serious and to act quickly and decisively is also significant. Unlike many of the other cases, the protestors seemed better organized and better equipped than the establishment to handle negotiations. The settlement was complicated because of the multiple government agencies involved in the administration of the center. The transient nature of the student body makes the persistence of the demands and the development of the negotiations even more interesting. One of the major features of the case is the fact that a grievance procedure was established as part of the agreement.

The threat of a strike proved to have enough coercive power to force the administration to undertake serious negotiations. This was undoubtedly reinforced by the early involvement of both a black and a white intervenor, part of whose contribution appeared to be convincing the administration of the seriousness of the situation. In this sense, there appears in this as in many other cases the latent problem of recognition. The administration response in the first three negotiating sessions, with a change in negotiators in each, appears to have been the result of a miscalculation as well as a failure to take the student organization seriously. The further involvement of the black and the white intervenors in reaching a settlement is unique in this case. The fact that both were local men, with knowledge of the city and the personalities involved and expertise in the mediational area was probably quite important.

The agreement itself provides many interesting facets. A three-man arbitration panel was established with the unique feature that the third party was paid from sources outside the city.

INTERMEDIATE SCHOOL 201, NEW YORK CITY

This case is summarized more briefly than others in this book because it has been included in an earlier volume of case studies on racial negotiations.[3] It was used in that article by a black participant-observer to develop a particular position on negotiations in racial disputes from the viewpoint of blacks.

The incident analyzed occurred in the fall of 1966. I.S. 201 was a new school located within a black community. There had been previous attempts by the black community to get some assurances from the administration and the board of education that white students would be transported into the district so that the new school would be desegregated. These attempts failed and there was considerable feeling in the black community that this failure constituted a breach of faith by the establishment. This failure led the community to demand community involvement in the new school. Several community meetings were held and it was decided that the community would demand the appointment of a black principal to be selected by them and the establishment of a policy-determining community committee. They further decided that they would boycott the school unless their demands were met. At one of these meetings, ten persons were elected as community representatives. The board of education, fearing a confrontation when faced with the parents' threat of a boycott, elected to postpone the opening of the new school.

Subsequently, the superintendent of schools agreed to meet with the community representatives. For about a week, discussions, in a format that suggested negotiations, were held and resulted in an agreement between the superintendent and the black community representatives to replace the white principal; to name a black assistant principal as an interim principal; and to utilize the I.S. 201 negotiation committee as a planning committee during the transition in order to (1) select a new principal, and (2) plan for a more meaningful role for the parent/community leaders in school affairs. A school-community committee was to be established.

These agreements were later nullified. Both the board of education and the United Federation of Teachers refused to honor the terms worked out by the superintendent. Even the teachers—both black

---

[3] This summary has been taken from a case study prepared for this project by Preston Wilcox of Afram Associates, New York City. A more complete discussion of this case is to be found in: Preston Wilcox, "To Negotiate or Not to Negotiate," Part 2 of *Racial Conflict and Negotiations: Perspectives and First Case Studies*, ed. W. E. Chalmers and G. W. Cormick (Ann Arbor, Michigan: Institute of Labor and Industrial Relations, 1971).

and white—of the school refused to support the superintendent's actions.

This was an early attempt to establish some first steps in community control. However, the positions taken and the promises apparently made by the superintendent were overridden. Faced with the repudiation of the agreement, the community was neither sufficiently well-organized nor did it have sufficient power to require the negotiations to be accepted and the agreement honored. This school later became one of the three experimental community-controlled districts funded by the Ford Foundation.

A CENTRAL CITY COLLEGE SYSTEM

This case presents yet another facet of the public education system.[4] It concerns the efforts of one of the black communities in a major northern city to obtain a new college within a federated system of city colleges that would be located in their community and be designed to meet the community needs. The confrontation occurred between a coalition of black organizations and the central board and chancellor of the Federation of City Colleges. What is presented here is a brief summary of the events and issues that were involved.

Formal negotiations started in March 1968, and continued until the end of September 1969, between the administration and one set of representatives of the black community. Agreement had been reached on several issues at this point but an impasse existed on one central point. Negotiations were broken off and were never resumed with this first set of black representatives. Subsequently, in March 1970, the administration reached agreement on the final point at issue with a different set of black representatives. Thus, the total negotiating process covered a period of almost two years.

The city supported, with state and city contributions, a network of two-year community colleges and four-year, degree-granting colleges. A central board administered these institutions and was charged with the added responsibility of making decisions on expansions of the system. The section of the city involved in the dispute comprised approximately a half-million people, more than 90 percent of whom were black. There were also a rapidly expanding Puerto Rican population and a continuous loss of whites to other sections of the city and to the

---

[4] This summary has been taken from a case study prepared for this project by Donald Watkins of Brooklyn College.

suburbs. The educational needs of the area were great. One study estimated that 85 percent of those persons completing secondary school emerged with a general or commercial diploma rather than an academic one. Only about one-third of the graduates of the high schools serving the area qualified for admission to college under traditional standards.

Although the actual negotiations and definition of the issues did not occur until 1968, this large black community had made previous demands on the city's higher education system. As early as 1964, many residents, including their elected officials, had organized to request that a projected two-year community college be located within their district. The request was not supported by the major political figure in the area and was passed over by the central administration in favor of a location in a middle-income, white district. This district had considerable status and its supporters were more powerful than those mustered by the black community. A furor was created at the final 1964 hearings when a white opponent of the black community's request asked, "Why send students to areas of degradation and blight?" This remark was later stricken from the record, but the decision went against the black community. However, a small branch of the new college was set up in the black community; it accommodated only a few hundred students and was considered by the residents as an appendage rather than the college they were seeking.

From that point on, the residents and their organizations worked to get their major political representative actively engaged with them in securing a college for the community. They educated this representative by taking him on a tour of the community, pointing out their needs, and showing him a site that they considered appropriate. These measures were successful and by February 1966, they succeeded in gaining his support for the placement of a college in the area. Other important political figures were also convinced and the pressures on the central administration increased. However, in February 1967, the higher education board announced a decision to open another four-year college in a predominantly white district. This decision was appealed to both the board and the mayor but no change was made.

During this same period, one organized grouping within the black community moved to set up plans for a college that would provide two-year and four-year programs, innovate educational approaches, and respond to the needs of that community. They hoped to obtain private financing for this institution but this plan was thwarted by requirements of potential donors (largely foundations) that the funds would have to be handled by an existing university or college system. The board did take some limited note of these efforts. In February

1967, coincident with the announcement of the new four-year college, the board announced plans for an additional two-year college to be opened by September 1969, with no site mentioned. In the fall of 1967, the plans prepared by the community group were shown to the officials of the city university system. These plans called for an autonomous governing body and a two- and four-year program. In late November, the board announced its plans for the additional community college to be located in or near a poverty area, oriented toward meeting the needs of the disadvantaged, with an admissions policy that would vary from that of other institutions in the system. No site was mentioned. In mid-December, the chancellor committed the new community college to the area in question. In late January 1968, the board appointed a presidential search committee for the new institution. In early February, the plans for the new community college, described as innovative and community-oriented, were announced by the chancellor at a large press conference. Almost immediately, a part of the local community, organized into an ad hoc committee, took note that the decision had been made by a "white decision-making structure." It called for involvement of the black community and objected to the establishment of any such institution without such involvement. A community-wide meeting was called by this and other groups in February. Interest was high and, although called on short notice, nearly 500 people attended. Two staff members representing the chancellor attended the meeting, but were unable to answer many of the questions asked and they acknowledged that they were not authorized to speak for the board. As a consequence of the meeting a coalition which included representatives from a very broad and diverse number of organizations within the black community, was established.

The Negotiations

On the administration side, the search committee established by the board held its first meeting several days after the coalition had been formed. Its two staff representatives reported the proceedings of the community meeting, apparently without fully conveying the hostile tone of that meeting. The committee thus felt that here was some misunderstanding that could be cleared up if the community were informed about the functioning of the college system. They therefore proposed to meet with representatives of the community groups to inform them; to ask their views on college goals, possible sites, and selection criteria for the president; and to ask that several delegates sit with the committee as it sought a president. (These delegates were to have a nonvoting status.)

On the community side, the original meeting was followed by a workshop meeting that tackled specific questions and established a steering committee. Two issues were decided by the group at this point: first, that the institution should be a four-year college and second, that there should be community control. A later meeting of the coalition affirmed these points. In mid-March, the coalition representatives and the search committee met for the first time.

The invitation to the March meeting provided a kind of recognition since it was extended to the steering committee of the coalition and provided that they would select their representatives. The first meeting was attended by representatives from every organization that was a part of the coalition. Decisions made at this point were important to the rest of the negotiations. The coalition expressed displeasure at the procedures that had been followed in establishing the new college; and they demanded that all of their organizations be allowed to send representatives, and that the charge to the committee be expanded to include other issues in addition to the selection of the president. The search committee indicated that it would report these demands to the full board and committed itself to try to get the board to enlarge the five-man search committee to include an equal number of community representatives to be selected by the coalition. The coalition agreed to this smaller number of representatives.

The full board met on March 25, and the position of the coalition was transmitted to them by the search committee. The board adopted a resolution that expanded the function of the search committee to plan for development; expanded the committee to include five coalition representatives; and charged the present committee to inform the coalition representatives of the resolution and set up a series of meetings. Thus, the coalition had won an extension of the committee agenda and representation on the committee but the board did not respond to the two substantive issues of community control and four-year college. Coalition members assumed that their representatives would have voting rights, although this was *not* specifically conceded by the board.

The first formal meeting of the search committee and the coalition was held at the end of April. The resulting agreement on procedures essentially implemented the earlier resolution of the full board. Some items were perceived differently by the parties and were to provide some difficulties in the later negotiations. Specifically, while it was agreed that there would be five coalition representatives with an equal voice for all, and that there would be no unilateral action taken by either side, particularly on the selection of the president, the voting status of the coalition members was still unclear. It was agreed that there would be a governing board with community representation so that the community would have a voice in governing the new college. The composition of that body and whether it would be responsible to the full board or to the community were not decided. It was also agreed that the coalition steering committee plans would be presented unaltered to the full board and that the question of a four-year degree-granting institution would be explored.

The remainder of spring 1968 was spent by both parties preparing for the hard negotiations. The coalition held meetings, made progress reports, and elected the five representatives for the search committee. They decided that they needed to do their own fact finding and demanded financial support from the board for this activity. This demand was met later, although there were delays and some acrimony before a coalition office was opened at the end of June. The negotiating team was to have authority to act, but was to clear its actions with the steering committee whenever possible.

The meeting in early June established an agenda that was an essential victory for the coalition. The first discussions centered around the role and nature of the governing body and the four-year question rather than on the board's proposal of orientation to the nature of the community college system. Throughout these and later discussions, the board members of the search committee insisted that a change from the projected state-approved two-year college to a four-year college would require new and different authorization.

Meetings continued until January 1969, and a series of important decisions was reached, sometimes fairly painfully. Issues resolved included the site, name, admissions policies, and the kinds and variety of curricula. The issues that proved to be most difficult to settle were community control, the nature of the college, and the selection of the president.

Community Control

There were differences on the issue of community control within the coalition, ranging from those who wanted the city to turn money over to the community board to spend, to those who felt that the college would be inside the federated college structure and that representation was the best that could be arranged. Ultimately, while the coalition negotiating team demanded control and autonomy, the members temporarily accepted a community governing board that would have community and higher board representatives and as much autonomy as possible under the college system. This position was reached fairly early and was never expanded significantly.

Nature of the College

From the beginning, the community had demanded a four-year, community-oriented institution. From the beginning, the official proposal had been for a community college—basically a two-year institution. The official position was that funds had been authorized for a two-year institution and a change would require new authorization from the state. The first modification of this position was the agreement that the board officials would investigate the possibilities of including some four-year programs within the two-year institutional structure, even though there would be no change in the authorization.

Later, the original official position changed radically after investigation and the central board administrators persuaded the board to accept the four-year plan that they had earlier labeled as impossible. But all of these steps were taken unilaterally with neither the involvement of nor communication to the black representatives until the plan was virtually a fait accompli. The establishment representatives expected gratitude, and met anger and distrust.

GENERAL CHARACTERISTICS OF SCHOOL CASES

The Parties

The organization of public education ranges from the teacher to state boards of education, although most confrontations have directly involved an administrator and/or a local board of education. For the most part the negotiating function rests with the administrator, although his power to function with authority may be severely limited as is evidenced in the I.S. 201 case of a community demand for control. In many of the cases of student challenges, the organizational pattern usually calls for the high school principal to carry on discussions with the students. In the cases studied in Detroit, however, this was not the pattern either because the challenge was to the principal, or because the principal did not wish to carry on discussions with students. Thus, in most of those cases, the negotiator for the schools was at a higher administrative level.

However, the administration is generally reluctant to negotiate with students, and frequently views this as violating the traditional student-institution relationship. The concept of sharing decisions with students is not yet widely accepted and the existing gap is organizational and generational as well as racial.

In cases of parental or community challenge, the tendency seems to be for the superintendent and/or the board of education to speak for the establishment. Again, the concept of sharing decision-making authority with others is strongly resisted and the professionals tend to resist the lay community in determining educational policy. The I.S. 201 and the community college cases were of this order.

In general, the establishment spokesman speaks for those parties interested in maintaining the status quo. The predominantly white board, administrators, and principals and teachers, individually and as organizations, are basically concerned with maintaining the existing patterns of the educational establishment.

The Black Challengers

In the high school cases that we studied, the protestors were black students who were either pressing a grievance against the system or insisting on rule or curriculum changes. At some point in the proceedings, some parental or community groups were also involved but, on the whole, the challenges were made and pressed by black students within a particular school.

In the skills center situation, the challenge came from somewhat more mature students. The other cases involved protests by parents and community organizations formed into loose coalitions, as in the community college case. In each of the situations, the challenge was for a change from the status quo toward a relevant education achieved through community control.

The Issues[5]

Some of the major issues entering into school conflicts are:

1. *Reallocation of Resources.* The claim is made and documented in many cases that schools in primarily black residential areas receive smaller allocations of available funds than do those in pri-

[5] In this sector, perhaps even more than in others, it is important to stress the variable and changing character of some of the racial conflicts. Our cases involve black students, black parents, local black communities, and the formal structures of white-dominated school boards. We have not been able to include those clashes between white and black students and between white and black parents even though these now appear to be occurring with increasing frequency. These additional forms of school racial conflicts dramatize the resistance to change and underline the inflexibility of the educational system in the face of black frustrations.

marily white neighborhoods. Special federal funds have partially alleviated this situation but no major shifts of resources have taken place. If the funds are fixed, the pressures from white parents in opposition to any cutback in funds allocated to their schools are more effective than those of black parents in ghetto areas for an increase in allocations.

2. *Quality of Education.* It is alleged that classes are larger, personnel less well-trained and less permanent, educational materials less available, the physical plant less desirable, and the educational process less effective in schools in black communities. Professional educators tend to respond by declaring the students less educable, a position that angers many in black communities. Many black protagonists also insist that the professionals have not dealt with the identity needs of many of their students and, indeed, have exacerbated the problems because of their social perspectives.

3. *Black Personnel.* Black students and their parents place a high priority on increasing the number of black personnel in their schools. They insist that many white teachers are racially prejudiced and incapable of understanding the problems of black children, and that black children need the presence of black teachers to bolster their self-images and black identity.

4. *Community Controls.* The move to the concept of community control reflects a desire to have a voice in allocating resources and in guiding the educational function that has been so badly performed for black children.[6]

5. *Other Issues.* Some of the issues are much more specific and deal with in-school problems such as discipline, dress codes, administrative sanctions for black-related programs and activities, and the like.

Most typically, the focus on in-school problems and the demands for a more relevant curriculum and more sympathetic and empthatic personnel tend to originate from student groups, while questions of

[6] In none of our cases was there a contest between ethnic groups as to leadership in the challenge to the school system. In some situations, an accommodation between group representatives is reached and an ad hoc coalition is formed to press for changes in the educational system. In other cases, however, rival spokesmen appear, the demand for community control is compromised, and the capacity to challenge the system is seriously impaired.

control, resource allocation, and general quality of education tend to originate from parents and/or community groups. While they appear to be very different on the surface and have different sets of protagonists, fundamentally all of these issues stem from the strong feeling, based on considerable evidence and shared by students and parents, that the schools are unresponsive to the needs of the black students and the black community and must be made to change.

Coercive Pressures

The coercive measures available to the black students and their parents are limited and costly.[7] Students, particularly those from lower economic levels, are almost entirely dependent on the public school system for an education. Indeed, they are legally required to attend school and their parents can be held accountable for their presence. A student boycott may have greater direct disadvantages for the challengers than for the establishment that is the target since the black student will be disrupting his educational process. Disruption or violence within the school also exacts a high price from the black student since it includes the possibility that the protestors may face suspension or even legal action. Even for parents and students who consider that the education is poor, these penalties may be viewed as a significant sacrifice and may make it difficult to sustain the pressure.

Coercive student pressures, however, may embarrass school officials and even stimulate their concern for the student. They may also be unwilling to accept disruption by black students and fear escalation of the conflict and the consequences of using the police.

Parent and community groups are not, of course, so easily disciplined. But even these groups have relatively limited coercive powers unless an adequate number can be organized to put considerable pressure on the system. On the other hand, school officials have great power to resist student pressures by indicating sympathy with the grievance but pleading their inability to act because of funds, licensing

[7] Our case studies have not focused directly on the degree to which black groups have used political pressures on school administrators, school boards, and city and state legislatures. Nevertheless, it is reasonable to speculate that, in each of our cases, the school authorities were concerned with the political implications of the black challenges. On the one hand, it is expected that these political figures are concerned with retaining or developing as much black political support as possible. On the other hand, in these situations, each board and administration appears to be concerned even more strongly with white constituencies. The consequences of these conflicting political pressures and the organizational and professional characteristics of each of our cases are reflected in the interactions that have been examined.

rules, terms of contracts with the teachers' unions, jurisdiction of a state board, and other restrictions. The hierarchical structure of the system and the overlapping authorities provide fertile ground for buck-passing and delaying tactics. The system also has access to more direct pressures, including disciplinary procedures such as suspension or expulsion from the school or filing charges against the protesting students in the local courts.

Moreover, the school system may be subjected to pressures from other segments of the community to oppose the demands of the challengers. If the demands require a reallocation of funds from predominantly white to predominantly black schools, the pressures from the white community are likely to be stronger and more effective than those that can be applied by the black community.

However, pressures from the black students and the black community, particularly if they involve shutting down a school by boycott or by disruptive tactics, have the potential of persuading the school authorities to recognize and negotiate with the black leaders. A student strike threatens the image of success in public education that is so important to the professionals. The central board may judge that a long-term failure to operate a school in a black residential area would not be accepted by the community in general. Also, during strikes the board risks a loss of state revenues that are allocated according to a days-of-school formula.

One of the major problems to be met in school cases is the basic reluctance of professional school personnel to negotiate with outsiders even though they are clients of the system. Where students are concerned, administrators and teachers tend to be wary of negotiating because they see such activity as undermining the discipline of the classroom and the school and weakening professional prerogatives to determine the content and method of education to be offered to the community. Part of this resistance, of course, arises from the generation gap and a resulting reluctance to accept the authority of the school system and tends to be nonracial in character.

Issues raised when these groups confront the school constitute a fundamental challenge to the educational system and its definition. Basically, the black protesting groups demand the right to an educational system that *they* define as responsive to the needs of the black community. The resulting issues directly involve the central school organization and the interrelationships of local and state education boards and local and state political structures. For example, substantive issues of education, teacher assignment, and selection of principals and curriculum concern the unions of teachers and administrators. New building construction or school repairs involve building contractors, building trades unions, and business organizations that provide supplies and services to the school system.

The problem of professionalization is paramount and has increased the distance between the school and the parent. As described by Fantini:

> There has been an inverse correlation between professionalization and parents' involvement. . . . Even well-educated, middle-class parents who seek to engage in *meaningful* school decisions are deterred short of effectiveness by the inertial mass of the system or by the aura of professional exclusivity. . . . Most parents visit school only in response to trouble.
>
> Although, as suggested, the parent has never been a true partner in the education process, at least the concept of lay and local control of public education has a long historical tradition. But the tradition has been diluted and is largely impotent against the force of a professional monopoly.[8]

Fantini notes that parents are not ignored but that their participation is elaborately planned as an exercise in community relations to make the system work more smoothly. He concludes:

> . . . The existing concept of parent and community participation in education is basically misdirected toward supporting the schools' status quo.[9]

As a result of this process, parents have little or no continuing contact with the system and little expertise in how to make the system respond to their demands.

Disruption tends to challenge the legitimacy of the system. In discussing the education system as it operates in large urban centers, Hamilton notes:

> The important point here is that loyalty, allegiance, is predicted on performance. What decision-makers *say* is not of primary importance, but it is important what black people *believe*. Do they *believe* that the school systems are operating in their behalf? Do they *believe* that the schools are *legitimate* in terms of educating their children and inculcating in them a proper sense of values? With the end product (i.e., their children graduating from high school as functional illiterates) clearly before their eyes at home and with volumes of reports documenting lack of payoff, it is not difficult to conclude that black people have good reason to question the legitimacy of the educational systems.

---

[8] Mario D. Fantini, "Intervention Alternatives for Urban Education" in *Equal Educational Opportunity*, ed. Harvard Educational Review (Cambridge, Massachusetts, 1969), p. 245.

[9] Fantini, p. 247.

They begin to question the entire process because they are aware that the schools, while not educating their children, are at the same time supporting a particularly unacceptable situation. They know that the schools are one of the major institutions for socializing their children into the dominant value structure of the society.[10]

This dissatisfaction is the basis for black reactions to authority and discipline and for demands for community control of schools.

Negotiating Styles and Processes

It was exceedingly difficult for the black challengers to penetrate administrative barriers in order to carry on meaningful negotiations. In each of the cases involving high school students, the actual negotiating was finally carried out by a district rather than by a local administrator, and included some black adults who represented one or more community groups.

There appeared to be much fear that the traditional student-teacher-principal relationship would be threatened by student participation in decision making. In the skills center case, it took considerable pressure from the black congressman before the legitimacy of the student organization was recognized and negotiations began. In community-based challenges like those in I.S. 201 in New York City and the community college, many efforts and coercive threats had to be made before the establishment representatives recognized the legitimacy of the groups and the necessity of negotiations. In the first instance, there was some challenge to the process by which the negotiators were elected. Almost throughout the entire negotiating process in the latter case, the central board continued to question the degree to which the negotiators for the black community really represented that community. Agreement was not reached in that case until the original group of black negotiators had been ignored and a new group was chosen and recognized by the board.

Because of overlapping authorities, it is difficult for a protesting group to find the right person with whom to bargain. In the I.S. 201 case, the protest group reached an agreement with the superintendent of schools, but that agreement was abrogated by the school board. In several of the cases, the establishment side tended to bring in a unilateral plan, which presumably considered the demands that were

---

[10] Charles V. Hamilton, "Race and Education: A Search for Legitimacy," op. cit., p. 190.

being made, only to be surprised to find that the challengers were unhappy with the result. This behavior, of course, indicated that the establishment accepted a consultative role for the challengers but not their direct involvement in decision making.

Some researchers have observed that, in general, school principals and superintendents are relatively inexperienced in the process of negotiations. Broadly-based community groups and ad hoc coalitions allied for a particular school issue may also lack negotiating experience.

Results of Negotiations

Our data in this area are modest and our conclusions are tentative. Based on the cases that we have examined, it appears that it is possible for a black student group, particularly if joined by parents, to negotiate some changes within their own school if they are able to mount sufficient pressures to influence the central school board and if their demands are relatively modest. Because many student demands concern personnel and finances and because they charge that white administrators and/or teachers act in a racist style, final negotiations tend to take place with some representative of the central school board. But the changes that were made in the Detroit schools in our studies were essentially minimal and the structures and attitudes that produced the conflict remained. In 1971, some of these same schools were again embroiled in disputes severe enough to force temporary school closings.

Our data seem to indicate that exceptional circumstances are needed for a local black community group to negotiate even some degree of shared control over the educational policies and practices of a unit of a city-wide school system even when that unit is located within their own black community. The leverage available to black community leaders is hardly more than that available to local black student groups. In the I.S. 201 case, the black community was unable to sustain enough pressure to force implementation of an agreement that they thought had been reached. In the community college situation, the central educational authority apparently considered that it needed to accept the insistence of the local community and involve it in planning the new college. However, on a crucial issue in the development of the new college, the board decided that it would ignore community spokesmen and would work out understandings with others who were more cooperative with the board. This maneuver of dividing the black community was successful and the original group of leaders could not sustain their impetus.

GENERAL PERSPECTIVES

As we have noted, efforts of black students and their communities to force changes in school systems stem from widespread dissatisfaction with the educational quality of their schools and the judgment that the systems will be adequate only when black interests are met. Establishment response, which seems to be based on avoiding disruptions, widens racial conflicts. The structure of the central board, the external pressures to which it responds, and important internal pressures work to maintain the status quo. Fundamentally, the educational criteria on which the whole system operates and by which it is judged derive from a common set of educational perspectives that are strongly supported by bureaucratic structures and powerful professional organizations.

It appears highly unlikely that black leaders, who draw support only from limited, localized black community groups, can negotiate significant changes from central school boards. Central boards probably will not recognize such local leaders as spokesmen for all black interests and will not voluntarily delegate to such groups control over educational, personnel, and other policies within local school units. The current explorations of decentralization patterns in various cities do not seem to provide a basis for black community control. Even school systems that appear to accept some local community involvement also have many resistances and rigidities, as shown by limited experiments with local community control. Central decisions on the allocation of resources for instruction, buildings, equipment, and many other local needs are, currently at least, beyond local control. Also, the criteria for evaluating teacher and pupil performance are still beyond the reach of the local community.

Our data and analyses, then, suggest that change through negotiations provides a route for the *temporary* adjustment of some racial conflict but only within limits of established central board policies and administrative procedures. Given the organizational patterns and structures of forces summarized in this chapter, there seems to be little prospect that this process can yield long-term, basic changes in school racial policies and practices.

CHAPTER 6

Public Welfare

The complex welfare system in the United States includes a wide variety of public and private programs. The case studies in this sector, however, represent one phase of the overall public assistance programs and do not focus on private welfare activities or the role of the federal government, although city and state governments were directly involved in each dispute.

All three of the cases deal with confrontations between the clients and the welfare establishment in the largest of the categorical aid programs, the Aid to Families of Dependent Children program (AFDC or ADC) administered by a city, county, or state authority. Because of the size of this particular public assistance program and because the clients involved have some limited degree of organization, we judged that these patterns represent the kinds of welfare crises found in the North during 1968-70.

These cases present more uniformity than those in other sectors. Each started with demands by ADC mothers for changes in payments for special grants and each included a strong black leadership affiliated with the National Welfare Rights Organization (NWRO). In all three cases, the protestors applied coercive pressures against the welfare administrators and each of the protesting groups won some concessions. The issues and confrontations were used as organizing devices by the NWRO.

142   Racial Negotiations

The differences among the cases derive more from the physical location of the confrontations than from the issues involved. The Ann Arbor confrontation occurred in a small city and included strong university student support for the black protestors. A second case occurred in a large northern city with a relatively small black population. The third case, which took place in New York City, originated with a loose federation of local NWRO affiliates and ended with state legislative action.

In this sector more than in any other, the factor of race was difficult to isolate and determine. While a large percentage of the members and leaders of the NWRO is black, the organization defines its functions around welfare issues rather than around the issues of race. However, racial characteristics were examined in the three cases. To assist in understanding the case reports, a brief overview of the public assistance system follows.

BACKGROUND

At the present time there is considerable impetus to change the basic structure of the public welfare system in the United States. The material included here refers to the system as it existed at the time of the confrontations reported in the three case studies.

Eligibility for public assistance is defined in relationship to a series of categories such as the blind, the disabled, the aged, and families with dependent children. The programs rely heavy on eligibility criteria to determine who may receive assistance. Where physical disabilities are involved, eligibility is relatively easy to determine. The criteria are less clear for other programs including ADC. Guidelines are set by federal, state, and local governments and financing is available from all three sources.

The system is organized to perform functions that were formulated in the earliest development of the welfare state and have not changed fundamentally despite the great expansion of categories of aid, funding, and administrative machinery. It is intended to provide minimum financial and psychological support for those who are unable to take care of themselves. Most recipients of ADC are female household heads who are blocked from entry into the labor force for various reasons.

[1] *Improving the Public Welfare System*, Committee for Economic Development, April 1970, New York, New York.

In 1970, a Committee for Economic Development report indicated that ADC included more than half of all public assistance recipients.[1] The report noted the large disparities among states as to the amounts paid. At the time of the report, more than 20 states did not accept all of the federal funds available because of "reluctance or inability to appropriate matching funds." Standards for amounts paid to ADC families varied widely, as did the provision of special grants for various items.

All three of the cases reported here deal with special grants. In Ann Arbor, the request was for additional money for school clothes; in Central City furniture allowances were demanded; and in New York, the protestors attempted to gain all of the special grants available by law for as many clients as possible. Special grants are not automatic since, in most states, the client must apply and the caseworker must approve the application and the amount. The system does not assume that there will be universal application or approval and the funds for such universality are not immediately available to the welfare administrators.

In the view of most of its students, the welfare system is based on the concept of dependency. It assumes that the client who is unable to provide for himself is also unable to manage his affairs and needs a variety of social services, which are usually performed by the caseworker. The special grants, frequently made in the form of vouchers rather than cash, are a further extension of this dependency doctrine. Theoretically, ADC payments are made equally to all who qualify. An attempt to introduce flexibility and individualization has led some states to a series of special supplementary grants. The guidelines for these special grants are complex and vague and provide wide latitude to the caseworker. These supplemental allowances, then, led to considerable disparity in the standard of living prevailing among ADC clients even within the same community. In each of the cases NWRO attempted to increase membership by providing information and assistance in obtaining supplementary allowances. In New York, this led to a demand that the system be made to "work to rule" and produce for each client all that was coming to them. In Ann Arbor, the protesting group tired to achieve a favored status for its membership. A further complicating factor is the degree to which overlapping authorities were involved. Demands submitted to individual caseworkers were referred to supervisors and then to a variety of city, county, and state authorities, each of whom preferred that someone else make the ultimate decision.

In summary, the welfare system is vulnerable to attack by its clients. Increasingly, clients, aided by NWRO, have rejected the concept of dependency. New social workers in the field reflect this changing view. However, the system is largely administered by professionals whose discretionary decisions produce inequities. Further, these professional caseworkers and administrators are reluctant to yield either their operating criteria or their supervisory roles. Administrators feel strong public pressures to live within budgets that cannot possibly be stretched to pay everyone adequate benefits, and may make payments only to those who become aware of their eligibility and who file claims, thus increasing the inequities among clients. Finally, some white politicians and their constituencies feel that the system is too costly and too generous in providing more benefits than the poor deserve. It is also possible that an element of white racism is involved.

WASHTENAW COUNTY CLOTHING ALLOWANCE DISPUTE

Although the attempt of a group of ADC recipients in Washtenaw County, Michigan, to secure supplementary allowances for school clothing during September 1968 had been long in the making, the confrontation, negotiations, and settlement lasted only seven days.[2] Like participants in the other two cases in this category, the organized ADC recipients demanded supplementary or special allowances rather than challenging the basic formula of welfare payments and sought to gain additional payments and to use this campaign as a means for adding membership to their organization. Unlike most of the ADC disputes in 1968, the action took place in a medium-sized city rather than in a large urban center. Thus, the incident provided a good opportunity to analyze the community and political forces impinging on the conflict-negotiation process in a relatively small political unit.

Background

Washtenaw County lies in southeastern Michigan and has a complex industrial mix. The largest employers are two major state-sponsored universities but substantial employment is also generated by an automobile manufacturer and satellite companies, hospitals, and other

---

[2] This summary was prepared from an unpublished case study by Louis A. Ferman, with the assistance of Jeffery Davidson.

public institutions and small industrial parks housing the "think tanks" of industrial units in technical fields. The county seat, Ann Arbor, is the home of The University of Michigan and combines some of the attributes of a university town with those of a bedroom community for Detroit. It is estimated that 60 percent of Ann Arbor's population has had some college education.

The black population of the county dates back to the World War II period when large numbers of unskilled workers were brought to the area to man defense jobs in the Ford Willow Run complex. These unskilled workers occupied contiguous but largely segregated areas around Ypsilanti and Willow Run Village. Following the shutdown of defense industries in the county in 1945, many of the whites returned to their southern homes and many blacks migrated to Detroit, Toledo, and Cleveland seeking better jobs. The unskilled black and white populations that remained were supported by low-wage employment or unemployment compensation. New industries in the county demanded highly skilled people and this group of workers lived on marginal jobs, unemployment compensation, and, finally, welfare benefits.

In 1968 the ADC program in Washtenaw County served a monthly average of 600 families. In August 1968, the month before the confrontation, 614 families were receiving ADC funds that totaled $122,427. The average ADC family of four received $2,212 per year, a figure that was below the national poverty level. Included in this figure were the total estimated needs (excluding medical and dental care). The clothes allowance per child included in this amount was $9 per month.

Prior to 1965, each city and township in the state controlled its own welfare program. After that time, the state of Michigan asssumed control of the program, setting guidelines but providing discretionary authority to each county. Workers in the local welfare authority were employed by the state civil service and county welfare expenditures, namely emergency assistance and relief, were viewed as supplementary to the state grants. State welfare funds were received by the elected 39-member Board of County Supervisors, which passed on these monies and the county supplements to the three-member Social Services Welfare Board (SSWB), which included two members appointed by the supervisors and one by the governor. In principle, once these funds were released to the SSWB by the supervisors, the authority to set priorities and spend funds rested with that board. In actual fact, however, most of the decisions in Washtenaw County were made by the county welfare director who had held the position for 20 years at the time of the confrontation.

The ADC Clients

The relationship between the ADC mothers and the welfare authority had a long and unhappy history. The complaints were fourfold. First, most ADC recipients lived in and around Ypsilanti and Willow Run Village while the welfare office was some distance away in Ann Arbor. As early as 1958 there was considerable agitation for a supplementary welfare office that would be more accessible to the clients since regular public transport was not available between the two cities. A new office was opened in early 1960 but its location had been established without considering the clients' suggestions and they did not consider it suitable. A second cause of disaffection dealt with caseworker practices, particularly those that included recommendations for supplementary allowances. Criteria for these were never defined and were left to the discretionary authority of the individual caseworker. From the client's point of view these recommendations were arbitrary and were used, it was alleged, as a tool to reward the compliant and punish the protestor. The third complaint arose when a citizen's advisory panel, which included ADC representation, made a series of recommendations to the Social Services Welfare Board, but these were largely ignored. Finally, there were complaints that the system of allowances based on a universalistic idea of a fixed amount per child or per family was unresponsive to individual need.

Early attempts to organize ADC clients had met with little successs. The longest-lived, an organization called Humanizing Existing Welfare (HEW), was formed in 1966. The thirty members, of whom six were white, met only sporadically and were largely a discussion rather than an action group. In February 1968, however, two ADC recipients from Ypsilanti decided to form a local chapter of the NWRO, a national organization that had developed in the middle sixties as part of the movement of the poor and black for civil rights and income. They consulted with NWRO organizers in Detroit and with some social work students at The University of Michigan and established a local chapter. In the spring of 1968, a delegation went to the state capital to protest a proposed 25 percent reduction in state ADC payments. In March, they were represented in the Poor People's March in Washington, D.C., having raised their own funds to cover the expenses. During the summer four of the members attended a series of WRO workshops in Chicago and Washington. At these workshops, they received information about federal and state laws governing welfare payments and heard discussions about projected campaigns including one for school clothing. Inspired by these contacts, the group continued to try to organize and, by August, had approximately 30 members—all of whom were black.

In August 1968, some of the members of the local WRO chapter met to discuss plans. The school year was approaching, the need for school clothing was urgent, and some of the clients had been questioning their caseworkers about this issue since June. It was decided to make the allowance for school clothing a first order of business. Some of the clients had decided that they would not enroll their children in school until the clothing problem was resolved. At the end of August, the HEW group joined the WRO in the fight and the two groups esssentially merged in this campaign.

The Confrontation

On August 29, seven ADC mothers and a small number of students from The University of Michigan who had provided assistance in formulating demands, went to the welfare office in the Washtenaw County Building in Ann Arbor to discuss the school clothing issue. At that time, they were met by an assistant welfare director who informed them that the director was not in his office. The group tried to make an appointment for the following day but had to settle for September 3. They were assured that they would be able to speak with the director and the three-member Social Services Welfare Board who had full legal authority over the county's welfare operations.

As a preliminary to that meeting, the group distributed clothing forms to all ADC recipients in the community. These forms, prepared by the leaders of the group and some students from the School of Social Work listed the kinds of clothing needed by school-age children and prices of these items in local stores.

As scheduled, approximately 30 ADC mothers with their children and a few advisors arrived on the morning of September 3 at the welfare office. This first encounter did not start well. The director alleged that there had been a prior agreement that the group would be limited to ten. The attempt to limit the number of women participating in the discussions aroused considerable anger and the director finally agreed to meet the total group.

The major position taken by the protestors was that welfare payments were based on a 1961 cost-of-living index, that a $9 per-month per-child clothing allowance was inadequate, and that clients had to spend from the food and housing money to clothe their children. A flat grant was opposed since it was alleged that some children needed more than others. The initial demand was that each child's needs, as indicated on the prepared forms, be met no matter what the cost.

The initial response was that the current funds were insufficient to meet this demand and that only the County Board of Supervisors could appropriate more money. The protestors tried to insist that the welfare director arrange a meeting between the supervisors and themselves. The director refused to do so and left the building, thus terminating the discussion.

After a series of abortive meetings and negotiations at various levels of authority—caseworkers, the assistant director of welfare, the welfare director, the Social Services Board, the Board of Supervisors, and the Ways and Means Committee of that board—the protestors staged a sit-in in the County Building on September 5. They were joined by students from The University of Michigan and Eastern Michigan University. At the high point of participation about 1,000 students were involved. Although the sit-in was peaceful and nondestructive, armed police accompanied by dogs were stationed inside and outside the County Building and 200 persons, mostly students, were arrested during the sit-in.

The confrontation involved city officials of Ann Arbor and Ypsilanti, an around-the-clock meeting of a special committee of the Board of Supervisors, a fact-finding panel that included the Dean of The University of Michigan School of Social Work, the black mayor of Ypsilanti, and the manager of the local office of the Michigan Bell Telephone Company. Although the WRO originally demanded that supplementary clothing allowances be based on a needs formula, this was modified to a demand for a flat payment of $70 per child. The fact-finding panel counterproposed a formula that offered each ADC mother in the county an immediate $40 allowance per child that could later be supplemented by additional funds based on need and not to exceed $30. The fact-finders returned with the proposal that the total available funds of $91,000 be allocated to the 1,300 school-age ADC children in the county on the basis of an affidavit of need filed by the mother and that all cases be handled within a 30-day period. If all filed, this amounted to $70 per child, as proposed by the WRO. Any unexpected funds were to be allocated on the basis of need after that time. This proposal was accepted and some saw this as total victory since it seemed to be identical with the last proposal made by WRO. WRO saw it as only a partial victory, however. The funds were distributed quickly, although in voucher form. They were made available to all county welfare recipients folllowing notification of their availability by the welfare department and thus there were very few unexpended funds available.

CAPITAL CITY WELFARE

In the capital city of a major eastern industrial state, a coalition of client organizations of ADC recipients challenged the welfare establishment of the city and state in a large-scale confrontation and subsequent negotiations in the summer of 1968.[3] The confrontation started in July, and terminated weeks later after some negotiations. As in most of the cases under study in this project, a series of earlier events led to the climate in which the confrontation occurred.

By the summer of 1968, welfare rules, regulations, and programs had come under attack from a number of sources. There had been some changes in the kinds of rules that prevailed but the basic essentials and philosophy of welfare remained the same. The amount of administrative red tape; the harshness of investigatory procedures, including the practice of making a midnight visit to search for a man in the homes of families that were receiving ADC; and the general attitude of caseworkers toward applicants and clients changed significantly as a result of a series of court rulings, a growing flexibility in the approach of caseworkers, and increasing militancy on the part of welfare clients.

At this time, considerable nationwide emphasis was placed on basic reform in the welfare system, and NWRO had launched a series of confrontations designed to organize welfare recipients and to change the dependency system of welfare that placed welfare workers in loco parentis to their clients. The welfare load and its costs had been rising steeply throughout the 1960s. Welfare costs had become the source of major financial crises for many cities and there was an increasing tendency for clients to demand more benefits and for the public to become more resentful of the burden these costs seemed to represent.

General Characteristics

The Parties

At the time of the incident, the welfare establishment was centered in the state department of public welfare, which dealt with ADC as well as with other welfare programs. The department was headed by a commissioner who administered the program through local offices throughout the state. On the eve of the confrontation, July 1, a new

[3] This summary was prepared from an unpublished case study by Michael J. Piore, assisted by DonCosta Seawell.

150 *Racial Negotiations*

welfare reform act had given the state full control over local offices. This was designed to curtail local authority, but, says Piore, "... at the time of the confrontation, the local offices were still operating with some autonomy, and the shift in control left considerable ambiguity about the locus of authority in the local office."

The welfare commissioner was responsible to the governor, which interjected a political note into the establishment's reaction since during this period, the governor was campaigning to become the vice-presidential candidate of his party and his major concern was to prevent the confrontation from becoming a liability in that campaign. In addition, the commissioner was responsive to members of the state legislature who controlled both the department's appropriation and substantive legislation affecting welfare. The federal government never became involved in the actual confrontation and negotiations although the supplemental allowances that were at issue were an optional feature of the federal program.

Three client groups were involved in the confrontation: the NWRO, the State Welfare Rights Organization (SWRO), and Mothers for Adequate Welfare (MAW). Like SWRO, MAW was a statewide coalition of local chapters but its structure was even looser and less formal than that of SWRO.

The Issues

The supplemental allowance program, which was the specific point of attack in the confrontation, was a program designed to supplement the basic monthly allowances of welfare families in certain categories of unusual or nonrecurring need. The two most prominent categories were household furnishings and clothing. Under certain circumstances, grants could also be made for food, rent, and utilities. These grants were awarded at the discretion of the caseworkers under guidelines established by the state department of public assistance. In part, grants were designed to individualize the program and, therefore, at the time of the confrontation, the guidelines gave wide latitude to individual caseworkers in determining client eligibility, specific items of furniture (or clothing) allowable, and the quality and the price to be paid for the items approved. Inevitably, the supplemental allowances led to considerable inequalities in the standard of living prevailing among different ADC clients within the state. In part, this inequality was due to the variations in program administration by local public welfare boards and the move to state control was designed to set a state standard applicable to all. A part of this inequality, however, occurred within local districts and could be attributed to wide differences in the ways individual caseworkers interpreted and applied the general guidelines.

The initial issue was the individual requests of a large number of clients for furniture grants. Later in the confrontation, related issues included uniformity of standards for the determination of furniture allowances; the items, quality, and prices specified in the uniform standards; and the procedures through which the standards were to be established.

This confrontation gained support from the NWRO attempt in the summer of 1968 to demonstrate, through a series of confrontations, the absurdity of the welfare system by demanding for every client each of the benefits to which a consistent, uniform application of existing regulations would have entitled him.

The Principal Events

On July 22, 1968, clients marched on two local welfare offices in the capital's black ghetto and applied en masse for special furniture grants. With their applications they left an ultimatum demanding action within one week. The department responded by attempting to process the requests within the one-week period. Despite some delay and considerable confusion, the caseworkers spent a good part of the week in the field reviewing furniture requests, and a large number of requests were actually granted.

One week after the first episode, the client groups returned to the local offices in the capital to review the welfare department's response to their initial demands. At the same time, predominantly white welfare groups elsewhere in the state marched on their local offices with large numbers of individual requests and demanded action within the week as the groups in the capital city had done the week before. The important events in this phase of the confrontation occurred at one of the capital city's offices where the clients occupied the basement and attempted to argue with department officials about the disposition of their requests on a case-by-case basis. These discussions continued throughout the afternoon and early evening, first with local officials and then, at the insistence of the clients, with officials of the city and state, including the state commissioner and a representative of the governor. Finally, the individual furniture claims were all processed but the clients then demanded telephones. The commissioner, in desperation, granted this last demand and the clients left the building. The following day, the commissioner put a freeze on further furniture allowances from this or any other office throughout the state until the department could establish a set of price and item guidelines. He also withdrew his earlier approval of telephones.

152 Racial Negotiations

The last phase of the confrontation centered upon the guidelines and the procedures for establishing them. Both the department and the welfare clients drew up a set of guidelines. The latter developed their guidelines through a detailed process of comparative shopping and interchapter discussion. The departmental guidelines announced the following week fell short of the clients' list in both the prices and the number of items included. The promulgation of departmental lists precipitated a sleep-in in welfare offices throughout the state that continued for about two weeks, varying in levels of attendance and in militancy from one office to another and within each office over the course of time. The sleep-ins resulted in a series of meetings over the period, which led to an end of the occupation of the welfare offices and an agreement by the commissioner to establish a special committee with extensive SWRO representation that would review and revise the guidelines.

The Results

Negotiations occurred when the welfare department negotiated specific furniture applications with the clients and their representatives in the second phase of the confrontation. The department later discussed the issues surrounding uniform guidelines and eventually concluded a limited agreement upon a procedure for the review of a set of guidelines that it had first established unilaterally. In Piore's view, however,

> The final settlement . . . was largely a face-saving device enabling the SWRO to call an end to the militant phase of the furniture drive. The confrontation served to harden the position of the welfare department in its dealings with the clients and, since the agreement at the end of the summer of 1968, no real negotiations have occurred.

The significance of these limited results will be discussed later in the analytical section of this chapter.

THE WELFARE RIGHTS ORGANIZATION AND NEW YORK CITY: SPECIAL GRANT DISPUTE

This dispute centered around a system of special grants available in New York City to ADC mothers, which were used by the WRO as a means of expanding income to welfare recipients and as the basis for an organizing campaign.[4] Although the dispute had roots going back

---

[4] This case was analyzed by Professor Herbert Semmel, assisted by Lawrence Cumberbatch.

to July 1966, the case studied covers a period from early 1968 until the end of September.

In New York City, as in many other communities, special grants were paid only after recipients applied for them. Most recipients knew little about their rights and it was not generally the practice of caseworkers to advise them. Processing special grant applications required a great deal of paperwork and time and resulted in relatively small sums. Caseworkers preferred to use the special grant as a discretionary device to help out a particular family in an emergency or to reward cooperative clients. Few ever attempted to bring their clients up to minimum standards, that is, to give a family money for each item of furniture and clothing for which the family was eligible. In February 1968, with total ADC welfare recipients in New York City numbering about 900,000, the monthly expenditure for special grants for furniture and clothing was one million dollars, a rate of $12 per recipient per year.

WRO began using demands for special grants and minimum standards as a thrust for an organizing campaign in July 1966. Following public demonstrations at City Hall in 1966, the welfare commissioner ordered caseworkers to inform clients of their rights to special grants. In September 1966, there were sit-ins demanding school clothing at welfare centers, but the campaign was not sustained. The issue was raised again in July 1967, with a public demonstration outside City Hall and a sit-in in at least one Brooklyn welfare office.

Early in 1968, WRO started a large-scale organizing drive, promising welfare mothers instant money by assisting them in getting special grants to which most were legally entitled. Although the number of mothers applying was only a small percentage of the total possible applicants for such grants, an administrative crisis occurred at the local welfare centers because caseworkers had insufficient time to process the applications under existing procedures. These procedures called for checking the client's file to see what special grants had been given in the past, verifying the need for the requested furniture and household goods generally through a home visit, and approving the grant by the case supervisor.

The WRO demanded immediate payment based on the legality of its claims and the long denial of members' rights. Organizers would bring hundreds of welfare mothers to a welfare center, tie up the office, and demand payment based on application forms prepared in advance by WRO workers. On April 18, 1968, there were demonstrations in at least six centers, with as many as 400 at one Brooklyn center. These demonstrations because de facto sit-ins when mothers stayed in the office until they received payment. Caseworkers in these offices reported average payments of $300-400 per family, with payments of up to $1,200 reported in exceptional cases.

Demonstration sit-ins at welfare centers continued regularly through May and June, resulting in heavy psychological and physical pressure on caseworkers. The initial reaction of city officials was payment and tolerance. A de facto change in procedures occurred at the center level and was tacitly approved by the department, probably with the consent of Mayor John Lindsay. Verification procedures for special grants were abandoned; checks were issued to applicants on the spot, and caseworkers were encouraged to work overtime to process every applicant who came to the center. At the same time clients were permitted to remain in the centers overnight and, in a few cases, over weekends. WRO kept all applicants in the center until all claims were processed, thus maintaining pressure on the caseworkers. The result was that special grant payments hit $11.5 million in May 1968. The city began moving to meet the problem by switching to a flat grant above the monthly allowance, a proposal that had been under study for at least six months but that might not have been utilized had the demonstrators not forced their hand.

By the end of June, WRO learned of the flat grant proposal from friendly caseworkers and demanded and received meetings with city and state officials to protest. By June, the caseworkers union also was demanding changes in procedures to simplify special grants, a return to order in the centers, and police protection. An organization of guards at welfare centers threatened to strike unless they were allowed to wear guns and were given full police officer status. On June 29, a weekend sit-in began in the office of the city welfare commissioner and resulted in the arrest of 11 persons, including the chairman of WRO in New York City. There were arrests of some who sat in at other centers during July. August appeared to be quieter.

On August 27, the commissioner announced elimination of most special grants and a substitution of a quarterly flat grant of $25 per recipient at a cost of close to $10,000,000 per year. WRO responded with demonstrations, sit-ins, and, for the first time, some property damage at some of the centers. Large numbers demonstrated at as many as 25 centers on one day until the middle of September, with a number of arrests. The city announced a get-tough policy but only made arrests when a crowd got out-of-hand. By the middle of September the demonstrations began losing momentum and the special grant dispute was essentially over by the end of that month. By November, WRO was talking about a rent strike and demanding credit for welfare recipients in department stores. In March 1969, the state legislature abolished the flat grant entirely and, in addition, made cuts in some welfare budgets, depending on family size and age of children.

During the entire period there were two separate issues, the procedures and speed in processing special grant applications and the decision made at the city-wide level, with approval of state welfare officials, to switch to a flat grant. The WRO exerted a little power at this level and no real negotiations took place on this issue.

The establishment involved in this dispute was essentially the administration of New York City, specifically the Department of Social Services. While never directly involved, however, both state and federal governments could be considered as background parties to the dispute since most of the funds derived from the federal government were given to the state, which essentially had the power to nullify the results of the confrontation by changing the rules at the state level. For the most part, the WRO was represented in the negotiations by local representatives, two city-wide representatives, and occasionally the executive director of NWRO.

The racial characteristics of the confrontation are complex and hard to analyze. On the establishment side, there is a great deal of general public prejudice against welfare mothers, some based on racial stereotypes. On the other hand, the administrative structure in New York City included a number of blacks and some Puerto Ricans among the caseworkers, supervisors, community organization specialists, and top officials of the Department of Social Services. In New York City, 47 percent of the ADC mothers were black and 40 percent were Puerto Rican at the time of our study. Although many Puerto Rican mothers participated in the demonstrations, the WRO local leadership was predominantly black. Thus, while the issues in the New York confrontations could be considered nonracial, the confrontation itself had strong racial characteristics.

The coercive potential of the challengers was substantial when focused on limited issues at the local centers; it was very limited when applied to policy issues considered by the city administration. The protestors could and did succeed in tying up operations at the various local welfare centers by their sit-ins demanding special grants. In most cases, they were asking that they be given what the welfare laws provided should be theirs, a tactic comparable to the "work-to-rule" sometimes used by organized labor.

At first, the city moved cautiously despite the disruptions. Once it became clear that there was almost no overt support from the black community, the risks appeared to be less serious to the city administration. However, city officials were reluctant to engage in mass arrests of welfare mothers since there was a real problem of child care if these mothers were held in jail for any length of time. The negotiation process at the welfare center level resulted from the coercive tactics of WRO in bringing large numbers of women to the centers. In some centers, agreement was reached about the first major issue, the processing of applications, and the caseworker was empowered to write checks without home visits and without supervisor approval. A second isssue arose because there was not enough staff to handle the requests, even on this basis. Varying kinds of accommodations were worked out: mothers were allowed to stay overnight to be first in line in the morning, numbers were given to ensure the same result, and caseworkers were encouraged to work overtime.

The principal negotiator for the Department of Social Services at a center was generally the director of the center who was joined by one or two of the supervisory personnel. The WRO side usually included a leader of the local affiliate, one or two of the mothers directly involved, and, if available, a representative of the city-wide WRO staff. The negotiations at the center level were of the simplest kind; the agreements were oral, de facto, and differed from center to center.

In several of the negotiations between center directors and local protestors, some community organization specialists, hired by the Department of Welfare, acted almost as mediators or interpreters. The specialists' job description called on them to transmit departmental policy to the clients and also to act as client advocates. Therefore, these roles were carried out as a function of the individual's personality and convictions. Since their role was ambivalent they emphasized different aspects of the conflict.

Further conflicts appeared during the discusssions between the WRO and the Department of Social Services. Although the NWRO and its leadership was predominantly black and most of New York's WRO membership was composed of minority group members, a large percentage of the black and Puerto Rican welfare mothers were not WRO members and did not join in the action at the local centers. Throughout the discussions with the welfare commission, there was no evidence of support for the ADC mothers from their city-wide minority communities.

At the level of the city welfare administration, according to Semmel,

The term 'negotiations' is placed in quotations because, in fact, there were no negotiations although there were frequent meetings between top officials of the Department of Social Services and top officials of WRO. . . . Essentially, the pattern would be a series of demands by WRO, a response by department officials as to what was possible under existing laws and regulations . . . and, possibly, a promise to do whatever possible and, finally, an exchange or recrimination. . . .

The Welfare Department was usually represented by the commissioner, deputy commissioner, and several other administrators including the general counsel. On the WRO side, meetings involved the national director, two city-wide representatives, a lawyer or two for WRO, some leaders of local affiliates, and occasionally a few welfare mothers. Semmel notes that while WRO planned for these sessions, the administrative response was usually to "defer for further study," a technique that was very frustrating to the WRO negotiators.

The flat grant system had been under consideration prior to the WRO drive but was finally acted upon unilaterally by the city without any real discussion with WRO officials. Indeed, WRO learned of the proposal through unofficial channels. This kind of unilateral decision was much resented by the protestors. Semmel notes:

It is probably a fair conclusion that the failure of any real negotiation in meetings between the department officials and WRO officials was based on the evaluation of the city officials that WRO was nothing more than a special interest pressure group that had little following. The department concluded with some accuracy that WRO could not demonstrate the level of coercive power generally present in situations where true negotiations develop.

The issue of formal recognition of WRO as a bargaining representative of ADC mothers was essentially a secondary one, although it was an added goal of WRO. The city rejected formal recognition on the grounds of WRO's limited membership and because there were competing welfare groups. The city moved to widen its consultative procedures particularly at the center level by directing local center administrators to select members for consultative advisory committtees. Whenever the city negotiated with WRO at the center level, there was de facto recognition of the right of WRO to bargain for those physically present at the center, but no formal recognition of WRO as spokesman for all welfare clients. WRO lacked the coercive power to force such formal recognition.

In some cases WRO members became active in the community advisory committees to the Department of Welfare. However, Semmel notes that this organization was oriented to the administration's point of view and that "the community advisory committees were reminiscent of company unions in the pre-Wagner Act days." The degree of control of the center director over these committees varied depending on his style and personality. A WRO official said of the committees: "... there is no point in making a fight to take over something that is nothing. The CAC are advisors; they have no power. WRO is talking about real community control of welfare boards."

In summary, in its drive for individualized special grants, the New York WRO at first significantly improved the payment levels for all who responded to their efforts. In this way, they also substantially expanded their membership and organizational base. When the city administrators shifted to flat grants the payments to ADC mothers were extended further, although those who had not supported the WRO also benefitted. The later action at the state level wiped out these monetary advantages and the WRO found itself with little political capacity to oppose such a move.

Although significant racial variables influence the position of welfare clients and the welfare administration, the WRO has been concerned with welfare rather than racial issues, particularly at the national level. Indeed, based on the activities of its local units, the NWRO has been campaigning at the federal level for a total change in the welfare system.

GENERAL CHARACTERISTICS

The Parties

The complex establishment in the public welfare arena includes social caseworkers; local and district administrators; centralized administrative bodies; various political groups at the city, county, and state levels; and state legislatures empowered to allocate funds and determine general policies. In each of the cases, negotiations were carried out primarily at the local levels with some city- or county-wide involvement. In Ann Arbor, various political figures were involved. In the capital city, the change from local to statewide authority was confusing. In New York, most of the immediate negotiations involved individual welfare centers with some movement to the city administrator. Even within these varying groups, there were different views of the legitimacy of the demands, the seriousness of the coercive threats, and the resources available. The general philosophy of welfare within the United States was in such a state of flux that establishment responses varied widely.[5]

The Challengers

In the ADC cases studied, the protestors were primarly black ADC mothers who were organized as a continuing unit of a national organization. While the membership of the national organization and its local affiliates was *not* based on color but on economic status, for the most part the members and the leaders were black in all three of the cases. In Ann Arbor, the protestors won the support of large numbers of white university students and technical assistance from some university personnel and the legal aid society.

However, the primary emphasis of the NWRO and the local organizations was on the nonracial characteristics of the dependency status that the system imposed on all of its clients, the urgency of their children's needs, and the injustices perpetrated by the system. Thus, there is more uncertainty regarding the role of race in these disputes than in other sectors we have studied. The main negotiators in each of the cases were black ADC mothers, some of whom had been trained in NWRO-run workshops. For the most part, they took the position that they were seeking their rights. This attitude was reinforced by the frequent admissions of caseworkers and others within the welfare establishment that the demands were indeed reasonable. Of course, this view was counterbalanced by the insistence of the various welfare authorities that there simply were not enough funds available to meet the demands.

The Issues and the Coercive Pressures

In addition to the general budget balancing pressures on legislators and the concern of many citizens that the welfare system has accepted, and even increased, the dependency of growing numbers of its clients, many of the working poor who do not qualify for or request

[5] Three recent books examine the welfare system in considerable detail: Piven, Frances Fox and Richard A. Cloward, *Regulating the Poor: The Functions of Public Welfare* (New York: Pantheon, 1971); Steiner, Gilbert Y., *The State of Welfare* (Washington: The Brookings Institution, 1971); and Stein, Bruno, *On Relief: The Economics of Poverty and Public Welfare* (New York: Basic Books, 1971).

welfare grants believe that ADC clients receive as much for not working as they receive for diligent efforts within the economic system. On the other hand, many welfare mothers feel strongly that they are not receiving enough for their minimum needs, that money is doled out to them by a highly demeaning system, and that neither they nor their spokesmen are even consulted in the development and administration of the welfare process.

Our cases suggest that this kind of a system with its limited resources, discretionary judgments, and concepts of dependency has the potential for overt conflict. Our cases focus on one or another application by caseworkers of a specific element of the categorical assistance program—Aid for Dependent Children. In each of the three cases, the local leaders of the welfare mothers organized pressure on the system by assisting and encouraging more mothers to file for larger supplementary grants. They encouraged extra demands which were submitted to local administrative offices and caused major bottlenecks within the system. The caseworkers could not carefully examine each claim; the administrative machinery in the local office could not function fast enough; and the offices became overcrowded with claimants.

This process suggests that if enough claimants are encouraged to act, if they receive assistance in preparing logical claims, and if the claims fall within guidelines that have been used to make previous sizable grants, inadequacies in the welfare system are revealed. The present welfare system is too cumbersome to react quickly or to permit the application of its own investigative procedures. When responses by the caseworkers and the local administrators are decentralized, more resources may be allocated than are actually available. If a client group began to make extended claims and if everyone who came within the guidelines also filed such claims, the system would break down.

The first step in the crisis in each situation was the organization of these claims by welfare mothers. In each case, the core group of mothers was black and most of the local organizers and representatives were black. Our scholars and the leaders of the NWRO report that this color identification apparently helped to build an organizational unity within the groups of welfare mothers. Also, their unity was enhanced by their mutual perception of the welfare system as being dominated by whites who perpetuated negative racial stereotypes and stigmatized clients, viewing them as dependent blacks.

On the other hand, all of our case studies report an organizational emphasis among welfare clients based not only on blackness but also on their mutual status. Thus, different local groupings of white and Puerto Rican welfare mothers cooperated within a generalized approach that did not emphasize color. This focus is emphasized in the official statements of the NWRO.

Our scholars had some difficulty in determining how much of the establishment response to the demands of these client organizations was based on racial factors. Although the major administrators were white, they did not identify white racist reactions in themselves. On the other hand, the central administrators, politicians, and legislators who were responsible for resource allocation and general policies certainly felt pressures from those who characterized welfare programs, especially ADC programs, as supporting undeserving blacks. A somewhat more easily identified white reaction was the fear that the blacks would riot. This fear appears in some form in all three cases.

Despite differences among the cases, there were essential similarities in the issues pressed by the clients and their leaders. They resented the concept of dependency and sought to establish their right to a minimum income. They objected to the investigative processes that pried into their personal affairs and suggested that their income decisions should be made for them. As they became aware of the extreme inequalities in the treatment of different individuals with the same characteristics, they insisted on equal allocations for all in the same circumstances. They judged that the system was far too slow in responding to the requests they were forced to initiate and, perhaps most importantly, they considered that the amounts finally received were far from adequate.

The mothers and their leaders applied two major forms of pressure to the system. First, they recruited large numbers of additional claimants for supplementary grants and swamped the system with claims that came within the guidelines of the administration but that could not be handled rapidly if there were to be investigations of need before responding to each claim. Second, they moved to sit-ins in the administrative offices to bring the system to a temporary halt, to dramatize their grievances, and to intimidate administrators and politicians. In Ann Arbor, non-client pressures from university students added to the concern of public officials that disorder would follow.

In two of the three cases, administrators and politicians hesitated to respond to sit-ins by using police and threatening court action, which they feared might escalate the conflict because the protestors were black and because they were mothers. In each case, their self-restraint did not last long. In one case, it should be noted, counterpressures against the claimants also developed from the organized caseworkers and local order-keeping employees in the welfare offices. The capacity of the ADC mothers to sustain their pressures was severely limited.

They had to leave their children unattended or keep them out of school and had to get to the offices where the sit-ins or pickets were operating. Even as an organized group, they lacked the political power necessary to make public officials respond to their demands. In New York City, for example, because there was little open support for the welfare mothers from the rest of the black community, the mayor, who owed his election in large part to the vote of that community, was able to discount the mothers as a future political influence. On the other hand, the ability of the welfare establishment to shift the locus of the decision-making process from one level to another, and to organize the public for an economy approach, generated considerable support for resistance to the pressures of the protestors.

Negotiations

Brief but intensive negotiations took place in two of the three cases. In each of these, the administrators believed that the spokesmen for the protestors were responsible for the pressures against the establishment and that they would be able to suspend these pressures if an accommodation were reached. The techniques varied in these two cases. In Ann Arbor, informal as well as formal exploration took place between the protest leaders, the administrators, and the politicians responsible for resource allocation at the county and the state level. But the final formula was accepted by the establishment negotiators only after a professional panel had been used to give public credibility to the cost of the proposed additional grants. In the capital city case, the administrator ended a brief negotiating session by agreeing to procedural shortcuts and to increasing the amount of the grants, although he later withdrew his acceptance of an allowance for telephones.

No negotiating process as such occurred in the New York case. Also, no continuing procedures which accepted the protest leaders as the spokesmen for the clients were established in any of the cases. On the other hand, in the capital city and New York City cases, spokesmen for the protestors were able to perform a consultative role as the administrators and legislators made additional decisions affecting the issues that had been raised.

In the New York City case, community organization specialists acted as contacts with the clients on behalf of the welfare administration. These specialists, who were predominantly black, assigned to black communities were a part of the administration but aided individual clients when they had trouble securing proper treatment and when they sought to press nonwelfare agencies for assistance.

When faced with the need to reestablish the smooth running of the organization and the fear that they will be held accountable for the exacerbation of social conflict, welfare administrators are likely to deal with the protest leaders no matter how reluctantly. Faced with the need to convert coercive pressure into welfare improvements, the protest leaders will be ready to seek a settlement through negotiations, if one appears to be possible.

NEGOTIATION RESULTS

In each of the three cases, there was an immediate and significant expansion of the welfare payments made to the clients who were protesting. More clients filed claims and received large supplementary grants during and immediately after the overt conflict and negotiations. In each of the three cases, some claims were processed more rapidly and the emphasis on the individual caseworker's judgment and investigation of the needs and circumstances of a particular family was reduced. In no case, however, did these actions represent a shift away from the dependency concept and approach.

The consequences for the clients of these challenges and brief negotiations patterns are well-illustrated in the New York City case. Faced with rapidly rising relief costs and the need for procedures that could keep up with the claims, the administration countered the demand for extended supplementary grants by introducing a uniform flat grant above the monthly allowance. Although this action greatly reduced the delays in making such payments, it actually reduced the amount of supplemental grants that could be and were received by those who had most vigorously pressed their specific claims. Later, the system responded with a legislative decision to reduce the funds available for all mothers and to eliminate the special grants on which the whole pressure for increases had focused.

Membership temporarily expanded in the client organizations as the groups demonstrated their ability to press claims. When the system reacted to these pressures with a somewhat greater use of flat grants, this organizing momentum abated. Since the representative character of the organization was only temporarily and sketchily established, an organizational base for continued development was not achieved.

Within the welfare system itself, the pressures caused some changes. A limited shift away from the individualized case-need approach occurred. The guidelines applicable to each caseworker were tightened in the hope of achieving a closer approximation of fairness for claimants. On the other hand, politicians, including central administrators and legislators, became increasingly concerned about the public image of the system and developed greater determination to avoid rising relief costs if possible.

Additional consequences included the restoration of relative, and perhaps temporary, peace in those specific situations. But local client-related bases for a national organization of welfare mothers that could serve as a nucleus for many different kinds of pressures on administrators and legislators were established. In general, the results of the negotiations were announced as a unilateral decision of the administrator in order to preserve the image of a system that does not accept the role of clients in the decision-making process. Since recognition is thus avoided, the agreement suspending the conflict is unlikely to include any provision for ongoing machinery through which the protest leaders could act as spokesmen for all of the clients or for those who have become members of their welfare rights organization.

Whatever the terms of an agreement entered into with the protest leaders, decision makers at higher levels of the system are likely to react independently. General administrative or legislative decisions may modify the guidelines and even the patterns of categorical grants and outdate the gains made in local negotiations and agreements. Restrictions or even reductions in legislative budget allocations may require that administrators find new and different approaches to reducing the benefits to welfare clients.

CONCLUSIONS

These three cases suggest that, at least during 1968-70 in northern areas, the use of negotiating processes may have restored peace temporarily but did little to resolve racial conflicts or make the changes in the welfare system desired by many recipients. One of the important aspects of our data is the finding that race played a less obvious part, provided a more uncertain rallying point for discontent, and drew less resistance from the establishment than was apparent in other situations that we have studied. Most of the clients and their leaders who participated in these cases were black. However, they emphasized issues of poverty and basic changes in the welfare system rather than race as such.

The whole welfare system, dominated by white chief administrators and white politicians who are responsive to white voters, reacted with prejudice against black mothers and displayed a generalized fear. Indeed, the black leaders effectively used these white fears and yet attempted to avoid the kind of white polarization that would strengthen opposition to their efforts. However, the primary efforts of legislators and administrators were directed toward maintaining the dependency characteristics of relief and restricting the commitment of government funds to the poor.

The second important conclusion drawn from our data is that the coercive resources that the welfare mothers could use to force immediate improvements in the system were quite limited. Thus, they had difficulty in mounting strong pressure against the system even when their cause contained the prospect of expanded benefits for the protestors.

The ability of black mothers to develop and use negotiating maneuvers within their own organizations and in face-to-face exchanges with the white establishment was also limited. It is extremely difficult to develop a strong, continuing organization to hold the poor together and to represent their interests within the system. Traditionally, of course, this has been true of other organizations in other times in America. However, because of their experiences in dealing with whites, black mothers can interpret the meanings of administrative responses. Indeed, they may have a communications advantage compared with the administrators with whom they are dealing.

A third major aspect of our general conclusion is that welfare client organizations are arrayed against an enormously powerful establishment whose resources include the opportunity to penalize the dissenter and to heighten the risks of anyone who moves into conflict with the establishment, the use of police forces to suppress opposition, and the power of chief administrators and legislators to change the rules and to reduce the available resources. On balance, then, such an unequal alignment of forces suggests that only minor procedureal and temporary improvements can be expected through this route. One of the major gains for the clients, however, may be increased pride and emotional independence.

A fourth major aspect of our general conclusions points to future processes of change. The NWRO has helped groups of welfare mothers press their claims for supplemental grants and for equity within the system and has also founded a base for a national continuing organization through these approaches. This leadership and continuity has already influenced a number of welfare administrators to accept NWRO as a spokesman for their clients. From this base, the black leaders of the NWRO are also able to speak with some authority within black coalitions concerned with many racial issues.

These conclusions, of course, are limited. Although the NWRO is the only national organization of welfare recipients, it is far from being *the* accepted representative for all welfare clients. Although its black leaders participate in black coalitions, it is by no means able to join as a part of a *single* black coalition speaking on behalf of the whole black community. The significance of the NWRO lies within other nonnegotiations processes for change in American society on behalf of blacks. Some important advantages for blacks have already opened through court decisions in which the NWRO has played an important part. Although these decisions lie beyond the scope of our particular study, it is useful to summarize them to put our racial negotiations conclusions in perspective. Presumably, these court decisions are based on the expansion and application of two fundamentals: welfare clients have constitutional rights that should not be violated by legislatures or by administrators, and the image of a benevolent government that looks after its needy citizens must apply equally to all in appropriate categories. At the time of this writing, it appeared to be doubtful whether courts or legislatures would interpret and extend these protections much further.

Over the last five years, there has been an enormous expansion in monies made available for relief payments, particularly in aid to dependent children, as political units decided that it was appropriate to expand the range of the welfare state. Although NWRO as such has played only a minor part in this expansion, it has been functioning as a spokesman in this field. At the time of this writing, it appeared that there could be a reversal of this trend in welfare allocations. Proposals were before Congress to substantially change the dependency emphasis on which the system has been built and to force detailed changes in the system. In a larger sense, the success of the confrontations and negotiations in this sector was in the degree to which the leaders and the mothers built a base and established the legitimacy of the NWRO to articulate the needs of the poor in legislative, executive, and judicial processes on welfare and related issues.

CONTRASTS TO OTHER SECTORS

There are several ways in which these cases contrast with those in other sectors: (1) The cases were more uniform; (2) There was stronger emphasis on the general relationship of establishment to client, and less on race as such; (3) The pathway for negotiations of small gains appeared to be relatively easy; (4) The system could recover and restrict gains more easily than could the other sectors by making overriding political decisions that were largely beyond the reach of the protestors; (5) Within the welfare institution, a new national organization was already giving general guidance to local protest actions so that welfare clients had more potential for an indigenous sustained national leadership than did any other protest groups we studied; and (6) As the leadership attained national status, it developed the capacity to speak for a much larger and inchoate black and white constituency.

In some ways, the cases studied in this category are the most baffling to analyze meaningfully. The gains were achieved with less difficulty than in other sectors but were much more ephemeral. However, it was one of the few situations other than public employment where an established ongoing organization existed to provide the focus for the protestors. The welfare recipients acted without strong support from either the general community or the black community. They lacked political power as a group and had little disruptive power except through physical means that were relatively easy to contain. Because they move frequently, lack group identity, and have been trained into dependency, hopelessness, and apathy, poor people are difficult to organize and hold together. They are extremely vulnerable to fear and pressure since they are not likely to have any financial support without their welfare payments.

Our cases may be difficult to analyze because the welfare system and its rationale are in such a confused state. While studies in this area seem to agree that the present system is demeaning, inadequate, and administratively overburdened, there is little consensus about how it should be changed or the probable consequences of the proposed changes. Earlier attempts to link benefits to social services had little success. Later attempts to move recipients from welfare rolls to tax rolls also were unsuccessful, partly because needed social services were unavailable, crucial day care facilities were nonexistent, and the poor lacked skills for jobs with adequate pay.

In the final analysis, it is possible that political action and power are the most influential factors in attempts to make fundamental changes in the welfare system. Unfortunately, our case studies did not deal directly with this factor. Steiner's book includes a chapter that reviews special assistance programs to aged and disabled wartime veterans and their survivors. Because veterans have significant political power and society in general accepts the legitimacy of their claims, recipients of benefits under this program may get more assistance more easily than those in the welfare program. Veterans receive their benefits as a matter of right and are not conditioned to think of themselves as a burden on society. They are assisted, not investigated; they are believed, not doubted; they are assumed to be responsible, not dependent; they carry their benefits with them when they move. Steiner concludes "Veterans' pension is the relief program with the least rational justification but with the smoothest political path and with the most admirable administrative features."

It was not clear whether the Family Assistance Act which was pending at the time of writing would succeed in providing for the recipients more realistically and more humanely. However, NWRO is using most of its energies to influence political action at the state and national levels rather than supporting the kinds of limited local actions that were described in this chapter.

CHAPTER 7

Construction

The conflict between blacks and the organized elements of the construction industry is one of the most dramatic and continuous racial confrontations. Many blacks believe that the dismal black-white ratios on skilled jobs and the predominantly white membership of craft unions reflect racist attitudes of white unionists and contractors. White skilled craftsmen work at high wages on jobs that are largely government financed in the urban areas where blacks are concentrated. Black challengers to the industry are on the outside looking in, and the rules that affect the ratios of skilled blacks are made within a system in which they have played no part and where neither their services nor their purchases have been needed for the system's continuation. Black challenges pit black militants against white unionists and place traditional antagonists, the unions and the contractors, on the same side of the table, united against black demands.

BACKGROUND

Some perspective on each of these general characteristics can be gained by examining the data from a single city. Because the case discussed later in this chapter occurred in Chicago, the data cited are from that city, although parallel figures exist for other cities. In Chicago perhaps as much as 30 percent of the population is black, but, of all the journeymen working in 19 major crafts, only 2.7 percent

(2,349) are nonwhite.[1] Even this small number was unequally distributed among the crafts. In each of 11 of the trades, which include 55 percent of all of the city's craftsmen, less than 1 percent of the journeymen were black. On the other hand, higher ratios of minorities occurred in a few crafts that are at the lower end of the skilled wage rates (including 7 percent for roofers, 12 percent for plasterers, and 20 percent for cement masons). The black-white job ratios are closely paralleled by data on union membership. In Chicago during 1969, the average of blacks in those craft unions that reported was 3.3 percent, and the range was from 0.9 to 12.6 percent.[2]

Illustrations of the other basic characteristics appear in the way in which the Chicago confrontation developed. Members of the Black Coalition (a coalition of black organizations) staged most of their demonstrations on federally-financed projects within or near the south side and demanded that government representatives require changes in construction patterns. Before the Chicago confrontation the major organized involvement by blacks came through the "integrated" Urban League, which included as active members a white spokesman for the building trades unions and a prominent white contractor. Even the Urban League role was entirely limited to the recruiting and pre-induction phases of the industry, not to its essential rule making or procedures. All of the Chicago negotiations, from the first exploratory discussions to the final signing of an agreement, were carried on by representatives of the contractors and the unions on one side of the table and representatives of the Black Coalition on the other.

Characteristics of the Industry[3]

The Black Coalition's focus on training as well as on job placement can be understood by examining the manpower characteristics of the industry. Many of the jobs require extended training and experience before adequate proficiency is achieved. Since there is no ladder of promotion in the industry and the individual contractor or subcontractor is rarely willing to provide skill training, there should be a level of

[1] From a report of the Bureau of Labor Statistics, North Central Region, dated September 10, 1969. The category "nonwhite" is primarily black, but other data suggest that between 10 and 20 percent of these craftsmen are either Indians or have Spanish names.

[2] "Total and Minority Group Membership in Referral Unions in the Chicago SMSA, 1969." Equal Employment Opportunity Commission, Washington, D.C.

[3] Some of these characteristics have been analyzed in Derek C. Bok and John T. Dunlop, *Labor and the American Community* (New York: Simon and Shuster, 1970). Chapter 4.

proficiency that permits a contractor to assign a man to a particular kind of work.

There is very little supervision on the job, so the contractor depends largely on skilled workmen for adequate performance. Further, many construction projects require the use of a particular craft for a limited period, so workers have only brief employment with a single contractor and frequently move from one employer to another. In addition, the whole industry is subject to employment highs and lows, partly as a result of the changing flow of government and private decisions and partly because of the strong influence of cyclical changes in the economy. Finally, the technology of the industry is changing substantially and would change even more rapidly except for constraints imposed by the unions, which are frequently joined by contractors. These industry characteristics also explain craft union objections and specific programs.

The central goals of the craft unions are to protect the job opportunities of their members in an industry that is highly unstable, dramatically seasonal, and organized around short-time employment by separate specific craft subcontractors on different jobs; and to expand the wages and other benefits of these craftsmen. The first is done by limiting the supply of skilled craftsmen and by allocating jobs among union members. The latter is done by a bargaining process with local craft contractors or subcontractors that results in separate local collective agreements for each craft.

The individual craft unions establish and maintain such controls by insisting on a twofold classification of jobs: skilled journeymen and helpers and/or apprentices.[4] The structuring is enforced by rules limiting the ratios of one category versus the other that may be used by the contractor on any specific job and by elaborate jurisdictional rules that specify the work assignments that must go to a particular category of craftsmen. The union, then, can furnish the journeymen needed by running a hiring hall or, more simply, by enforcing the formal and informal rule that only union journeymen can be employed.

The union is able to limit the supply of skilled journeymen by certification and by other procedures for eligibility for union membership. These methods have been used by the unions to deal with the substantial flow of workers who have presented themselves as competent craftsmen but have not received formal training. In a recent study, it was found that significant numbers of working journeymen had learned

---

[4] This summary ignored the unskilled category—the common labor category—where many blacks are now concentrated and about which there is relatively little conflict.

their trade by just picking up their skills on the job, particularly during periods of relative labor shortages; in on-the-job training under nonunion contractors, particularly in home building; by acquiring extra experience as laborers; in training received in other industries or in the military; or by getting instruction from friends and relatives.[5]

Because some contractors and unions have wished to improve craft standards and because the unions have a particular interest in limiting the labor supply, they have collaborated in promoting apprenticeship systems in each of the crafts. These systems are operated by unions, contractors, boards of education, and the federal government, which severely restrict the supply of additional skilled labor. The following devices in apprenticeship programs support that end: educational, age, and "no police record" qualifications for enrollment into the program; screening processes that include a substantial emphasis on judgments derived from personal interviews; controls over school curriculums; the availability of apprenticeship jobs; and the length of time required to graduate, which is controlled by unions and contractors.

Unions state that their emphasis on apprenticeship rules is essentially nonracial. One representative of the Building Trades Council in Chicago is reported to have said, "We tried to explain to the Coalition the difference between discrimination and exclusion. The trades never went out of their way to discriminate against blacks but, as a matter of practice, did try to exclude all so they could control the numbers." It is obvious that such a distinction is not acceptable to the black community.

Racist Characteristics

Many discretionary elements have been built into the system and have been used to limit the involvement of blacks as journeymen. The unions have the discretion to determine who can be enrolled as an apprentice and who can be graduated; who can join the union and be

---

[5] Howard Foster, "Non-Apprentice Sources of Training in Construction." *Monthly Labor Review*, February 1970, Vol. 93, No. 2. The findings from this study are consistent with a study by Ray Marshall, *The Negro and Apprenticeship*, which, in 1963, showed that only some 40 percent of the craftsmen had learned their trade through a formal apprenticeship.

Another way to present the same position is to use the projections made for Chicago as to the needs for additional skilled manpower for the industry during the next five years. Combining retirement and death estimates with a conservative estimate of the growth needs of the industry for an expanded work force, there may well be a need for an average annual addition of about 2,500 skilled craftsmen to the Chicago building industry. The prospective supply of skilled journeymen who are now in the apprenticeship system, however, even assuming that all of them then become journeymen and work at the trade in Chicago, is only about 1,200, somewhat less than 50 percent of the projected need.

given the work permit card; and who is excluded altogether. The union agent determines who should be sent to what jobs by the union agent, and the contractor determines which workers are to be accepted. A general contractor decides which subcontractors he will use, and banks and other lending agencies can back or turn down the requests of black contractors.

Another set of factors deriving from those already cited can be characterized as the discretion exercised by blacks on whether to enter the system. Given the deliberate discriminatory actions of union leaders, hostile union memberships, unsympathetic and weak contractors, and a government that ignores its own requirements for affirmative action toward equal employment, blacks who otherwise might undertake the long training necessary for a skilled job have been unwilling to risk it.

Over the years the flow of blacks into the apprenticeship system and then into the union as journeymen assigned to jobs has been limited by union and contractor policies, by their own strong sense of discrimination within the system, and by the actions of others. The educational system has failed to provide an adequate educational base for blacks. School counseling programs have steered blacks away from such training on the assumptions that the youths are probably not equipped to learn a trade and that the unions and contractors are not ready to receive them (another example of the vicious circle).

This pattern of discretionary choices as to who is accepted and who is rejected by the system, in addition to the limited attractiveness of the present apprenticeship programs, adds another perspective to the question of the availability of skilled labor to meet industry's turnover and growth needs. In Chicago, for instance, there are limited numbers of apprentices now enrolled (about 1,500 per year) who might be available to join the industry's labor force, and only about 115 of those are black. Although the 1969 ratio (9.1 percent) is slightly higher than it was in 1968 and higher than the ratio in the unions and on the job, the absolute numbers are so small that changes in the ratios of accredited blacks in the unions and on the jobs by the continuation of such trends would be insignificant for many years to come.

The Parties

In this as in other sectors, organized interests in the institution and among the black challengers define and conduct the confrontation and possible subsequent negotiations. In construction cases the organizational structure of the institution provides special problems for a challenge from a group outside the system. In one sense, the institution is very loosely organized and combines unions and contractors that are highly decentralized. However, the constituent members of the loosely organized overall union structure are the tightly organized individual craft unions.

These overall organizations for the unions and the contractors have been developed to deal with each other, but they are not geared to the kind of negotiations necessitated by black challenges. Relevant government involvement in construction confrontations, on the other hand, is duplicated in welfare, school, and other cases we documented. This poses more complicated problems for black challengers, however, because, like black school children, black university students, or black welfare recipients, they have no firm base within the existing system.

Within a single city, general contractors and subcontractors are joined in a relatively loose federation that functions for a variety of incidental concerns including lobbying with city and state governments. The subcontractors are organized into separate associations that bargain with their counterpart craft unions, participate with the unions on apprenticeships, and occasionally function on jurisdictional and other matters. General contractors may also have a separate city-wide association. In general, authority to speak on behalf of the total industry is usually delegated to the city-wide general federation only on specific issues and within fairly narrow limits.

Because the individual contractor or subcontractor has at least nominal control over job opportunities for blacks, he becomes involved in racial confrontation. He hires his employees, makes work assignments on the basis of judgments of skill as well as other considerations, provides any on-the-job training, and is responsible to the customer for quality and time of performance. Each general contractor must comply with government equal employment requirements and must secure similar commitments from his subcontractors.

The formal authority for a whole series of job decisions is divided, therefore, among the subcontractors and their associations **and the** general contractors with some incidental responsibilities delegated to city-wide industry federations. But these employers have a lesser role in determining manpower policies than those in any other major industry because of the degree to which local unions have taken over this set of functions.

Unions

The separate craft unions have maintained their control of jobs by retaining responsibility for certification of workers' skills through the mechanism of acceptance into full membership and journeyman status and by supplying needed workers to contractors through a hiring hall. Most of them also exercise some control over the assignment of individual workers to specific jobs. The local business agents of the individual craft unions usually carry the authority for these decisions. These functions give considerable authority to the respective business agents, but, as in any political organization, each business agent must both influence the judgments of the rank and file membership, and be responsive to them.

Through the long-term use of collective bargaining, the unions and the contractors have jointly developed and now administer an elaborate set of rules for the employment patterns of the industry. These rules are usually drawn up separately for each trade by its union and contractor representatives. Across the industry, in one form or another, machinery for the adjudication of jurisdictional disputes had also been established. The local union and relevant contractors participate jointly in a formal apprenticeship program, although the selection process is usually dominated by the union and the training process may be subsidized by federal government agencies.

Any insistence on more skilled jobs for blacks is, thus, a challenge to a system in which both unions and contractors share decision-making responsibility. If rules are to be changed as a result of a black challenge, the changes must be made through the joint action of contractors and unions. The two can and do become collaborators, having their internal conflicts and problems but presenting agreed-upon positions in confrontations.

On issues involving the availability of jobs to blacks, the unions generally dominate even joint decisions. There are great seasonal and cyclical fluctuations in construction orders, and, since most of the costs of this instability are born by the workers, the unions have worked to establish and maintain almost complete control over the labor supply. The contractors, therefore, are so bound to the unions for their labor supply that they are not free to act on their own in changing employment patterns. Although an expansion of the labor supply might be to the contractors' interest, the unions see any substantial enlargement as a threat to their members and to their ability to dominate wage setting negotiations. This complex relationship between unions and contractors is confirmed by collective agreements and so firmly established that it is strongly resistant to change.

Black Coalitions

When a black coalition is formed to press demands for jobs it becomes a prospective participant in racial confrontations. Where this style is adopted, it marks a contrast to the cooperative approach carried on for years by organizations with white and black membership and leadership, including many local branches of the NAACP and the Urban League. While these earlier efforts met with considerable success in changing legal provisions by legislation and by the courts, a more militant black leadership insisted that the employment patterns in construction have been changed very little.

These coalitions are usually formed on an ad hoc basis, although some have developed from earlier groupings. They may include black contractors who have a specialized interest in securing a greater share of government-financed contracts or subcontracts. Only occasionally will they include a black industrial union of skilled and unskilled workers that is not affiliated with building trades councils or the AFL-CIO.

Coalitions of this sort range over a wide variety of organizations with different focuses and constituencies within the black community. They represent a generalized desire of the local black community for job opportunities in the high-paying, prestigious skilled building trades. Such a coalition is likely to insist that it speak on behalf of the whole black community in a dispute with a section of the white establishment. This claim may or may not be actively challenged by other black leaders, since within the wide spectrum of black perspectives and commitment to blackness there are many different views.

The question of recognition and legitimacy of the Black Coalition recurred throughout the Chicago negotiations. In giving testimony before a government panel, one of the representatives of the contractors put it this way: "... perhaps the panel can help us to locate or relate to someone in the black community who is willing to sit down and work out a constructive program . . . Perhaps they (the Black Coalition) don't really speak for the community."

The Black Coalition, on the other hand, tended to consider its de facto existence adequate proof of its legitimacy and considered that the choice of representatives was a matter for the black community, not the establishment, to settle. The depth of this feeling was made clear in various statements from varying representatives during the confrontation and negotiations. One extreme might be indicated by the response of a black leader approaching a construction site to shut it down. When asked for his credentials, he responded, ". . . I don't need credentials—these men are my credentials." A more moderate, but equally firm, position was taken by the Rev. Jesse Jackson in a letter written from jail after his arrest at one of the construction sites, "... We'll march, protest, break injunction, boycott, and use other forms of creative protest in order to be heard, recognized, respected, and allowed to participate."

The authority of a coalition in a confrontation with the construction industry, then, is a function of the extent to which blacks identify with the criticism of the establishment and the goals of the coalition, the extent to which the specific programs developed by the coalition appear to be realistic and better than alternatives that have been tried or proposed, and the extent to which the coalition claims to speak for blacks and its capacities to coerce the industry are accepted by unions, contractors, and government agencies.

Governments

In one form or another, the federal government is, or can be, involved in racial confrontations in construction. There are a number of existing federal programs, administered by various federal agencies, that *could* be manipulated to press contractors and unions to change their racial policies and practices. One of the federal tools is based on the section of the 1964 Civil Rights Act that gives the Justice Department the right to file suit if employers or unions engage in discriminatory employment practices or resist efforts at equal employment opportunity. Another federal tool is the use of administrative regulations in accordance with Executive Order 11246 of 1965, which requires not only nondiscrimination but also affirmative action provisions for any contractor doing business with the federal government. Only the latter has been seriously tried and is a factor in our current analysis.[6]

Of course, there are conflicting federal purposes in addition to the efforts to induce or require the construction industry and unions to adopt affirmative action programs. A most immediate one is the attitude taken by numerous government agencies, which indicates that enforcement against the unions is almost impossible to achieve and that requirements against employers cannot be pressed very far. A second is the concern to find ways to moderate inflationary tendencies generated within the industry. This concern produces various alternative federal perspectives: cutbacks in construction such as those made during the Chicago incident summarized below; some reduction in the bargaining capacity of the unions against contractors because of a larger supply of labor; and an adequate supply of labor to carry on

---

[6] The federal government has also spent a good deal of money in assisting local groups and educational institutions in developing training programs for many kinds of occupations. Some of them have undertaken pre-apprenticeship building trade programs. The control over the program objectives of such training can become an issue in the conflict between blacks and the construction industry. As of this writing, the federal government may also have begun efforts to require affirmative action approaches in apprenticeship programs.

projected future plans for massive rebuilding of the cities, especially as Model Cities might focus on new construction and on repairing old buildings. But there are also political responses to the capacities of the building trades unions and their allies within the AFL-CIO that affect federal as well as local government policies.

Even the regulations made under the executive order had little effect on the contractor and union patterns until the experimental development and application of the Philadelphia Plan.[7,8] Under this approach, ranges are written into bids for new building contracts financed by federal money, which specify for at least some individual crafts the number of minority craftsmen that must be employed. The determination of acceptable ranges for each craft and for each contract is to be based on a judgment of the current extent of minority group participation in the trade; the availability of minority group persons for employment in such trade; and the impact of the program on the existing labor force.[9]

From the point of view of key federal administrators, this approach also has serious difficulties. First, it substitutes a compulsory program for a voluntary one, even though there is real doubt whether the compulsory requirements can or will be administered with sufficient care to produce the results specified. Beyond this, there is a great reluctance to take such action if any alternative approach appears to hold promise. There is also the uncertainty of whether the program will survive two future tests: the legislative test of continued support for this use of the executive order, and the judicial test of conformity to the nondiscrimination phraseology of the 1964 act.

Faced with these difficulties and balancing the political pressures affecting the national administration, the Secretary of Labor an-

---

[7] An illustration of federal weakness and black frustration appears in the unsuccessful effort to use the contract compliance route in Chicago in 1962, when the federal government let contracts for the construction of a U.S. court house. In a judgment of the court in response to a suit, the judge found that blacks were discriminated against in getting into an apprenticeship system and into union membership. Yet, the federal government did not require corrective actions by union and contractor at that time. According to testimony given by Samuel J. Simmons, Assistant Secretary for Equal Opportunity of the Department of Housing and Urban Development in Chicago on September 26, 1969, the court determination did not "produce a prompt and widespread response from the construction industry."

[8] See particularly *The Congressional Digest*, March 1970; and Chapter 4, *Manpower Report of the President*, March 1970. For the legal background to the plan, see "Executive Order 11246: Executive Encroachment" by James E. Remmert, *American Bar Association Journal*, November 1969.

[9] Taken from a fact sheet prepared by the U.S. Department of Labor and distributed at the hearings in Chicago on September 26, 1969, in the case summarized here.

nounced that the federal government would welcome the development of city plans and that, if these plans appeared to meet the objectives of the act and of the executive order, they would be accepted.[10] The posture of the federal government was to press contractors and unions to achieve voluntary agreements with black challengers and with any program that met the purposes of the act and the regulations. No specific terms for such an agreement were formulated by the government either in general or in regard to a specific city, contract, or craft. Thus, to a very limited degree, the pressures of the federal government were added to those of the black community in attempts to change the employment patterns within the construction industry.

City governments are less likely to be operating from a local nondiscrimination or affirmative action law but may be concerned with racial employment patterns in the hope that they will aid economic, social, and political development of the inner cities. A local administration may be anxious to avoid vigorous friction and violent conflict between constituencies. A city government has a variety of resources that can be manipulated to affect the outcome of a racial confrontation in construction if it wishes: the discretions available to the police and prosecuting attorney, the degree of enforcement of building codes, the handling of craft licensing provisions, the awarding of construction and repair contracts, and more subtle political pressures.

Political administrators of federal and local policies are concerned with their interactions with the three groups immediately involved: the politically powerful building trades groups, the business interests of the contractors and those related to contractors, and various segments of the black community. In a more general sense, these political figures are concerned not only with peaceful patterns but also with fairness in the degree to which the government plays a role in the relationships between the black community and the construction industry. There are also tensions between the administrative and political organization of a city, on the one hand, and the federal government, on the other.

In summary, in each large city there is a construction industry composed of craft unions, contractors, and subcontractors; there is a city and federal government administration that is concerned, among other things, with peace and equal employment; and there is the potential of a black community coalition.

---

[10] A formal announcement to this effect was issued by the U.S. Department of Labor early in October, 1969.

What happens next? A challenge to the industry by that black coalition is a possibility.[11] Such a confrontation, the resulting negotiations, and the characteristics of possible agreements are suggested by a summary of what happened in Chicago during 1969-70.

A CONFRONTATION BETWEEN A BLACK COALITION AND THE CONSTRUCTION INDUSTRY IN CHICAGO, ILLINOIS

This case concerns the confrontation of the construction industry, employers, and unions, by a coalition of black organizations. It extended over a six month period from July 1969 through January 1970 and terminated in an agreement that has become known as The Chicago Plan.

At issue were demands by members of the coalition for entry by black workers into the construction industry at the journeyman level and the development of special training programs to prepare black workers for construction jobs. The coalition, which had been formed earlier to deal with other community issues, mounted a campaign to help more blacks enter the building industry. Although 12 organizations apparently represented the core of the coalition, the actual number of participating organizations approximated 60 when the controversy was at its height. The organizations involved covered a wide spectrum of ideology from "gang" groups to organizations such as The Westside Builders' Association, Operation Breadbasket, and the Souther Christian Leadership Council's national headquarters. On the other side were the Building Trades Council and all of its constituent craft unions, the Building Construction Employers Association, and the Builders Association of Chicago.

---

[11] Of course, alternative developments may occur in each of these cities: (1) there may be no organized effort to change the black-white ratios; (2) there may be organized efforts to incorporate blacks into existing systems by developing apprenticeship programs run exclusively by government agencies or by organizations in which some blacks play a part; (3) the government may seek to require affirmative action programs such as those the contractors and unions devise for themselves; (4) changes in black-white ratios may follow from educational developments, changing technology in the industry, or expanded markets for the industry that require modifications of union-management practices. From a variety of black and white perspectives, one of these alternatives may appear more desirable than the confrontation alternative with which we are concerned. As the reader is aware, we recognize that such alternative approaches enter into the judgments of each protagonist in a confrontation but we are not making any independent assessment of which is the most desirable of these approaches.

The precipitating incident appears to have occurred in April 1969, when the Westside Builders Association, a group of black building contractors, met with the Department of Urban Renewal. At that meeting, the builders claimed, they were promised a substantial amount of the subcontracting for a rehabilitation project in the ghetto. In early July, they realized that this promise was not going to be honored and that the contract had instead been awarded to a white construction company and that only white subcontractors were being asked to bid on the work to be done. The Westside Builders contacted the white construction company and were offered subcontracting amounting to less than four percent of the total. As a consequence of this situation, the construction coalition closed down the construction site on July 23. The day before, the coalition had participated in a demonstration at another construction site. Additionally, some members of the coalition had sat in at the office of the head of the Building Trades Council. They were arrested and charged with illegal trespassing. In the days following, several other construction sites were shut down. The intent of these demonstrations apparently was to show a concern for the lack of black employment in the building trades as well as for the position of the black subcontractors. A press conference was held and an initial demand for jobs was made.

After these events, the coalition became more tightly and highly organized and additional shutdowns occurred. Federal construction jobs were given first priority because of their susceptibility to pressure on the basis of administrative orders and the Civil Rights Act, but also because they provided an opportunity for federal intervention. The federal government first intervened through the Community Relations Services of the U.S. Department of Labor, and other government agencies.

In early August, an initial meeting took place between the coalition and the Building Association, followed almost immediately by a meeting of coalition, contractor, and union representatives. These first meetings were fruitless and on August 14, the contractors asked for court injunctions restraining the coalition leaders from mounting any demonstrations on building sites. The injunction process was expanded the following week. On August 21, the coalition agreed to put its demands in writing and the representative at the Building Trades Council said that he would recommend the agreements made to his constituent bodies. The groups decided to exchange proposals. A whole series of meetings, proposals, and counterproposals were made, and Chicago's Mayor Richard J. Daley finally intervened as a mediator. These efforts culminated in an agreeement known as The Chicago Plan.

Analysis

This case summary provides illustrative material for a more general analysis. The discussion preceding the case description describes the complex nature of the construction industry and the parties to the confrontation. In many ways this complexity is greater than that found in any of the other sectors analyzed.

These complexities include the fact that the establishment side was a combination of unions and managements and that the major part of the negotiations was carried out by representatives of central organizations made up of a number of different unions and contractors. On the side of the challengers, the organizational structure was almost as complex since it was comprised of representatives of a large number of diverse black organizations. While those organizations, in general, agreed upon the general thrust of obtaining more black representation in the building trades, they held different views on strategy and priorities. On both sides, diverse styles were found among the various representatives.

The Issues

If a confrontation develops, there may well be negotiations that focus on one or more of six sets of issues. The first of these, the authority of the spokesman for each side, may never be resolved to the complete satisfaction of both parties.

The black coalition is likely to insist on firm commitments from the contractor-union spokesman and their ability and willingness to execute any terms jointly agreed upon. The industry spokesmen will counter, however, by emphasizing the craft-by-craft characteristics of separate union-management agreements and apprenticeship rules, and the fact that council and association spokesmen can make *recommendations*, but have no authority to change either set of rules.

This difficulty is illustrated by the initial reaction of the representatives of the Building Trades Council when confronted with the original sit-in by some of the black challengers. In response to those challengers, they said, "... black pressure is misdirected when used against us. The Council does not negotiate contracts. It does not control the apprentice training systems developed between unions, contractors, the board of education, and the government. It does not recruit workers for any of the trades. It does not have a hiring hall."

In the case study prepared by McKersie, he noted:

In general, during these negotiations, the parties held dramatically different views of what the discussions were all about. The coalition viewed them as their 'Own Wagner Act.' In other words, they came to the bargaining table as negotiators seeking a firm agreement for their constituents. The Industry, for its part, wanted the discussions to be exploratory and advisory but not *formal* negotiations. They did accede in part to the Coalition's view of the discussion, but only to the extent of agreeing to *recommend* to their affiliated groups the understandings that had been reached at the bargaining tables. They vigorously objected to committing their organizations. In this sense, the union and employer representatives were 'go-betweens' or spokesmen without any real authority to commit anyone. They were 'under instructions' and possessed very little flexibility.

The industry spokesmen, moreover, are likely to challenge the representative claims of the black leaders and to doubt their ability to enter into binding commitments on behalf of the black community. Such a position is more likely, of course, if some blacks, whom the industry perceive as "more responsible," remain outside a coalition and press rival claims to represent the black community. In part, the black response will be to develop indications of their black legitimacy and also to search for methods and allies that permit them to gain recognition.

A second urgent conflict issue turns on proposals to expand the training of blacks. It is likely that the coalition will admit that too few blacks are sufficiently skilled to earn the high hourly rates of the industry and will focus on ways to train blacks to fit into the industry as skilled craftsmen. On this, there may be serious differences of tactical judgment within the black coalition. Some leaders, such as those in the Chicago Black Coalition, may insist that a basic change in the training system is essential to open up the industry for black workers. An alternative tactic may be to accept the apprenticeship system and to attempt to find ways to modify it, or more likely, to modify the black workers so that they will want to get into that system and be able to successfully achieve journeyman status through it.

If the former programmatic approach is pursued by a coalition, there will be a strong resistance by the unions and the contractors. To the unions, such a program will appear to be threatening the established apprenticeship system and all of the rules and expectations that are based on it. The unions will also resist the program because it could enlarge the inflow into the industry and endanger their control over the labor market.

The contractors are also likely to oppose this program despite the facts that their bargaining position, vis-a-vis the unions, would be improved by a larger supply of skilled labor and that there may be extreme shortages of skilled labor in a variety of the crafts as expansion occurs in the industry.

Another aspect of this issue over training programs concerns the degree of expertise that apprenticeship programs seek to develop. For black leaders, the present criteria necessary for graduation frequently appear to be far too elaborate. Numerous blacks appear to be functioning as craftsmen with knowledge developed by experience rather than by formal training and over half of all whites with journeyman status never completed an apprenticeship program. The contractors, however, are likely to decide that the black position is based largely on ignorance of the technical needs of the industry, and will claim that future foremen and subcontractors will need basic education in the trade.

A third urgent issue is the number of jobs that would become available to blacks. The complications of this question are obvious to the industry and are likely to become obvious to the black challengers as negotiations proceed since almost all construction jobs involve employment with a specific contractor for only brief periods and the total job pattern for any group of workers is a function of the level of construction activity. No individual contractor can guarantee the total number of jobs that can be shared by white and black journeymen. Even an estimate of the available jobs requires separate calculations for each craft and this must be based on technological and business forecasts. Finally, a projection of the number of black craftsmen available for future jobs involves estimates of how many would present themselves for training and how many would graduate.

All of these uncertainties lead industry protagonists to insist that it is meaningless for blacks to demand a guarantee of a specific number of jobs. Industry spokesmen argue that any commitment such as a quota would restrict job opportunities for whites and would require an undesirable preference for blacks.

On the other hand, the black community puts enormous pressure on its spokesmen to insist on assurances of the numbers of jobs that are going to be made available to blacks since there is little trust in white promises. This lack of trust has been supported by the record of discrimination and the existing low ratios of black workers years after equal employment laws and regulations have been adopted. Black leaders also feel that if blacks are going to be persuaded to enter training, they must have increased assurance that they will be accepted into union membership and be permitted to enter the job market.

There are three types of responses available to negotiators to meet these pressures: (1) to require numbers or ratios such as the system in the Philadelphia Plan (pressed at one point by one spokesman within the Chicago Black Coalition); (2) to set target figures for the numbers or ratios of black to white workers (such as those included in the first industry offer in Chicago); or (3) to identify target numbers to be incorporated into training programs (such as those specified to other sections of the final Chicago agreement).

A fourth set of issues concerns the existing rules and practices of the industry, especially the whole apprenticeship process from selection to graduation. Other issues are eligibility for union membership, the job assignment process that involves the role of the business agent in sending workers to the jobs, and the informal union-shop provisions that frequently prevail. Whatever the training and job promises of the industry, they are not likely to be kept unless contractors and unions accept the fact that these industry rules and practices will have to be changed. However, they are likely to resist these changes with great determination because they prefer the stabilized relationships that have been worked out over the years.

Here again, the negotiators have a number of choices: They may agree not to specify any changes in these rules, as they finally did in Chicago; they may agree on an end-result that could only be achieved by some changes in rules or practices but leave such modifications up to the unions and contractors as was done in Philadelphia; or they could incorporate some rule changes such as the proposal, which was rejected in the Chicago case, that only work-permit cards be issued until black numbers or ratios are achieved within the unions and on the jobs.

Fifth, there is a set of issues centering on the degree of coalition involvement in the decision-making process of the industry. As included in the original demands of the Chicago Black Coalition, this issue had strong emotional overtones and was necessary because, as one spokesman put it:

... We are asking that black people be trained by black people, or at least that the administration of any programs for black people be in the hands of black people. . . . We cannot allow [racists] to be in charge of the training of black people. . . . The average young black man doesn't trust white overseers, nor does he have any reason to. That's tragic, but it's true. . . .

We do not want in on an advisory capacity because we have learned that black people's advice is not taken seriously. We want to come in on decisions and have a voice in those decisions, carried out in this nation with pride. And the inner city is the black man's land.

The industry view as expressed by a union spokesman was equally firm:

In our discussions with some of the leadership of that group, their principal thrust appears to be control. And we don't believe that is something we should give them.

Negotiators can consider several responses to black demands for control or for participation. These could range from assigning exclusive responsibility to a coalition (such as the Chicago industry proposal that all recruitment functions be assigned to the Coalition) to different degrees of joint participation (such as the eventual Chicago formula that there could be discussions of changes in the training programs for individual crafts but adoption only if there was mutual agreement on the craft committees). They could include maintaining unilateral white decisions such as determining who to admit to union membership and to assign on a specific job (both of which were left unmodified in the Chicago agreement). There are, of course, many permutations of each of these categories of black involvement in decision making, any one of which may be considered by the negotiators.

Finally, there is a set of issues that involves policing the way in which the agreed upon policies are applied. If a coalition is to be involved in an enforcement effort, some procedures are required. These might include a mediational approach that leaves the final decisions within the industry decision-making structure, or the development of grievance and impartial arbitration machinery outside of that structure. In most of the construction cases this enforcement issue has not been pressed.

All of these issues require implicit judgments by each side about the future: Will a coalition or its replacement continue as an organized expression of black interests in contruction jobs? Will either the leadership for a coalition continue with the same perspectives that dominated the making of the original agreement? Will the conditions in the industry approximate those contemplated by the present negotiators? What will be the future postures of the city and federal governments? Will the necessity for black coercive potential continue in order to implement decisions and develop new policies? If so, will such black power exist? Or, by contrast, will opportunities arise for cooperative activities? If so, will both sides encourage joint development? All of these questions require predictions about the future and it is likely that these will vary among representatives of each of the two protagonists.

Coercive Pressures

As in other sectors, a black cry for justice becomes an effort by the black community to force an expansion of the number of black skilled jobs in the construction industry when black leaders have the capacity and determination to organize such coercion. Such an activity requires vigorous and wise organizing efforts and, inevitably, involves costs and risks to leaders and followers.

Some of the direct coercive methods available to blacks in other contexts are not meaningful here because the black community has no functional relation to the industry. Strike calls could not be effective because there are so few black workers who are important to the industry and white worker support for such an effort is very unlikely. A boycott against industry sales is not meaningful since the amount of direct sales of construction to blacks is insignificant and there is no likelihood that individual white purchasers would join blacks in this activity.

Thus, the black community approaches the system from the outside. The only *direct* interaction of blacks with the industry that is likely to force a change in policies or practices is the use of any device that can shut down the construction site, interrupting work and stimulating a fear of violence.

Of course, coercion by demonstration has built-in limitations. It requires many participants who are prepared to respond day after day. There is always the risk of repressive penalties if violence is initiated by police, white workers, or black demonstrators. On the other hand, the fear of violence can be a powerful coercive tool if it can be manipulated carefully.

Secondary sources of pressure include peers of the white industry leaders in the power structure of the cities and unions, local political figures, and national politicians. Any or all of these three groupings can be appealed to or threatened by the black community. They may be persuaded to join in a coalition and apply whatever degree of pressure they possess in their own self-interest. Peaceful demonstrations, the implied threat of less peaceful demonstrations, and the suggestion of the possibilities of violence may activate these persons to put pressure on the industry. Black leaders may feel that demonstrations that stop construction work, even temporarily, and indicate to others the urgency of feelings of injustice are much more promising than simple appeals to white workers, white contractors, or whites outside the industry.

The first response of the industry to black demands tends to be "retain the status quo." But the investment in the status quo is not limited to the unions and contractors. A preference for existing patterns is shared by members of other white groups who feel that their position would be threatened if black power developed from a confrontation with the construction industry. It is supported by local and national politicians who may have, with great effort, put together a working relationship with unionists and contractors and who have judged that black political support is not likely to be rewarding.

There are counterpressures on each of these political groups from others whose interest in political power as such is peripheral but who wish to correct the whole pattern of white discrimination. Politicians also must not alienate black support any more than is necessary and must respond to the fears of citizens who want their political leaders to find ways to avoid violence.

A demonstration stimulates each of these supplementary groups by dramatizing the degree of black commitment, defining issues differently and raising them to levels of political symbols, and creating the spectre of violence. The Chicago case and other illustrations indicate that these secondary pressures can reinforce the demands of the black demonstrators and provide some coercive muscle with which the blacks can approach a bargaining table.

The industrial relations system of building trade unions and contractors establishes rights and duties, procedural rules, and the balancing of benefits and costs to which all within the system are committed. These relationships are supported by laws and administrative rules and the availability of the police power of the state. The system is supported also by public and private purchases of construction.

Neither federal nor local governments have demonstrated much capacity or inclination to change the system, although it obviously produces high costs and inflexible responses to construction needs and continues widespread job discrimination against blacks. Any alliance of contractors and blacks to press for nondiscrimination and affirmative action is restricted by commitments to the functioning of the present rules and balance of forces.

Even more than for other sectors, then, the primary response in construction is a rejection of the demand of outsiders to get inside the system as an *organized* interest. Where such a refusal needs the police powers of the government, these are available to break up demonstrations and to block further demonstrations. In addition, the governmental allocation of resources, such as training for craftsmen, may be assigned to the industry and to those blacks who are prepared to operate within the existing system.

Government concern for equal opportunity expresses the need to develop a symbol of establishing and enforcing equality. Since the government is not able to achieve this alone, it may desire an agreement by black leaders to serve as symbolic proof that the industry is in substantial conformity because black spokesmen have accepted programs that can be expected to move toward equality.

Negotiating Interactions

A racial confrontation in construction usually starts with sharply conflicting positions and the possibility of disruptions. The problem for all concerned is whether and how the parties will find agreement from divergent positions and peace from disruption. The degree of change in the traditional practices and policies of the industry that would be made by the terms of an agreement is also a concern.

Three sets of factors appear to be most influential in determining the course of negotiations: (1) the shifting priorities of each side; (2) the attitudinal structuring; and (3) the capacities and choices of each side for coercion and for cooperation.

Consider the three categories of demands that are likely to be made by a coalition and rejected by the industry: to change specific rules and procedures, including the apprenticeship system and union membership restrictions; to guarantee specific numbers of skilled worker and trainee openings; and to rearrange the decision-making structure of the system to assign an important and continuing set of functions to the coalition. During the course of negotiations, each side will find it necessary to reassess the relative urgency with which it holds to each demand. The choices will be made as different leaders and influences become more or less prominent. These choices are also affected by changing perceptions of the likelihood of approaching various goals through the negotiations. In the Chicago case, there were clear, substantial shifts in priority positions within the Black Coalition that were also reflected in changes in leadership roles. The industry position, on the other hand, changed much less. However, it does appear that there was a greater readiness to accept larger Black Coalition roles within the industry during the early stages and under the early leadership in the industry group. When the leadership shifted to a hard-line union spokesman, there was more reluctance to accept the demand for promises of job openings or a participatory Black Coalition role.

Frequently, in the beginning of negotiations between the construction industry and a black coalition, each side views the other as hostile and unwilling to attempt to find a compromise that could be the basis for an agreement. Indeed, the industry representatives may accurately perceive that the challengers are so certain of the white racism of the industry that a coalition is not even trying to be realistic or to consider compromise. In the same way, a coalition may accurately view industry representatives as being unsympathetic to black efforts to gain economic and social status and unwilling to reach an understanding with militant black spokesmen. The rhetoric of each side is likely to reinforce these views.

These judgments may be modified during the course of negotiations. If they do not change; the possibilities for a meaningful agreement are slim. Changes may come about through greater familiarity with one another or, as in the Chicago case, more friendly and accommodating postures may be purposefully sought by some, even as others are making accommodation more difficult.

The second prominent attitudinal aspect of racial negotiations is each side's judgment about the degree to which the other side's spokesmen represent and express their group's position and can secure acceptance of the terms of an agreement. In the Chicago case, the contractors and union representatives suspected that the black coalition spokesmen were not really representing the black community. This suspicion is heightened by previous, more favorable experiences with other blacks who acted more cooperatively and by the belief that a cooperative attitude is the only posture that makes sense for blacks. These industry doubts and suspicions, as we noted in the Chicago case, may be modified, even though they may never be completely allayed.

The third general aspect of attitudinal structuring relates to accurate reading of the signals communicated from one side to the other. For the accommodation to take place successfully, both the threats and the offers of cooperation must be accurately understood. The efficiency of this communication process depends on the judgments of each side about the other side's representatives and is also affected by the differences that develop within a single side about perspectives and intentions. Most fundamentally, the efficiency of the communication process is affected by the degree to which each side adopts coercive or cooperative approaches to securing changes in the position of the other. This factor is so fundamental to the whole process that we deal with it separately.

Throughout the negotiating process each side assesses the degree of pressure that it will encounter as well as muster against the other. In the Chicago case, each recognized that the early coalition demonstrations at the construction site called for some concessions by the industry, while the extremely limited capacity of the injunction moved the power balance back toward the industry. The threat of federal imposition of the type of contract requirement instituted in Philadelphia caused the mayor and the industry to recognize some limited coercive power in the hands of the coalition. Each side also acknowledged the potential for violence, which both sides wished to avoid. This tool was available to the coalition particularly because of its youth gang affiliates and the image they created of black violence. On the other hand, both sides could use, but also feared, the consequences of the "hard hat" reaction of many union members. It moved the balance moderately to the advantage of the coalition because it prompted the mayor and the federal government to conclude that some concessions by the industry were urgently needed to reach an accommodated agreement without further white violence.

Offers of collaboration can also be made. For instance, the earliest industry offer in Chicago called for a role for the coalition in recruiting blacks into the apprenticeship program and in developing preapprenticeship programs. This was a modest suggestion that the coalition join in a cooperative effort and, insofar as the industry needed such an expanded inflow into the apprenticeship programs for its manpower needs and to improve its record, it was an offer of collaboration. At that stage of the negotiations the coalition rejected the offer as representing neither enough involvement, nor a package that would produce the results they sought.

A more significant development of this alternative approach occurred in Chicago in the final choices faced by the coalition. It had to decide how much of its priority should be put on obtaining firm industry commitments and how much effort should be expended in working out a friendly and cooperative relationship with the local craft unions and city-wide leaders. The agreement was finally achieved when, despairing of forcing firm commitments for rule changes, numbers of blacks employed, and a different training route, the coalition decided that it would try the alternative of collaborating within the structure of the industry to achieve, at least in some degree, the objectives it attempted to force in negotiations.

Third-Party Intervention

When there are black challenges to the construction industry, negotiations are possible only if each side is ready to accept the respective spokesmen as representatives of their interests. Even this preliminary issue may require the assistance of third parties, just as in the Chicago case it required the intervention of Mayor Daley to persuade the industry to accept the representativeness of the coalition.

Some additional mediational functions can be performed by a person who has no direct interest in the outcome of the dispute. In the Chicago case, there was intermediary assistance in arranging for sessions and chairing them, interpreting positions to the other side, and suggesting alternative solutions that might meet the needs of both sides. A supplementary role for a third-party intervenor, the role assumed when the intervenor has an interest in the outcome, was very important in Chicago and suggests its usefulness in other cities. Both the federal compliance office and the mayor wanted one outcome more than another; each wanted the negotiations to result in an agreement. The federal agency needed a basis for developing a record of enforcement of the equal employment and affirmative action contract provision even more than it needed an expansion of black employment in construction. The mayor needed agreement to underscore the fact that his local administration had achieved an understanding without the compulsory intervention of the federal government, and to lessen the danger of further violence and rioting.

Thus, the federal and the city governments were interested in finding some form of agreement regardless of the terms. The federal government did provide the coercive muscle that helped the coalition get an agreement from the industry; the mayor did provide pressures on both sides toward agreement. But neither grouping had independent standards on any of the three major categories of issues that they sought to press on the participants.

POSSIBLE RESULTS

The record on the experience with the confrontation-negotiation approach to change for blacks in the construction industry certainly is not complete. There is inadequate experience with what happens *after* a voluntary plan has been adopted. However, if one judges by press announcements and by formal documents of agreement, black coalitions have made progress by confrontations and subsequent negotiations. For instance, it appears that the Chicago Plan established the Black Coalition, at least in some minor degree, as a participant in the recruitment, training, and even the certification of blacks as skilled craftsmen. There is a minimal promise of admissions into the unions and a joint consideration, craft-by-craft, of the possibilities of different, or at least abbreviated, training plans.

But it is too early to assess any of these possibilities. At best, most of the plans contemplate an extended training period before many additional black craftsmen become available for journeymen jobs. Further, progress depends on a number of other things that may happen: changes in the market for construction; changes in government postures about discrimination in construction employment; and the extent to which blacks continue their pressures on the unions and contractors. Finally, there is a consequence, hard to evaluate without extended additional investigation, which has not been analyzed in our case or elsewhere. Black leaders as individuals may be added to the recruiting programs of the industry as they were in Chicago, or they may appear as representatives of black organizations that have undertaken a continuing organizational role of involvement within the industry.

Despite these uncertainties, however, it seems possible to speculate that, at least so far, the efforts of black leaders to pressure the industry provide only minimal prospects of significant change but that blacks have the added capacity to require some assistance in their efforts from city and federal governments. Even this added pressure (offset as it is by many other competing political considerations) has produced only modest results. Indeed, there has been almost no immediate change in the number of black craftsmen either on jobs or newly incorporated into the hiring hall patterns of the unions. Also, there has been no substantial modification in the apprenticeship system or in the criteria and procedures for admission into union membership. The number of blacks in the apprenticeship system may have increased somewhat, although how much this is a consequence of the direct involvement of a black coalition is unclear.

So far, it is not clear that there have been any important changes in the system of union-contractor controls on the labor market or in the training programs for those who seek to qualify as journeymen. Thus, there have been no changes in the criteria for eligibility to enter the apprenticeship system, the apprenticeship curriculum, the qualifications for graduation, and the procedures by which these are applied. The sharp, enforced distinction between journeymen and apprentice-trainees still remains. There have been no changes in union membership patterns and practices or in the hiring hall processes that have been used by local union business agents as a way to assign union members to a job with a contractor.

The date of the Chicago case and the general analyses appear to support a conclusion expressed in the Baron-Cassell case study:

> The basic problem of the case, that of finding ways to give black workers a greater share in the important construction industry, is the enormous resistance of institutions to any real change. Entrenched interests, entrenched bureaucracies, entrenched beliefs are all just that: entrenched. Efforts at change, even extensive efforts, are blunted, and anything less than extensive efforts are hopeless.

CHAPTER 8

Nonprofit Service Organizations

Churches, professional organizations, and social and recreational clubs are nonprofit organizations whose primary role is to provide assistance and service to their voluntary membership. Racial confrontations that have occurred in many such organizations have involved black and white professionals who differed on the direction of the professional activities and/or the desirability of a professional organization taking positions on social issues unrelated to its work.

Although only one case was studied in depth for this project, it included characteristics that seemed representative of many other such organizations. Therefore, it can be used to develop an understanding of a number of overt racial conflicts in this category. We studied and analyzed the conflict that appeared during the organization of the National Council of New Careers. In this case, a predominately white group of professionals was establishing an organization designed to develop programs for the benefit of a predominately black group of paraprofessionals. The conflict, therefore, was not based on racial factors alone; it also matched professionals versus paraprofessionals. For the black professional the situation was doubly difficult and involved competing loyalties.

FOUNDING CONFERENCE OF THE NATIONAL COUNCIL FOR NEW CAREERS

This case concerns a confrontation and subsequent negotiations that occurred at the founding conference of the National Council for New Careers in June 1968 at Wayne State University in Detroit.[1] The major events occurred over a four-day period, but the consequences have been traced over a longer period of time.

Background

The new careers idea originated in the early 1960s and had achieved considerable recognition and support by the time of the confrontation described here. The core of the new careers concept is the employment and utilization of noncredentialed workers as paraprofessionals[2] who are trained for entry-level employment in human service agencies and who, it is hoped, will move up a career ladder as rapidly as possible.

By 1968 new careers programs had been established in many cities and had enrolled several thousand trainees from the poverty population, most of them minority group members. Government and nonprofit agencies providing health, welfare, education, and other human services had accepted trainees and assumed responsibility for their progress.

This type of a program inevitably poses a challenge to the traditional concepts of the organization of such services and to the educational and other requirements built into the system of accrediting professionals. The conference described here was an attempt to form an organization that could operate to promote the new careers concept in some organized way.

The Planning Stage

Over a period of nine months in 1967-68, a predominantly white group of scholars and technicians, all with important professional and organizational positions, planned the establishment of a national organization. Their intention was to create an instrument to promote

[1] This summary and subsequent quotations in the analysis are taken from a more elaborate in-depth study prepared by Sumner A. Rosen as a part of the Racial Negotiations Project.

[2] The terms "paraprofessional," "nonprofessional," "subprofessional," and "new careerist" have all been used in the literature of this subject. We use the terms paraprofessional and new careerist.

changes in patterns of manpower utilization and training in human service agencies across the country to move them toward the new careers concepts developed in the early 1960s. The planning committee represented disparate groups that supported the new careers idea: professionals, professors, unionists, and two new careerists who agreed on the need for a national organization but differed in their approaches, priorities, and focuses on problem areas.

A small interim committee of white professionals took on the task of actually planning the conference. A planning meeting held in December was attended by approximately 65 people invited by the interim committee. The participants represented labor unions; professional, political, business, and civil rights organizations; foundations; and some state and federal offices. Since only a few paraprofessionals attended, the group was highly elitist and dominated by the professsionals.

Several issues that arose during these planning sessions were to be part of the confrontation at the June 1968 founding conference. The planning group tried to meet some of the problems, including the basic one of whether new careerists should be invited to the Detroit conference. The interim committee was expanded to include a few new careerists and several members of this group were included on the invitation list. However, the professionals conceived of their function as founding an organization that would serve new careerists, coordinate the professionals working in the area, and assume a supportive role for whatever kind of a separate organization the new careerists themselves might select. It was decided that the council would include persons in influential positions in the new careers field.

At this stage, the basic questions as to the role and scope of the organization were essentially settled with an emphasis on professionalism and influence. Some 500 invitations were sent but only a very few new careerists were included in that list.

The Confrontation

The conference was scheduled for June 20-23 at Wayne State University in Detroit. Before the opening session on the night of June 20, one of the press services informed the planning committee that a group of black paraprofessionals from Newark, N.J., would attend and protest their exclusion from the conference.

The opening session of the conference was scheduled to include a keynote speech and a panel of three black and two white new careerists. In order to expand the audience and establish some relationships with individuals based in Detroit, additional invitations to the opening sessions had been extended to people from antipoverty and community action programs. Thus, the audience included a number of people who had no background at all in the planning for the establishment of a New Careers Council.

Early in the session a group of blacks from Newark took seats in the front of the auditorium. One member of the group announced their intention to stay through the conference and demanded that they be given full voting rights. The audience support for the group came as a surprise to the conference conveners. One member of the planning committee finally suggested that "negotiations with our brothers from Newark" take place after the opening session and, with his assurance that he was willing to recognize legitimate demands, the opening meeting proceeded as scheduled.

The issues that emerged from a night of caucusing and discussion with the black protestors were: (1) the right of the new careerists to participate in the organization, including the right to vote; (2) control of council leadership; (3) control and allocation of council monies; (4) the role of an organization of new careerists.

The First Negotiations

Negotiations took place between the organizers of the conference and the emerging black leadership. The first major issue tackled was that of representation. The conference organizers tended to see the involvement of new careerists as peripheral and premature and conceived of the organization as a coalition of those in positions of power who were interested in new careers and could advance the concept in private and government circles.

The representation issue was further exacerbated by the challenge from some white professionals who were substituting for invited participants or attending because they had some interest in the organization, although they had not been invited. On June 21, the convening group reiterated its position that voting rights were limited to invited participants. Challenges from the floor to this position were first resolved by extending voting rights to substitute delegates. A vote on this issue carried by a large margin. Later in the session, the right to participate was further broadened to include everyone present who would pay the registration fee.

The remaining issues were those that were of major concern to the black paraprofessionals. After the vote on the rules for participation, the floor was opened to discussion of the key issue of the relationship of the National Council to the paraprofessionals. Considerable intervention from the floor by other blacks underscored the need to adjourn for lunch and to hold a meeting between the conference organizers and the whole paraprofessional group to determine whether the demands could be negotiated. The results of that meeting were to be presented to the total conference at the beginning of the afternoon session.

Negotiations of Black Demands

At the beginning of the negotiations there was no clear indication of the leadership of the black caucus. However, as the demands were presented and discussed, the leadership patterns, probably set by the many caucuses that had been held by the blacks, became clear and one individual emerged as the chairman of the negotiating meeting and the leader of the black group.

During this session, the conference organizers responded to factual questions, particularly those concerning financing, and to specific points raised by the protestors. It became clear that the price for the continuance of the conference without a walkout or further demonstrations was the provision of a strong participatory role for the paraprofessionals. The apparent willingness of the conference organizers to negotiate with the black challengers shifted the latter's emphasis from disruption to accommodation. The control question, a primary focus of the more militant blacks, was postponed and there was no strong push for a 51 percent controlling vote by the paraprofessionals, a demand that had been made in the morning session. Agreement was reached on five major points:

1. Two paraprofessionals would be recognized as voting delegates from each city represented.
2. Each such delegate would pay the regular $10 registration fee.
3. The conference would accept and articulate a mandate to assist in the organization of a movement of new careerists.
4. A workshop on the organization of new careerists would be added to the conference workshops scheduled for that afternoon.
5. Two paraprofessionals would be added to the convening-steering committee, and two to the nominating committee.

The first two points dealing with representation essentially spelled out the earlier decision of the total conference but were seen as a necessary recognition of the black group, assuring the paraprofessionals of representation and guaranteeing the conference organizers against a flood of large numbers of paraprofessionals from the Detroit area. The third point essentially changed the purpose of the newly formed council; the fourth modified the conference program to recognize that changed focus; and the fifth assured the paraprofessionals of a continuing voice in the council itself. The total conference quickly accepted, by vote, the five points agreed on and the first stage of the negotiations was completed.

Implementation of the Agreement

The leaders that emerged were solidified by the legitimization of the paraprofessionals' role in the conference and the National Council. The workshop on organizing new careerists drew virtually all of the paraprofessionals. During these sessions, a group of white radicals attempted unsuccessfully to join with the black paraprofessionals on ideological and programmatic grounds. However, the paraprofessionals preferred to pursue their own interests in their own way.

Most of the black professionals, by this time, had joined forces with the paraprofessionals, providing that group with some sophistication in organizational dynamics. There were times when even these black professionals were excluded from the caucus of the paraprofessionals. The workshop group of paraprofessionals continued to formulate a specific set of demands through the evening, leaving the formal evening session to the regulars—the white professionals.

The agenda called for the election of the officers and executive committee of the newly formed council to take place on Sunday morning. The conference organizers, fearing that attendance at the conference would be small on that last day, proposed to hold the elections on Saturday, a move that the paraprofessionals regarded as an attempt to stage the election before they had time to prepare and gain support for their own proposals.

The black caucus, therefore decided to boycott the Saturday morning session in order to prevent any compression of the timetable and reconvened their caucus instead. Four demands from this black caucus were presented at the Saturday afternoon session:

1. The bylaws of the council should provide for representation of paraprofessionals on all bodies of the council, the paraprofessionals to be selected at their own convening convention;
2. A new standing committee composed entirely of paraprofessionals should be added to the council;
3. This standing committee should receive $50,000 to organize paraprofessionals; and

4. Provision should be made for the council to absorb the costs of the convening convention mentioned under point 1.

The conference accepted these points as a workshop report rather than as demands and there was no move to debate or act upon them. This strategy was acceptable to the black caucus because one of the black professionals had emerged as a vigorous spokesman and candidate for the top leadership position of the council. His color identification and his statements of the functions and purposes of the proposed council in racial terms suggested to the paraprofessionals that the four points would be less important if this leadership and point of view could prevail.

Attention centered on the preparation of a slate to be presented to the conference on Sunday morning. Although the paraprofessionals were represented on the nominating committee, the black caucus continued to meet and prepare its own slate. The idea of co-chairmen began to be considered by both groups and was approved by the conference before elections were held.

The selection of a white professional by the nominating committee led the black caucus to decide that only a black professional would have the status to cope with such strength. Thus, all the paraprofessionals who were nominated for the co-chairmanship declined until the black professional favored by the caucus was nominated. This surprised the professionals who saw their suggestion for a black paraprofessional as co-chairman (which they considered to be true equality) rejected by the paraprofessionals. All of the candidates sponsored by the caucus were elected, giving the paraprofessionals three of the seven vice-chairmen and nine of the nineteen executive committeemen as well as their candidate for co-chairmanship.

Results

As a result of these actions, the structure and proposed function of the National Council was substantially changed. The paraprofessionals achieved voting status, a change of agenda, representation on key committees, and the co-chairmanship. Most importantly, these specific changes symbolized the recognition forced on the white professionals that they could no longer act to provide services for minority groups without the active participation of those groups.

The rhetoric, the demands, and the programmatic directions of the black paraprofessionals combined, in differing proportions and at different stages, explicit questions of race with programmatic demands of the new careerists as workers and participants in the new careers system. The final results, as expressed in the elections, mirror these emphases. The paraprofessionals emerged from the conference with a heightened confidence and group consciousness growing out of their victory over the establishment, ambitious national plans to organize their counterparts, and an enlarged formal role in the new organization. The conference organizers emerged divided and to a degree demoralized and incapable of further involvement in the organization. But these effects varied; some individuals drew new strength and insight and found confirmation of the underlying theoretical base of the new career concept in the effectiveness of the black paraprofessionals. The National Council for New Careers was, in fact, established at the conference but was unable to achieve very much thereafter, primarily because of the erosion of white support that took place during and after the conference. New careerists organizing has proceeded with some good results in certain cities but is still far short of any effective national organization.

This case seemed to have particular value since it involved the relationships between white professionals and black paraprofessionals; a challenge to an organization by the very groups for whose benefit it had been formed; the divided loyalties of black professionals between the largely white professional group and the largely black group of paraprofessionals; and the development of caucuses within each of the two major groups.

ANALYSIS

The Organization

The voluntary nature of an organization is a major determinant of many of the characteristics relevant to this analysis. Since such an organization must attract and hold its members, and its organizational image and outputs must be developed in terms of their values and interests. It is presumed that this membership exercises at least nominal control over policies and practices. The manipulation of the majority voting procedure through which this control is generally achieved may become the key to the black confrontation and the development of possible alternative positions by a white leadership group.

In practice, of course, the decision-making process tends to be highly concentrated in a small group of members whose dominant roles are based on the opportunities for self-realization and on a greater than average commitment to the formal purposes of the organization.

This small and relatively united leadership group tends to have firm ideas about the fundamental purposes and directions of the organization. To achieve those purposes they will have developed expertise in handling formal procedures, including voting, and will also be able to exercise considerable control over executive and administrative positions within the organization. While their positions may be unsalaried, they will have a considerable status stake in maintaining them. As long as the professional criteria built into the organization are consistent with the values of the majority of the membership and as long as members of the leadership group perform efficiently, they are unlikely to be challenged.

If, however, a group of members can formulate credible demands based on allegations of the failure of the organization to meet their interests adequately, there is a basis for uniting that group and enlisting support of its position from other members. Although there have been some challenges arising from so-called radicals within the professions in recent years, they are not the focus of this study. Our concern has been with the black members of professional and nonprofit organizations who represent a subgroup most likely to make and defend such challenges by defining the leadership orientation as "white and middle class" and by posing a black perspective and a need to "relate to the black experience."

The general organizational structure of a nonprofit organization has consequences relevant to the potential for racial confrontation and negotiation. In an organization such as the New Careers Council, the programs developed by the leadership groups may focus on relatively narrow purposes, draw from white middle-class values, and reflect a kind of white elitism, including a paternalistic attitude toward other members who are defined as being in a lower status level. For instance, in the cited case, Rosen concludes:

Most whites seem to have come to feel that struggles over power were somehow a massive diversion from the 'real' business of the conference, i.e., serious engagement with obstacles to the furtherance of new careers ideas and programs, and organizing to deal effectively with them. This expressed an elitism which, though perhaps not explicit, sees the professional class as a major and relatively self-sufficient instrument for the solution of problems of the sort present in the case of new careers. They would, therefore, share with some of the conveners the view that the paraprofessionals, while important, would play a secondary and responsive role.[3]

---

[3] The extracted materials are quotes from the Rosen study. They are incorporated here because of their insightfulness, not only for the individual case, but also for the speculative generalizations with which this chapter is concerned.

In contrast to the relatively uniform and narrow focus of the leadership group on the purposes and functions of the organization, the general membership (largely white) may well have a wide range of views on the organization's racial purposes and programs. The need to secure membership approval through voting procedures sets limits within which the leadership group must operate in designing and administering its programs. While this may somewhat restrict its flexibility in responding to black demands, the existence, commitment, and capacity of the small group also provide a basis for the negotiation of conflicting positions as well as for the ratification of any agreements through the voting procedures.

The Black Challengers

The challenge is likely to be expressed by some black members or potential members who probably accept, at least in some idealized form, the image of the functions of the organization but who judge that the organization has failed to focus on the needs of the black community. Because of their individual professional interest, however, and their involvement as voluntary members, their efforts are likely to be directed toward changing the organization to make it more effective and relevant, rather than toward destroying it.

As in other patterns that we have examined, the black challenge here, at least in part, is a function of a widely shared and apparently rising emphasis on black identity that affects a growing number of professionals and subprofessionals. This group may determine that there is a need for black unity among the black members of the organization as a process of self-realization and as a basis for changing organizational policies. Part of the emphasis on black identity can be expressed as a wish to participate in decisions that affect themselves and the black community. In the case we studied the identity emphasis also included a strong objection to the paternalistic posture of the white leadership.

The conference was one of several events that occurred in the late 1960s in which blacks used dramatic methods to tell whites that they would no longer permit their lives to be disposed of without their active participation. In this sense the conference represents one more nail in the coffin of paternalistic liberalism that flourished during the first euphoric period of the civil rights movement. Recent years have seen the emergence of black pride; with increasing frequency blacks have demonstrated their ability to act collectively and coherently against white-dominated groups that in the past have been able to make important decisions or take initiatives in the area of race relations without any challenge from "below."[4]

This demand for participation and/or control over decisions and institutions serving the interests of blacks and the black community has been found in numerous other cases in such sectors as schools, universities, welfare, and building trades. Blacks resent the condescension and paternalism in the nineteenth century liberalist obligation that the "haves" should help the "have-nots."

The paternalistic perspective, as Rosen suggests, may include a misreading of the apparent passivity of the black membership, and the white leaders of an organization may be unprepared for these black challenges, despite their political sophistication, skills as social scientists, and closeness to the urban scene.

Although the blacks involved in the New Careers case shared a common black experience, they fell into three quite different groupings. First, the black professionals who were already a part of the organization; second, the paraprofessionals who were seeking to become a part of the organization rather than just the recipients of its services; and third, the blacks who were neither new careerists nor professionals, but outsiders. Alternate positions on whether to work within the organization or to direct efforts to destroy it had to be resolved. As Rosen states:

> The basic tension within the black group developed between new careerists with a stake in the success of the proposed national organization and other blacks who lacked this stake and thus had little or nothing to lose by pressing the issue to a conclusion, even at the risk of destroying the conference and preventing the establishment of the organization.[5]

In the course of the dispute, the outsiders played an important role in originally defining the conflict, but the decision by the organizers to carry on negotiations with the black paraprofessionals led to the emergence of leadership from that group. Thereafter, the outsiders played a minor role in the confrontation and negotiations, although their continued presence at the sessions was construed by the white organizers as a continued threat to the life of the conference.

For this group of militant blacks with little immediate interest in New Careers programs and for the white radicals who shared their

---

[4] Ibid
[5] Ibid

position, the issue was molding the proposed organization into an instrument of social change. The majority of black and white participants in this case however, had more immediate short-term stakes in the New Careers program, and their hope of resolving the conflict prevailed over the ideological approach.

Blacks who are already established within an organization play a highly specialized role in conflicts such as this. In general, the central problem of professionals who tend to accept the organization's policies and programs is whether to join the protestors or to defend the establishment. This decision is apparently influenced by the degree to which each professional identifies with the general black position in America. Many members of this group responded by identifying with the black protestors or at least with their general directions and efforts.[6]

These established blacks can perform an extremely important role by providing the insights and perspectives on the operating mechanisms, problems, and purposes of the organization that are needed by the protesting group if their negotiating position is to be realistic and effective. In the New Careers conference case, black members of the establishment who had credentials and professional status also provided the protesting group with respectability once they clearly identified themselves with the protest's objectives, programs, and strategies.[7]

Negotiating Patterns

The Issues

The demands presented to the organization by black groups tend to fall into two general categories. The first includes a demand for reor-

---

[6] They were willing to do this because it gave them credentials and a sense of respect among the paraprofessional group, and because relating effectively to that group helped them to solve problems of identity, and of the emotional balance between their sense of themselves as professionals and their response to the appeals for black solidarity which the confrontation had played a part in creating.

[7] While the leadership credentials moved quite quickly to the paraprofessionals, they depended on black professionals for credibility and voting power. They could not adopt a consistent negotiating posture until they had satisfied themselves that they understood all of the key issues. In addition, the transition from seeing the conference as a single encounter to seeing it as an opportunity to change long-run relationships between professionals and paraprofessionals was assisted by the black professionals. They were able to convey a sense of the complexity of institutional behavior, of the differences among the several white factions, and of the process by which political change occurs, which was persuasive to the paraprofessionals.

dering the priorities of the organization and changing the policies and practices on the services provided to the membership. Issues in this category may focus on the degree to which the services of the organization are available to black members, the racial policies and practices of the organization in relation to its members, and the alleged inadequacy of the organization in providing services or otherwise relating to the black community.

The second category involves possible demands for greater black group participation in reordering organizational policies and priorities and developing programs to meet the new priorities. These demands challenge the degree to which black interests are represented in the decision-making process of the organization. They also challenge the ability of white professionals to understand and represent black constituent interests. Thus, they call for independent black involvement in policy making and administration.

The organizational leadership is likely to insist that the services are already institutionalized and generally sanctioned by the membership. It is also likely to object strongly to the black demands if they are pressed in racial terms on the basis that the organizational purposes and functions are presumed to have professional and not racial referents. The leaders will probably hold that appropriate machinery already exists for the expression of membership views and for an efficient response to membership needs and that it would be inappropriate to recognize a separate black interest in formulating and implementing policies.

As in some of the other sectors, each side has difficult choices to make if it must decide between or assign priorities to the original demands for black participation in decision-making or the demands for changes in the service outputs of the organization.

For many blacks there is a logical connection between the ideal of black equality and changes in decision-making procedures that are needed to guarantee that black members define the black interests to be served by the organization. There is an important risk in this position for blacks. Individual blacks who might be appointed by the organization to act as spokesmen for black interests may become co-opted and no longer express black interests and black determination; to avoid such co-optation, a continuing black organization may be needed to keep up the pressures, but there is no assurance that such an organization can be maintained.

To the organization's leaders, however, it is likely to appear quite illogical and, theoretically, much more damaging to the functioning of the organization in the long run if black representatives and a specialized black interest are recognized and structured into the organization. Yet if one judges that the overt conflict cannot be sustained by blacks and that continuing black pressure is unlikely, concessions that take time to implement pose little risk to the stability of the organization. Also, those who begin as spokesmen for separate black interests may fit into organization patterns as they gain organizational perspective.

Organization leaders, faced with the need for limited concessions, may prefer structural changes. Apparently, on balance, black leaders faced with a similar limited opportunity may make the same choice.

Coercive Pressures

The structure and decision-making process of the voluntary service organization distinguish it from the other sectors. This analysis assumes that there is a white elite leadership group that is able to negotiate with the protestors and translate agreements into organizational decisions because of its capacity to guide policy formation and implementation.

The coercive capacities of the black protestors include the capacity to develop doubts within many rank and file members as to whether the white-dominated organization is concerned with the specialized needs and interests of its black members; the ability to threaten the leader with damage to the organization's public image if the response is inadequate; an appeal to the conscience within the leadership group; and the ability to capitalize on the possible concerns of the leader about the discrepancies between the idealized purposes of the organization and its actual practices and accomplishments. These aspects of a black power position may be developed simply by demonstrating black unity behind the presentation of a set of black demands that appear to follow logically from these black and white concerns, provided that this black position is brought to the attention of the general membership and leadership with sufficient vividness.

In general, the key coercive device available to the black protestors is a confrontation staged when a substantial number of members are gathered to use the service of the organization or to take part in its decision-making processes. In such settings even a small black group, if sufficiently determined, can seriously interfere with normal organizational procedures. Because of the voluntary membership characteristics of the organization, disruptions are more effective in this sector than in other institutions.

The effectiveness of black pressures on the organization depends on the rapid emergence of leadership within the black caucus and the qualities of that leadership. Black leaders tend to emerge rather quickly if there have been prior contacts among the black protestors.

As Rosen points out:

> A great deal depended on the knowledge of one another which several members of the leadership group had acquired before the conference; without this experience . . . it is doubtful whether coherent leadership would have emerged so quickly or endured without being challenged by others. . . . The group achieved a high degree of coherence and effective leadership quite quickly and maintained both of these attributes consistently through the duration of the conference.[8]

A black protesting group operating with a degree of sophistication and substantial unity under adequate leadership is able to use racial themes effectively with the white leadership and white membership of a nonprofit organization. The white leadership also has significant resources to counter such black pressures. It may appeal to the white membership for the continuation of past policies and practices. It may announce modifications of its programs and policies (with or without a prior consultation with black spokesmen) in the hope that members will accept these responses as meeting the black challenges adequately. It may deny the general membership access to the positions being taken by the black protestors and/or use the police to suppress disruptions.

The white elite group cannot develop an operationally productive response to black demands unless it understands the objectives of the black group and its frustration about achieving them within white society. The white group must also understand the ways in which these objectives are being translated into specific demands by the black leader. Perhaps the white leaders should also understand their own reactions and their own stake in maintaining the status quo.

The leadership position can also be constrained by the members' votes, which reflect differing perspectives along two white membership categories: the "moderates" and the white "radicals." Moderate white members of the organization may hold a wide range of judgments about the appropriateness of black demands and tactics. They are unlikely to develop an organized position and, therefore, are unlikely to take a major role in constraining or challenging the existing white organization leadership.

For the white radical members the problems posed by the black protest can be more urgent. They may be concerned with finding common ground with the black protestors and with supporting their positions and pressures on the establishment. On the other hand, white radicals may view the black positions as being too narrowly

[8] Ibid

conceived, neither wide enough to embrace the particular concerns of disgruntled whites nor comprehensive enough to take account of fundamental causes and to propose sweeping solutions. In this case, the white radicals were unable to form a coalition with the black protestors, who rejected their perspectives and leadership in favor of their own.

Restraints on Both Sides

The coercive resources of each side, however, also involve some constraints. As in other cases in this study, the action and words of the black protestors may stimulate antagonistic whites to mobilize counterpressures to preserve the status quo. If this polarization is strong enough, it may outweigh the coercive pressures of the black protestors. In addition, if the members perceive the black protestors as destructive and unjustified in their challenges, other blacks and whites may have strong negative reactions that could weaken the black position. Moreover, the organization is already providing some services for the protesting black groups even though these may be considered inadequate. The denial, or threatened denial, of these services may pose important risks and, therefore, restrain the rhetoric and actions of the black protestors.

Similarly, if members perceive the white leader as unresponsive to black challenges, even relatively neutral white members might be stimulated to mobilize behind the black protestors. Such a reaction might occur if members learned that they were being denied access to knowledge of the black position, or if the leadership used police power to repress protest.

Negotiating Styles

Black members may first approach the organization's leader with an appeal for justice, asking that they apply the idealized objectives of the organization, including in a definition of these the kinds and quality of services that the organization is failing to perform for its black members. The organization may consider modifying policies and practices if it can be done practically and in agreement with the leaders' definitions of professional and/or organizational nonracial criteria, but also may insist that any more extensive concessions would violate its standards.

If, or when, this "reasonable" approach yields changes so minimal that they are unacceptable to the black protestors, each side may move to more coercive alignments. There may be black efforts to define the issues to enlist white support inside and outside the organization, and these may underline the "justice" of their demands and the "racism" of the organization in their discussions. Similarly, leaders of the organization can mobilize support by using the publicity resources already available to them from within the organization and by joining in discussions with blacks to illustrate their own reasonableness.

It may be difficult for each side to turn these conversations into structured negotiations with the identification of relative power positions and the expressions of relative determinations and priorities. For the organization such a process may violate the image of a democratic group with a nonracial commitment to equality. For the blacks the process may reveal major difficulties such as inadequate organization, uncertainty as to leadership, conflicting perceptions and policies, and the capability of any of the black leaders to deliver either disruption on the one hand or the acceptance of compromise positions on the other.

Negotiating Process

The specific demands of the black protestors are likely to be phrased in terms suggesting that power, decision-making authority, and perhaps economic resources are to be given up to some degree by the white leadership and claimed by the black group. The white leaders may initially respond in such a way as to continue this definition of the issues posed by the blacks. The negotiating process, then, may focus exclusively on the question of what redistribution of functions and power will be necessary and acceptable to bring the dispute to a conclusion.

At some later stage in the negotiations it may be possible for both sides to perceive the potential for the kind of an accommodation that would contribute to the positions of both. The blacks may perceive a need to strengthen the functioning of the organization, or its present leadership group may decide that some or much of the black position could be incorporated beneficially into the organization's policies and programs. In the New Careers conference, as Rosen points out:

The organizers were willing to accept or concede a great deal to assure the creation of the national organization that they had set out to build; the paraprofessionals came to see that they would need the professionals and the skills, contacts, and influence that they knew how to use, if their own emerging agenda of a national organization of paraprofessionals was to get off the ground. They were thus required to temper their exhilaration at the spectacle of their own success and effectiveness in confronting people who had always played roles of authority in their lives, 'really biting into their (the conveners') ass' as one of them put it, in order to prevent the alienation and withdrawal of a base that it was important to them to keep accessible.[9]

Results of Negotiations

In an abstract summary of this kind based on a single case with some unusual features, it is pointless to predict the results of all confrontations and negotiations between black members and established leaders of voluntary service organizations. The outcome of this case, however, and some of Rosen's insights, raise some useful speculations.

The black protest group in the New Careers Conference case won major concessions from the organizing group through the negotiations process. They were accorded voting rights, changes in the agenda to include sessions devoted to their interests, assistance for developing paraprofessional organizations, representation on nominating committees and on the key committees of the newly formed New Careers Council, and the election of their representative as co-chairman of the council. These were the immediate terms of the agreements reached between the protestors and the conference organizers. The long-term consequences of the negotiations are more difficult to evaluate.

Rosen's reflections on the drama that he has analyzed start from a specific aspect of the general problem of our racial analysis. In this case, as in all the others we have analyzed, blackness and whiteness are intermeshed with the particular focuses of the individuals and their roles within specific social contexts. Thus, in the New Careers case, the confrontation and the results involved black versus white and professional versus paraprofessional.

The case also included a basic disagreement as to the role such an organization *ought* to play. Many white professionals were problem-centered and expected the new organization to be concerned with the professional and the institutional problems that they faced as individuals. Others felt that the organization had a responsibility to become more actively involved in the broad social questions within their field.

Whatever the organizational consequences of the racial encounter, it is possible that black protestors and white leaders have been provided with an opportunity to expand their understanding of racial issues and of the limits within which an organization can, or is likely to, change. According to Rosen:

> Experience since the conference within the National Council itself strongly supports the view that both groups learned a great deal. Some professionals

[9] Ibid

who played a passive role during the conference and who have had little or no relationship with the Council tend to feel, when asked, that the process that occurred, which many frankly admit left them disoriented and disenchanted, was in retrospect necessary if New Careers was to move beyond its early period without making the basic error of disregarding the nature of the historical period we are in. Had this adjustment been anticipated and provided for, presumably the result would have been a far less disruptive, intense, and fragmented process for most of those present. But they do not blame the conveners for their failure; rather, they see the episode as a way of bringing about a necessary shift in thinking and seeing which, however painful, was clearly worthwhile.

Others, perhaps less insightful, still resent what they see as a planning failure and a lost opportunity to achieve a significant development in national awareness and involvement in new careers. Some, as we have seen, find the failure in the exclusion of new careerists from planning and participatory roles. Others make precisely the opposite criticism—that the conference should have been confined to professionals and should have established an organization that was prepared to have cordial fraternal relations with organizations of new careerists, but with no merging of the two or common membership. This view implies a somewhat narrower, more instrumental, and less socially involved definition of new careers than the one that animated most of the conveners and that clearly affected the paraprofessionals, as well as a somewhat more traditional view of organizational methods and goals than is perhaps appropriate in dealing with issues that directly affect black economic and social well-being.[10]

It is possible that affiliation with the organization may be strengthened or weakened as a result of a confrontation. Partial success in achieving changes in organizational policies and practices, particularly if some black involvement in decision making has resulted, may enlarge the commitment of black members of the organization. Perhaps the view that only insignificant changes have been accomplished may move blacks in the opposite direction. It is also possible that blacks who have put together a strong protest may not be able to sustain such pressures after an original crisis incident has passed and that concessions to blacks by the white leadership may result in the disaffection of white members who object to the resolution of the confrontation.

Attempts of predominantly white organizations to define and write programs for blacks, without involving those blacks in the process, appear to contain the seeds of destruction. However well-meaning or professionally knowledgeable the whites may be, it is almost certain that such programming without black participation will not be acceptable to the blacks. Such programs may be oriented to white values, white perspectives, and white perceptions. Further, it is almost certain that exclusion of blacks will deprive the planners of essential

[10] Ibid

black perspectives and will be viewed as paternalistic by blacks. Here, as in some other cases, there are core issues of recognition and control.

In addition to these probable results, one can identify some major possibilities and factors to be considered in a more specific prediction of the consequences of confrontations in voluntary service organizations.

1. How wide is the gap between the existing organizational policies and procedures and the definitions of organizational relevance adopted by a substantial part of the black membership? The wider the gap the more likely the racial challenge.

2. How determined is each side to press the conflict? Does the discrepancy between the degrees of determination of the two sides affect the amount of change toward a black position?

3. How urgently do black members need the organization, as compared to the organization's needs for black members? Again, the answer here will influence the consequences of the confrontation. It appears likely that, as in the New Careers case, the black professional may prefer to stay within the system, finding an accommodation within an organization of his professional peers. On the other hand, his own experiences and his social context may continue as an emphasis on his personal and professional black identity.

Future confrontations may arise in the relationships of professionals to paraprofessionals. The growing group of paraprofessionals in fields such as social work, education, medical institutions, and others will tend to be largely black, while the professionals will be predominatly white. The black professional will find it increasingly necessary to determine his role. In the long run he may be able to provide the bridge between professional and paraprofessional and between black and white.

CHAPTER 9

Characteristics of Racial Negotiations

Each of the six preceding chapters has dealt with racial confrontations and negotiations in a different sector. This chapter focuses on those generalizations that cut across sector lines and summarizes the characteristics of the conflicting parties, their coercive potentials, possible negotiating interactions, and the limits within which change is likely to be achieved through negotiated agreements.

In Chapter 1, and in separately published pieces, contrasts between the usual labor-management negotiations and those found in our case studies have been noted.[1] As illustrated in the earlier chapters, these contrasts appear most sharply in the sectors that have institutional patterns different from those of managements that employ workers and deal with their unions. Even in these sectors, black protest appears to be quite different from job consciousness.

An additional fundamental contrast is the absence of accepted rules for the interactions. In none of our cases does the establishment immediately accept a duty to bargain with the black protestors. There are no federal laws providing or administering such rules, nor is there enough experience to make negotiations an acceptable and expected response without benefit of law. As the leaders of the black coalition which confronted the construction industry in Chicago saw it, they

---

[1] "Collective Bargaining in Racial Disputes?", *Racial Conflict and Negotiations: Perspectives and First Case Studies*, ibid.

were attempting to build their own "little Wagner Act" with only limited support from the city and federal governments. In contrast to union-management patterns, neither the establishment nor the black protest group started with a negotiating posture. For different reasons, the first reactions of each side were quite likely to be nonnegotiable positions. The coalition dominated by the black students of San Francisco State, for instance, presented 15 demands that the college administration held were nonnegotiable when it refused to acknowledge the need to negotiate with the students.

Despite these and other deviations from the union-management analogy, our case and sector analyses appear to have been aided by using that analogy to identify two parties engaged in organized conflict, that is, the black challengers and the establishment being challenged. Although we used this two-party concept, we found that our data yielded different information about the characteristics of the parties and the nature of their interactions than that usually considered in the union-management analogy.

CHARACTERISTICS OF THE TWO PARTIES

The White Establishment

It is probable that establishment decision makers will be reluctant to accept demands for substantially different patterns of operation and that numerous internal and external forces will support them in their rejection of black demands. In its outputs and in its procedures, the establishment represents the status quo, and the challengers are those who would unstabilize, or revolutionize, the institution. Consequently, under many different circumstances, the establishment is able to call on the support of the government—police administration officials, courts, and even legislatures—in resisting black pressures for change.

In varying degrees there are aspects of each establishment for which we use the summarizing phrase "white racism": decision makers whose perspectives and judgments include anti-black prejudices; outputs that are geared to white groups; and effectiveness criteria that are white-oriented.

A preliminary statement of the research design, however, implies a conceptualization of an establishment as a monolithic organization. The case data and the sector analyses indicate some of the major ways in which this oversimplification must be modified to describe more accurately how specific establishments function in a real world.

Characteristics of Racial Negotiations 217

This kind of modification, as discussed below, also must be developed to elaborate on the conceptualization of the black protestors. They too will be described, not as a monolithic expression of black interest, but as embracing a wide variety of complex and uncertain black leadership-constituency relationships and the even more complex relationships of leaders and followers to the black community.

Even the formal structure of each establishment has a variety of authority levels and operates at a number of decision-making points. Thus, the challenges of blacks differ depending on the level and location of decision making that they are attacking. The resistance capacities of the establishment differ among different levels and responsibilities within the total organization as well.

Further, the goal orientations of the establishment, on closer examination, are not monolithic and logically coherent. All of its participants do not share a common evaluation of its functions, nor is there a complete consensus on the ways the establishment should achieve even those symbolic expressions of its functions that are accepted. Various power centers approach their own roles within the establishment with somewhat different values and contribute to variations in the decisions of other units within the organization as well. Indeed, the whole organization is held together and continues to function in a more or less common direction largely due to the participants' needs for accommodations and the ways they adjust their internal relationships.

These internal differences in perspectives and in goal orientations affect the protestors' views of the establishment and the establishment's responses to the challenges. It is possible that the values and perspectives of some individuals and units may be closer to those of the black challengers than to establishment objectives. These individuals and units become potential allies of the challengers.

Finally, at a point in time, one establishment may be described and compared with others by the degree to which its managerial style involves centralization or decentralization of decision-making responsibility. But even this pattern will vary depending on the problem area and the relationship of the establishment to its changing environment. Particularly relevant to this study, then, is the analysis explored by Ferman who indicates in Chapter 6 that a challenge by protestors may cause a shift in administrative style—perhaps toward greater decentralization of authority and an expansion of administrative flexibility.

In most cases reported here the establishment has a close relationship to one or another government unit. This fact apparently gives rise to a number of special establishment characteristics that affect its responses to black demands. In Chapter 2, we noted that the general political connections of some establishments set limits within which establishment leaders must operate. This general proposition is illustrated in cases where school boards, welfare agencies, public universities, and city governments act as employers. It appears more remotely in hospitals which receive federal support and in the construction industry which is affected by federal employment regulations. In most of these cases, the controls operate through resource allocation, although with such allocations the executives of the government-supported unit may be following some general guidelines.

In our cases this relationship also was affected by the symbols used to support establishment positions. One prominent symbol was sovereignty, applied as an assumption that the authority assigned by the government unit to a set of establishment executives could not be shared through a negotiations process. Of course, the reality was quite different, and the cases reveal executives who did in fact negotiate with black protestors while preserving the fiction that they were consulting rather than bargaining and the resolution of the conflict was unilaterally determined by those with the governmentally assigned authority.

A second consequence of the governmental character that emerges is that these units perform an extremely important government function by relating in a specialized way to the needs and pressures of groups of citizens. Indeed, this process is much more flexible than a generalized law applicable equally to all citizens, or even the administrative responses to various pressures that interpret the general rules of the law to the advantage of some groups as compared to others. In our cases, the government, through its subunits, is responding to those blacks whose interests have been organized into a conflict pressure by specific black leaders and their constituencies.

A third implication is one that also will affect the analysis of third-party roles that appears in Chapter 10. The governmental process involves a variety of ways of accommodating a wide range of conflicting interests. A school board or a public university, for instance, has a government referrent that represents the accommodation of many interests to which the governmental process is constantly adjusting. Yet, as the executives of the government establishment deal with the black protestors, they are functioning as a single organized establishment and as the spokesmen of the accommodated interests of many groupings represented in the governmental process. The establishment side may be supported in the resulting confrontation and negotiations by an elaborate and multiple constituency that may represent divergent views and interests even more widely than do the constituencies represented by the black leaders.

The Black Protestors

The analyses of the cases confirm the generalized characteristics of black protest advanced in Chapter 2. In each of our cases, black protest is organized around the discrimination and black identity focuses that merge into a challenge to the policies and practices of specific establishments. The black protestors are likely to be united by these focuses and by shared perspectives about particular establishments. They may believe that the establishment, which is supposed to be supplying them with services or jobs, is racist and that the decision makers are prejudiced against blacks. They may be convinced that the establishment is failing to live up to its own theoretical commitments to justice and equality. They may view white spokesmen's descriptions of the purposes of the establishment and its relations to its black clients and employees as idealizations that are contradicted by their own experiences. For some, protest is an effort to bring reality into line with rhetoric.

As in every social movement the black protestors are organized by a limited number of activists committed to a particular program. The relationship between leadership and constituency is a function of the size of the groups and degree of their interactions, the shared identity of the potential constituency, the leadership qualities, and the degree to which the leadership presents an accepted ideology and a credible program that links the ideology to the functioning of the establishment that is under attack.

In most of our cases the black protestors developed the organized base for their challenge only at the time of the confrontation. In some cases, however, their challenge was introduced by a functioning organization with a very limited membership. As the leader of such a group purposefully developed a set of issues that appeared to summarize the frustrations and hopes of a larger black constituency, they developed a wider and more committed following while pressing these demands on the establishment. In other cases neither an organization nor a leadership existed until some action of the establishment brought into focus the objections of a number of blacks and triggered their development.

In such situations the leadership-constituency relationship may be tenuous because no stable organization has been developed and because many black followers may not be sure that the call to action by the black leaders will produce satisfactory results. They may expect the white responses to be wholly negative and repressive, or they may be unwilling to accept the risks of extended sacrifices accompanying a bitter struggle with superior power.

The character of the protesting organization is also a function of the issues chosen and the kinds of appeals that these issues make to potential black supporters. As we have noted, the key element in the choice of issues is the relationship between protestors and potential protestors and the establishment and their objections to the way they are treated by the establishment.

Several other aspects of the issue-selection process affect the possible support and potential power that can be expressed and applied by the protest leadership. One leadership problem is to phrase demands so that they are broad enough to speak meaningfully to black frustrations and narrow enough to appear relevant to the specific establishment being challenged. To understate the grievances is to fail to arouse the support and commitment of a constituency that must be prepared to carry on a difficult conflict. To take positions that are beyond the scope of the particular establishment is to provide the basis for a confrontation but not the opportunity for a negotiated change.

A third complex problem in issue formulation involves the appropriate distinction to be made between human dignity and black self-respect, and supportive services and affirmative action. Black leaders will insist that the equality of the human spirit and personality is not to be denied. They will resent any implication of subnormal characteristics among their individual constituents. On the other hand, they may demand programs to correct the consequences of discrimination against blacks by the particular establishment of the white society. This distinction is not difficult for black leaders to make although they may find some problems in its rhetorical expression. It may well be a distinction that the whites in positions of power have difficulty understanding.

A fourth factor that affects the degree to which constituents rally behind black leaders relates to the emphasis on participation and resource distribution. Followers and potential followers who are concerned with black identity and the development of independent black positions must emphasize demands for a decision-making process that will function to meet black interest. Those who are concerned primarily with the discriminatory actions and outputs of the establishment must formulate demands that focus on reallocation of resources. These two perspectives make it almost certain that the development of constituency support will be based on the selection and elaboration of issues around both thrusts. Indeed, in many circumstances, the leaders and the followers are likely to feel that neither adequate redistribution of resources nor increased quality of outputs will occur unless blacks get involved in the decision making of the establishment.

The above analysis suggests that one set of demands will be expressed by the term "control," perhaps phrased as "black control" or "community control." The appearance and meaning of such a demand will depend on the kind of institution (sector) within which the black protest leadership is operating and the range of power of the black protestors. Blacks may judge that the white establishment cannot or will not function in the black interest and demand that black groups take control of the relevant units of the large-scale establishments that are supposed to service the local community. This philosophy is demonstrated by demands for local school units, black studies and social centers on college campuses, and the responsibility for administration of police activities, delivery of health services, model cities programs, and other areas.

Finally, in analyzing the interrelationship between issue development and leadership support, it should be noted that no formulation of demands is preceived by either leaders or followers as the achievement of equality. It is assumed that, even if all demands are fully accepted and fulfilled, more progress must be made over the years before full equality is achieved. However, support from followers depends, at least in part, on whether they believe that these demands are likely to produce a meaningful start toward the equality they seek.

Power Positions

This speculative summary has been abstracted from the diverse actions and perspectives of individuals and groups in our case studies and is a simplification of the complex data. Nevertheless, it appears to be helpful, as a way to determine patterns of uniformity within these cases. Since the negotiating posture of the two sides in the cases depended more on coercive capacities than on a preference for mutual problem solving, this section focuses first on the power position of each side and then on the relationship between these positions.

The Power Position of Each Side

The capacity of the establishment to resist black demands is solidly based in the preference for the status quo by each individual and group involved in its functioning. Their commitments to existing arrangements stem from the roles they have achieved and the rewards they are receiving. Outside groupings and power centers also are interested in the functions and outputs of the establishment, and these groups may be prepared to rally to its assistance when the establishment is threatened by an unstabilizing demand and to assist in enforcing the present rules and procedures.

These positions are logically related to a value judgment that the objectives of society and of specific establishments should aim to eliminate color as a basis for institutional and personal actions. Any acceptance of black demands by a school, a university, or a welfare establishment, for instance, is resisted because it is seen as the subversion of the social objective of equality.

In addition, whites in and outside establishment organizations may decide that black power is dangerous and must be resisted and that concessions made to black demands will be an unstabilizing factor that will threaten established black-white relationships. The coercive or resistive capacity of the establishment is limited by several factors, however. Fear of the violent action or reaction to a complete and overt rejection of the protestors' demands is present whether or not the black leaders refer to the possibility of riots, and even though it is clear that riots as such can neither be produced nor stopped by the leaders. It is not uncommon for white decision makers and othere influential figures to assume that a negative response will bring violence and to hope that an affirmative response will make riots less likely in the future.

A solid establishment refusal to change its procedures and outputs because of black demands is also cracked by the effect of white conscience. White decision makers may believe that black Americans have been mistreated over the years and that their own establishment has played a part in such discrimination. Therefore, some individual white decision makers who are prepared to make concessions to blacks, probably within quite narrow limits, always use the term "equal treatment" rather than "preferential treatment."

White decision makers are the victims of their own rhetoric to some degree. They have defined the functions of their own organizations and appealed for acceptance and support of these definitions in idealized terms. When black demands appear to underline the degree to which reality falls short of the idealization, there is a tendency to concede the need for modifications of establishment policies and practices in these directions. Idealizations about organizations have usually been non-racial in character, however, and have supported the proposition that all who are similarly affected by the failures of the system have an equal claim for modifications of the system.

The capacity of organized blacks to press demands on establishments can be summarized with even less certainty. There are few analytical reports of such incidents and there is almost no body of developed theory about such black organizations. In addition, because black experiences reported in our cases reflect the trial and error approaches of many different black leaders and followers, generalization is difficult.

Black capacity to press an establishment is apparently a function of the issues chosen, since that choice will affect the degree of constituent support, the amount of commitment the leaders can generate, and the vigor with which the establishment resists. Reciprocally, the issues selected are also a function of the degree of power that might be generated. Specific demands are likely to be formulated based on the judgment by blacks of what are reasonable and practical steps toward equality. Because these are viewed as modest first steps, a strong black constituency is likely to feel that they ought to be achievable.

Black capacity to press an establishment is also a function of issue selection in another way. Issues can focus at various levels within the establishment. The more general the policy change that is demanded, the higher within the establishment power structure it may be necessary to go. A wide policy focus may be beyond the reach of the coercive capacity of the black protestors. One of the complex factors affecting the coercive power of the black leaders is the tenuous character of their relationship to a constituency. If no progress in the direction of the black demands occurs or appears likely, the constituency may become discouraged.

It may be possible to expand black coercive capacity by obtaining support from blacks and whites not directly involved in the conflict. Some of these individuals may be inside the establishment and, depending on their status and decision-making power, can play an important role in affecting the establishment position. They may be extremely useful in providing insights on the perspectives and operations of the establishment and thus help to formulate tactics and improve the accuracy of the perceptions of the black protestors.

Some other groupings also may be willing to strengthen the black coercive position without seeking to modify its tactics or philosophy.[2] Some of these are outside, but immediately related to, the establishment. At San Francisco State and at The University of Michigan, the white students rallied to add important coercive muscle to the black pressures against the respective establishments but did not participate

---

[2] We have classified allies as those additional groupings who feel common cause and concern about the outcome and are, therefore, prepared to lend influence or pressure without directly participating in the modification of demands or in tactical decisions. Those involved in a coalition bring to it their own interests.

in deciding upon the tactics or positions that their black allies were pursuing. On the other hand, allies providing this type of support may pressure the blacks to modify their tactics or positions. In some of our cases government units were anxious to restore peace and were prepared to press each side to change its position toward whatever terms could produce a settlement.

Finally, black power can be extended to a wider base through a coalition. The respective interests of coalition members must be similar enough to unite them against a common enemy. In such cases black power is increased by a formal or informal internal negotiations process in which the expanded alliance accepts some common targets, attempts to achieve those common demands, and agrees not to settle for less except by common consent. Such an alliance, for instance, was formed in the early days of the San Francisco State conflict and was signaled by the addition of five Third World Liberation Front demands to the ten that the black students had already formulated.

The Relative Power Positions

The preceding summary suggests that coercive power tends to be heavy on the side of the establishment with its ongoing operations, stable relationships, and relative acceptance and support from the society at large. In contrast, ad hoc black leaders face great difficulty in mustering enough pressure to threaten the functioning of the establishment. This generalization appears to apply despite the fact that the establishment may admit that modest concessions and an advisory or consultative role for blacks in decision making are appropriate. It also appears to be accurate despite the widespread black perceptions of the racist character of American society.

If this summary is an accurate approximation of relative power, it is not surprising that blacks are able to force the issue in only a few cases by structuring overt racial conflict with an establishment. The combination of conflicting pressures, hopes, and expectations only occasionally produces leadership-constituency demands with sufficient power to be taken seriously by the establishment.

In the negotiating process itself, the characteristics of the parties, the kinds of black demands, and the relative degree of power largely control the negotiating strategy of each side and the timing and level of agreement terms. During the course of any extended racial negotiations there may be many changes in the relative power of the two sides that are explained by their interactions and by any number of different external events. Bargaining strategies must be based on each side's power positions and predictions of the impact of events.

THE NEGOTIATING PROCESS

Alternate Strategies

Our cases suggest that neither side enters into a negotiating relationship with the other if any viable alternative is available and promises adequate results. Because negotiation only occurs if blacks initiate such a demand, it is important to note the alternate strategic choices available to black leaders. These have been summarized in Chapter 2: the use of the courts, the development and use of political muscle, the organization of training and other services that can help black individuals fit into and advance within the system, and the development of black units that carry on independent activities.

Black leaders may talk of challenging establishments and may even formulate and present some demands but they are unable to press the establishment further. The black protestors capitulate whenever it appears that a rejection by the establishment cannot be modified. They also frequently capitulate even when black anger is not brought into specific focus as in a riot or rebellion or when the demands are far beyond the coercive capacity of the blacks but compromise is unacceptable.

The establishment, on the other hand, can choose repression by using its own disciplinary devices as an alternative to negotiation. It assumes that there is no validity to black claims and that suppressing the dispute can be accomplished successfully and without any negative long-run consequences.

The concept of agitating outside is used to justify repressive tactics against any person whom the establishment defines as having no interest in the relations between protestors and the establishment. As tendencies for polarization in racial confrontations increase, the pressures for repressive responses become stronger. This kind of coercion, of course, is not available to black protestors.

Refusals to Negotiate

Even when the establishment does not choose repression and the black leaders are unwilling to capitulate, the two conflicting parties may be reluctant to negotiate. While the establishment rarely uses the term "nonnegotiable," its leaders frequently start from nonnegotiable positions. For them, any dilution of their basic control or any alteration in the basic structure of the particular institution is essentially unacceptable. In each establishment there is a stabilized structure of forces, roles, and accepted decision-making processes on policies and their administration. In addition, forces that impinge on the establishment from the outside have varying degrees of influence on its policies and practices. Many of these relationships would have to be realigned if an additional group were granted a participatory role in decision-making policy, its implementation, and/or the monitoring of results. Pressures inside and outside the establishment will resist any changes of output patterns or decision-making machinery.

Establishment leaders, however, may offer alternative responses to the black protest leaders. Since the black demands are based, at least in part, on the functioning of the establishment in relation to its clients or employees and since the establishment idealization is that it relates to its employees or clients on a nonracial basis, a first response is likely to be referral of the protestors to the existing machinery so that they can present and discuss their complaints or proposals in accordance with existing proper procedures. If the black protestors insist on defining their protest in racial terms, the establishment may accept the specialized character of the complainants and complaints, but may respond by simply enlarging the existing grievance machinery.

Both of these responses involve an acceptance of the protestors as participating in a *consultative* function to the establishment, but not in the decision-making processes. This does almost no violence to the existing decision-making patterns, defines potential racial conflicts as amenable to adjustment within the established procedures of the institution, and aims to provide for accommodation within the status quo.

Another establishment strategy is to refuse to accept the protest leaders as spokesmen for black interests. The establishment may have serious doubts about whether those who offer to speak for black interests should be recognized as having that authority. In almost all of our cases there was no clear process by which the black community demonstrated that it chose these black spokesmen and decided on the positions that they presented. The establishment also is quite likely to judge that it has already attuned its functions to the appropriate black interests—to the degree that such adjustments of policy and practice are consistent with its other pressures. These "adequate" adjustments may have developed from less organized signals that came from other black clients or employees. The signals may have originated from black subadministrators within the establishment who also recognized the legitimate claims of nonblack clients or employees. To recognize the protestors as the legitimate representatives of black interests, then, would appear to repudiate those blacks who have been functioning as black interpreters within the organization.

The establishment may also consider negotiations with the black protest leaders to be impractical because they do not have the authority to carry out negotiations. It may judge that the leaders are unable to modify their positions as they acquire different perspectives about establishment policies and problems, to persuade their constituents of more reasonable postures, or to follow through on the basis of any potential agreements.

Black leaders may have equally strong objections to negotiations, but for quite different reasons. They may say that their demands are nonnegotiable. One meaning of this phrase is: "We have reduced our demands to a first, but obviously practical, step toward equality and we *will not* reduce them any more." This may be a very useful bargaining move but, insofar as it recognizes (at least implicitly) that progress *toward* equality is a function of what is practical, it can and sometimes does open the door to subsequent explorations of just what *is* practical, particularly when relevant coercive power and establishment practices and constraints are added to the considerations.

Although the concept of nonnegotiability can be logically shifted to negotiability and although this may be an important route for prospective negotiators and third party intervenors, the gap between what is morally right in the eyes of the protestors and what is practical in the judgment of the establishment may be too wide.

Blacks also apply the label nonnegotiable to their view of fundamental human rights which a man *must not* compromise or trade off. These rights may be generated by the culture, the Constitution, or religious beliefs. If the establishment response is judged as continuing or imposing an inferior status on black representatives, it may be rejected and not negotiated. In the case of individuals this concept may refer to their fundamental rights to a black identity. In a collective sense the same concept refers to the right of blacks to define their own interests and select their own representatives. Thus, the establishment's recognition of protest leaders as legitimate black spokesmen representing black-defined interests is nonnegotiable.

Blacks may also doubt whether the white representatives are empowered to make binding commitments on behalf of the establishment. They may refuse to deal with an agent of the establishment if his role is limited to an exploration of black positions and may negotiate only with a central power authority.

The third hesitancy of black leaders about entering negotiations is more pragmatic, but may be just as rational and powerful. Chances of a successful conclusion to such negotiations may be extremely limited. This criterion of success is, of course, not a question of whether peace can be restored or maintained but whether black objectives can be substantially advanced. If the establishment indicates that it is not likely to be moved by logical argument or the moral force of the demands, if the process requires the development and matching of coercive pressure, and if the leaders judge that comparatively little black power can be developed, it is logical to refuse to negotiate. This is especially true if the black leaders fear being accused of acquiescing to insignificant changes in establishment policies. A refusal to negotiate may also dramatize to their constituents that a later and more aggressive commitment will be necessary before any substantive changes can be achieved.

When the prospects for meaningful negotiations appear to be dim, black leaders might adopt an alternative nonnegotiation posture. Our earlier discussion summarized an establishment nonnegotiation posture based on the assumption that appropriate black spokesmen were already in functioning positions. Alternatively, the establishment may offer a black leader either a personal or an organizational role that would operate under the general policy and administrative directions of the establishment, but be viewed as providing an opportunity to press black interests. This form of co-optation poses a problem for the leader as to whether both can be advanced simultaneously even if only in a limited way. For those black leaders who decide that co-optation is "immoral" but who also view their power resources as being extremely limited, nonnegotiable demands may be a way of avoiding an undesirable commitment.

Face-to-Face Interactions

Either of two contrasting judgments by the chief white decision makers may lead to their commitment to attempt negotiations. They may decide that the coercive position of the black protestors is so weak or the level of demand so minimal that the process can be concluded without any significant difficulty for the establishment in resources allocation or in procedural changes. White decision makers may also predict that the successful conclusion of such an agreement will dissipate the black pressures, at least for a period of time and, therefore, that benefits outweigh costs.

An alternative judgment is that the coercive capacity of the black protestors is presently or potentially so strong that the establishment would be seriously affected by refusing to negotiate. Even contrary to their preferences, the decision makers may be forced to attempt negotiations as the potentially less costly alternative to continuing to reject black demands. Under such circumstances it may be the establishment spokesmen who reach out, directly or through an intervenor, to persuade the black leaders to negotiate. It is possible, of course, that although the leaders see no advantages in negotiating, other forces will prevail to move the organization to the negotiating table.

Black leaders may enter negotiations for a variety of reasons. In some cases they may make a gesture of negotiating when they really only seek a preliminary exploration of the practices and attitudes of the establishment. They may adopt a negotiating posture in an effort to expand individual and group prestige by participating in a challenge to the white antagonist. Compared to life-experiences filled with designations of inferiority by whites, these gestures may have meaning for the individual and for the group, although there is neither intention nor hope of producing an agreement.

Black leaders may seek to use these bargaining interactions to explore whether or not there is sufficient flexibility in the establishment to make agreement possible. Within this approach there may be a reformulation of demands to test any potentials for agreement. One such step is to move away from generalized rhetoric and develop more specific demands that involve the practical functioning of the establishment.

The negotiating process also can be utilized as a way to build the power position of the protestors. While the negotiations are proceeding, the leaders may attempt to enlist outside support and even to develop coalitions. The black leaders may prefer to move slowly in the negotiations, seek out those within the establishment who are sympathetic to their demands, and give them time to influence establishment positions.

Finally, of course, leaders who are sophisticated in collective bargaining processes may accept offers to negotiate because they are sure that they have or can build enough power to force important concessions from the establishment even though some of their demands would have to be compromised. A negotiating approach, then, can avoid further costs and risks to their constituents, their organizational relationships, and to the establishment whose modified functioning they wish to preserve.

Difficulties and Potentials of the Negotiating Process

We have already noted that one side or the other may be reluctant to negotiate. The first issue is whether each side will commit itself to the negotiations process and whether each judges the other's spokesmen to be adequate representatives of their respective positions.

Throughout the entire negotiations a series of probings changes the perceptions of each side as to the other's coercive position. Issue by issue, there is usually a continuous reassessment of the extent to which each side is prepared to accept risks or actual costs rather than the terms of agreement being suggested. Such judgments about the other side are based on its verbal threats or promises, purposefully announced actions, and the appraisal and reappraisal of its internal and environmental positions. Each side decides whether to bargain and what positions to take, based on predictions of factors that can best be assessed by participants who have had experience in relating to each other or in dealing with this type of conflict.

The changing judgments of each side are a central element in the negotiations process. This means that the participants are dealing not with reality but with perceptions of reality. Much of this process turns on the efficiency of communications, a factor common to nonracial negotiations as well. Since the outcome depends on the opponent's judgment of the opposing side's determination and resources, bluff is inevitably a factor in the process. The relevant judgments of each side about the position of the other are based not only on face-to-face interactions, but also on attempts to read meanings into the other's actions in order to infer every change in the environmental constraints.

Some additional communication problems are specifically applicable to racial negotiations. The white spokesmen may have difficulty understanding the degree to which blacks are motivated to search for black identity and to demand recognition of their blackness. This difficulty is even greater for white spokesmen who psychologically arrange their own perceptions around those values in which the highest form of social adjustment is achieved by affording equal opportunity to all segments of the society. This view rejects the idea of special or preferential treatment to achieve such equality and also rejects a specialized black interest because it seems to lead to a kind of cultural pluralism. Within our culture most white Americans have not yet developed any clear alternative perspective to the melting pot concept. They share no common reference points, therefore, with blacks who seek to gain and retain black identity within a pluralistic society and who attempt to make institutions serve black interest.

Black spokesmen, on the other hand, have a different set of communications problems. One is that their stereotyping of white spokesmen matches the stereotyping of blacks by whites. Blacks also experience difficulty in understanding the actual (as compared to the idealized) symbolic operations of the establishment—its values, decision-making structure, and centers of power. Moreover, since each set of spokesmen is likely to begin negotiations with a deep suspicion of the motives of the other, there is apt to be considerable distortion of signals in interpreting the communications from the other side.

As an overt racial conflict develops into a negotiation exploration, as the probing by each of the other's position continues, and as communication proceeds, the demands and responses will also shift. The black side may move from generalized demands based on the moral position of achieving rights to demands based on the judgment of how much it will be able to get from the establishment. These formulations become increasingly precise for two reasons. First, as the negotiations proceed, the black leaders learn enough about the functioning of the establishment to be able to define their immediate objectives. Second, as they abandon hope that the establishment will recognize and adapt to the justice of their general demands, they find it necessary to define a basis from which actions, not promises, will result.

Shifts in the demand and response positions of the two sides also will occur during the negotiations as allies are added or lost by either side, or as coalitions are formed or break down. If allies have been added or lost, the issues may not be changed but the power alignment may shift enough to alter the outcome. On the other hand, if either side moves into a new coalition, issues as well as relative power may change within the negotiating pattern.

Since the overt racial conflict and resulting negotiations are likely to be a new experience for the participants, it is probable that the lines of support for the establishment positions will be changing over the period of the negotiations. Some who may prefer a position that is more or less responsive than the one that their representatives are adopting may move toward, or away from, agreement with the protestors as negotiations proceed.

Changes in support for the black position also may influence the black leaders. Some of this dissent may be based on alternate ideological commitments to change and may become particularly strong if the prospects of success seem dim. On the other hand, some dissenting positions could lead to a preference for a less intransigent bargaining position or a less aggressive use of coercion. This alternative emphasis may gain strength if the early negotiating position does not appear to be achieving its objectives.

Our data do not give any firm guide on the relative skills of one side or the other in handling the negotiations process. Although the white establishment leaders are likely to have had more experience in some kinds of organizational conflict and adjustment, the black leaders will have had more experience assessing the positions of whites. In any event our cases suggest ten ways used by negotiators as they attempt to change the other's positions:

1. Applying some criterion of justice to exhort both parties;

2. Appealing to the self-interest of the other side;
3. Developing implications of technical possibilities and/or difficulties;
4. Moderating emotional intensities to create flexibility of personal interaction;
5. Exploring alternative methods of achieving the same general objectives that may be less threatening or costly to the other side;
6. Adapting positions of either side so that they more nearly conform to the organizational structures and processes of the other side;
7. Formulating central positions that most nearly conform to already accepted symbols and avoiding symbols that appear most threatening;
8. Timing the modification of positions and the introduction of added data;
9. Setting meaningful deadlines; and
10. Threatening to apply or withhold raw power.

Not surprisingly, our data suggest the difficulties and importance of the attitudinal structuring between protagonists who have not yet developed a rapport and whose original postures are likely to be based on personal and institutional stereotypes. In addition to the manipulation of coercive power and its uses at the bargaining table, changes in attitudinal structuring can make some differences in the outcome of the negotiations.

Our data suggest that progress toward agreement can move faster and further if suspicion can give way to trust and if antagonisms can be replaced by a shared need to reach an agreement. Finally, both of these general modifications of attitude can be consciously developed or accentuated to some degree.

In most of our cases, establishment spokesmen hoped that conflict could be turned into cooperation in the negotiations and that what they perceived as common interests and needs would stimulate a common participation in solving the problems of the establishment. Yet, for most of our cases, the negotiations (like most union-management bargaining, for that matter) became largely an effort to adjust the conflict with the least cost to each side. A cooperative approach seldom appeared because there was mutual suspicion and distrust; the protestors judged that they had no obligation to assist an establishment that had been treating blacks so inequitably; and the establishment saw little point in aiding protest leaders whom they preferred not to recognize and whose roles within the establishment they were most reluctant to expand.

Considering these variables in the interactions across the bargaining table, it may be possible to identify moves made by each side that bring the parties closer to agreement. The degree of concession made by each side is a subtle problem. There may be movement on issues deemed unimportant to one side, with little movement on the crucial ones. There may be apparent movement which actually indicates only that the original position was not firm. There may be tentative explorations of possible positions that are only trial balloons, which can be withdrawn or modified as the reactions of the other side are assessed. Judgments must converge if agreement is to be reached, but the movement this will require from each side, the issues that must be negotiated, and the variations in approaches and attitudes from the original positions will differ greatly from case to case.

RESULTS OF NEGOTIATIONS

In the last analysis the process of overt racial conflict and negotiations is initiated by black protestors to induce changes in establishment actions. In response the establishment seeks to limit its concessions to those that appear to be consistent and useful to the effective functioning of the organization. Indeed, the speculations of each side on how the process might be concluded and what might be the terms of agreement can strongly affect whether negotiations are even begun and how they are conducted. Why did the two sides come to an agreement (if they did)? Why did they adopt the terms that they did? What are the long-run implications of their agreement?

Terms of Agreement

One objective of the protestors is to secure a commitment from the establishment to modify its outputs, services to clients, or employment practices. Since both sides are likely to view such demands as requiring a shift in favor of black claimants compared to those now benefiting most from the functioning of the establishment, the gain for blacks may be viewed as a loss for others. It is, in other words, a reallocation of benefits. In most of the cases in which agreement was reached, relatively small but identifiable changes of this kind did occur. In some cases such changes in outputs and services applied to all elements that had any relation to the establishment, although it was more likely that the changes affected a subunit within the larger establishment, or even only the group of black protestors and not others who also may have tried to press claims on the institution.

Although we use the phrase "agreement between the two negotiating sides," the public announcement in our cases usually appeared as a unilateral statement made by agents of the establishment, implying that its decision-making processes had not been modified and that no new grouping had been added within the structure.

Long-Range Consequences

Although our case reports include only a brief summary of later developments, it was presumed that the achievement of an agreement represented a solution that, for the moment at least, took the heat out of the conflict. In each of our cases the agreement temporarily quieted the conflict only because it included a promise by blacks to withdraw threats and actions and a promise by the establishment that was accepted by the black leaders as encompassing as much change as then appeared to be achieveable.

In none of our cases did the black protestors attain the degree of community control that some sought. Neither did they achieve a change in establishment rules that would specify a formal role for the black interests. In only a few cases was there an expectation that the leaders who had participated in making the original agreement would be accepted as playing even a consultative role in future establishment decisions.

In some cases a specialized outcome of the confrontation and agreement was an expansion of the role of the black administrator. Apparently, executives of some establishments assumed that such a person would function as the in-house representative of the blacks, although such a perspective was seldom shared by the protestors.

It can be predicted that blacks will continue to charge that they are not being treated fairly even within the rules and policies of the establishment. Indeed, this tendency to challenge alleged discriminatory acts is likely to be more extensive if the previous activity is viewed as a successful black challenge to the establishment. Further, there may be additional challenges if it seems that the terms of the agreement have not been properly implemented for some individuals or groups. Thus, the negotiators may predict a rising number of internal racial conflicts and may consider providing mechanisms to handle these complaints. This could be done by establishing some continuing processes that might be labeled "grievance machinery." Although only a few of the cases included such machinery, it may be useful to speculate about various approaches to this system.

The agreement might specify that any challenges by blacks are to be handled within whatever procedures already exist. Or, if none exist, a procedure might be projected under which all complainants might submit their grievances to higher authorities within the establishment. A second approach might be to regard the black leaders as having a continuing relationship to their black constituencies, assigning to them the function of representing the black complainants within the grievance machinery. Finally, the arrangement might include some device for the involvement of an outside neutral who could be appealed to if the black complainant was not satisfied with the adjustment of his grievance. This supplementary procedure could assign a fact-finding and mediational role to the neutral, or it could include a pledge that the parties would accept and apply his arbitrational award.

Although much of the pressure that led to the conflicts and negotiations came from the individual and group complaints of racial discrimination referred to above, they included demands for changes in general policies. The negotiator might have anticipated further demands for more policy changes since, obviously, black aspirations would not have been satisfied in a first agreement. One such plan would provide for continuing *consultation* as new problems arose and new demands were formulated. Such an approach would assume that the establishment could be depended on to meet new black needs adequately and that blacks could be counted on to achieve an understanding of the needs and policies of the establishment. This consultative approach could take one of several alternative forms.

The procedure could be a simple adaptation of structures already established for groups that recommend changes in establishment policies and practices. The negotiated agreement would provide that the black leaders of the protesting group would be free to join other groups within the existing consultative machinery. Or the negotiators could agree that there are specialized policy and administrative problems in the relations between blacks and the establishment and, therefore, the agreement might provide for consultation between black leaders and establishment spokesmen on appropriate occasions.

As an alternative or a supplement to the consultative process, the negotiators might judge that additional black challenges probably would be made later by the present black leaders and might require the same kind of a negotiating process. This projection could lead to a provision pledging the use of the process when it was necessary in the future. In addition, the negotiators could decide that some of the general policies or approaches agreed to in settling the conflict could best be *implemented* by the involvement of the black spokesmen. One of the crucial judgments of the establishment and the black negotiators is whether the black protest leaders are going to share the responsibility, holding the establishment accountable for the decisions incorporated within the agreement that concludes the conflict.

One approach to the functioning of black protestors as implementors of establishment policies would be to specify the organizational work that the black representatives would perform and their relations to the rest of the organization. Alternatively, it could be agreed that a subunit of the establishment would be under the control of the black protestors while drawing resources from the central structure of the establishment. This was the original proposal of the Black Coalition in Chicago and is a pattern urged by black militants for schools and other ghetto-located establishments.

Problems in Consideration of Continuing Machinery

The first problem faced by each side in negotiations aimed toward introducing any continuing machinery is deciding whether the existing black leadership-constituency relationship will continue to be sufficiently viable for the establishment to accept these leaders as the representatives of black interests. Such decisions by each of the two sides are a function of the predicted response of the constituents to the terms of the settlement, the characteristics of the black leaders, and the degree to which the establishment is expected to adapt to new policies and practices.

The second problem involves the judgment of each side as to the kinds of issues and environmental characteristics that may contribute to the next racial conflict affecting the establishment. Continuing machinery or understandings will be meaningful only if the establishment commitment is quite firm yet flexible, if the black leadership is stable yet also flexible, and if the sets of pressures in the new situation appear to be manageable by the same processes as the current conflict. In considering whether to take a position on a specific form of continuing machinery, each side must decide how much of its bargaining resources to apply to this set of issues—in other words, how high a priority it will assign to this set of issues as compared to other disputed issues.

Viewed from the perspective of the functioning of establishments, the negotiations that we studied resulted in little change in rules and essentially no change in the power bases of the establishment. For some of the protestors, however, the negotiations provided a meaningful opportunity to challenge the establishment. Such a perspective assumes that a sufficient rallying of black pressure will continue the efforts toward equality, although in almost all of the cases studied the organization that put the protest together did not survive to play a continuing role in representing black interests in the establishment.

THE BLACK ADMINISTRATOR

The original research design of the case studies did not focus on the particular role of a black administrator. The case records, however, suggest that such individuals can have an important impact on the development and consequences of confrontations and negotiations. Data from the individual case studies have been abstracted and used to formulate some speculative analyses of the significance of this role.

In many establishments one or more persons are responsible for the relationships with black employees, clients, and neighbors. Usually these persons have a black skin, although the degree of their identity with blackness is not predictable either from their skin color or from their role assignment.

This speculative analysis begins with an exploration of the possible characteristics of the role of such a person when the establishments are *not* being challenged by black protestors. Implicit in this problem is the distinction between the assumed usual functioning of the establishment to all others, on one hand, and the special characteristics of the relationship to the black community, on the other. It should be noted that the black grouping relevant to this analysis is not the black community as such, but a specific group of black employees, black clients, or black neighbors.

Four different role definitions can be distinguished. The first two are based on the assumption that it is basic establishment policy to treat blacks just like everyone else. This assumption of equal treatment leads to two different but interrelated functions for the black administrators that derive from allegations that the equal treatment policy is being violated. After investigation, the black administrator has one of two roles to play.

In the event that he judges that the alleged discrimination is *perceptual* and not *real*, he explains and hopefully changes that perception. This role assumes that the establishment is, in fact, operating satisfactorily under an equality policy and that a clearing of misunderstandings is needed. Since no establishment behavioral change is required, the problem is solved once the misunderstandings are corrected.

Alternatively, investigation may reveal that, despite the establishment policy, de facto unequal treatment does exist. That is, the establishment's implementation of the equal treatment policy falls short of policy directives. The black administrator's role becomes one of clearing any misunderstandings as to the real intent of the establishment. If this fails, he may then be required to carry the role further, alerting others within the establishment to the violations and perhaps also playing a significant role in correcting existing discriminatory actions.

A third role definition is based on a different interpretation of the equality principle. This is the assumption that equality is the functioning of the establishment and in its outputs can only be achieved by according differential or special treatment to blacks. In this formulation, equality is a *goal* rather than a *method*, and the simple application of the same rules to everyone will not lead to equal treatment. The individual holding this view, therefore, must identify these discrepancies, develop proposals for changes in the establishment's operations, and convince the organization of their validity.

Finally, there is a fourth alternative role definition when interests conflict and cannot be fully reconciled in any single set of policies and administrative acts. It is assumed that conflicting interests can be accommodated with some advantages and some disadvantages for each party. Under this definition of the patterns of conflicting interests, the black administrator's role could be to help the establishment achieve an accommodation of the interests of both.

The first three definitions view the appropriate role of a black administrator as simultaneously serving both black and establishment interests. The fourth considers that the administrator is required to strike some kind of balance between conflicting interests as the basis for his own criteria for action.

Each of the role definitions suggested above implies that the participants can identify the interests of the establishment and the interest of blacks. The interests of the establishment are complex, but for the purposes of this particular analysis it is assumed that a set of policy directions and administrative styles and actions are signaled to all participants by the executive officers. In an ongoing and stable organizational pattern this general assumption appears to be reasonable. Of course, within the organization the signals may be misread by some and, in any case, may result in varying degrees of support or opposition.

If the establishment interests are not precise, the characteristics of the black interest are even less easily identifiable; it is less likely that there will be a concensus among the participants about them. As has been noted in other chapters, there is no concensus among blacks as to the dimensions and characteristics of the black community or their immediate or long-run programmatic interests. Instead, various leaders and potential leaders present themselves as spokesmen for a black interest and seek support from members of the black community for their position.

Whatever role is assigned to the black administrator, some but not all blacks will share his judgments of the relevant black interests. The administrator may define black interests out of his own experiences and may formulate what he believes to be the preferable black interest on the basis of his personal strategic and programmatic judgments. Obviously, he cannot expect unanimous support for this personalized perspective.

On the other hand, he may be guided primarily by the judgments of specific black groupings in defining the relevant black interest in the functioning of the establishment. During most of the time, however, no formal organizational unit is recognized as speaking for the blacks in relation to the establishment. Even if the black administrator preferred such guidance, therefore, he rarely has a clear signal based on a black consensus to which he can respond with any certainty.

In addition to defining the black interest, the black administrator also has to make judgments on the *practical* aspects of the ways in which the establishment relates to blacks. The role he assumes will depend on his strategic judgments of what is realistic as compared to what is ideal. He will need to draw on his own resources to determine what can reasonably be achieved within the establishment he services. This is a difficult process, and if he is perceived as sponsoring programs that are far short of what "ought" to be, he may alienate the group he is trying to help.

There is one more step in this development of alternative role definitions of the black administrator. The analysis must be shifted from the real to the perceptual, that is, the operative role must be defined as the participants perceive it. There is no reason to assume that persons within the organization agree on the black administrator's role or that the black administrator defines his role as do superiors and peers. There is no reason to assume that any particular grouping of blacks necessarily shares a common definition of what the administrator's role should be or how it is being performed.

Thus, the black administrator's expectations of his role are uncertain and perhaps quite different from those held by the relevant groupings. In reality these roles are overlapping and may change within an establishment as the issues and situations change. The role to be played by a black administrator is derived from the intent of the establishment in appointing him to the job. In some cases the establishment may perceive such an appointment as insurance against allegations of discrimination. Within that definition his role is primarily to "cool it" by convincing the protestors that establishment policy is correct. He is to represent the establishment interests to the protestors and to explain those interests in a way that will gain acceptance for the establishment. Blacks, on the other hand, may view such a role as that of "house nigger" and reject both the role and the individual. They might prefer to see the administrator representing and interpreting black interests to the establishment and acting to change the establishment in the ways they desire. Such a dichotomy of definition almost inevitably leads to frustration if not schizophrenia by all involved and perhaps affects the black administrator most of all.

What role does the black administrator choose when a confrontation is developing? He may consider that the establishment is proceeding as well as could be expected to service black interests and that he should seek ways to support the establishment posture and to reject the protestors' developing challenge. He may decide that the black protestors are developing pressures that may succeed in producing changes in establishment policies and practices that he has been unable to achieve and he may seek to find ways to assist them to press for such changes.

Of course, real life is not that simple. But among the enormous variations in the perspectives and actions of all the participants, a few possibilities seem to emerge. The black administrator may support establishment functions of which he is a part and underline the impracticality of the idealized statements about the black community and the expectations of change held by the protest leaders. The black administrator may judge that the establishment has *not* fully met its obligations to blacks and may share their concern for greater and faster steps toward equality. In other words, in greater or lesser degree, the individual black administrator is quite likely to have internal tensions as he seeks to function as best he can in both camps.

There may be considerable divergence in the perceptions of reality held by the establishment executives and the black administrator. Many of the white policy makers and administrators are likely to affirm a nonracial treatment for all alike and to believe that, by and large, this describes how their establishment is functioning. The black administrator, on the other hand, is more likely to judge that performance is short of what it ought to be, even if he adopts the idealized nonracial policy position.

This speculative analysis of the role of black administrators has some general implications for confrontations and negotiations. As confrontations are developing, the black administrator who shares the judgments of the protestors may use their pressures to secure modifications of establishment practices that he had not been able to obtain. Such an achievement, however, is quite likely to be only a step in the direction sought by the protestors. Modest change may even be considered to be a hindrance rather than an achievement by those who hope for substantial establishment change.

Considerable tension may develop between the black administrator and the protestors. The administrator may doubt that the protestors have appropriately expressed black interests, that they represent the groupings of the black community, and that they are realistic in their demands. The protestors, on the other hand, may challenge the administrator's role as a spokesman for black interests and may consider that realism requires a challenge to the establishment accompanied by the development of more pressure for change.

If those tensions do appear, the black administrator may play no direct role in the confrontation and possible negotiations. On the other hand, he may participate in various ways, with or without official establishment sanction. If he has a foot in both camps or, to change the simile, if his heart is with the protestors and his head is with the establishment, he may be able to interpret the perspectives and problems of each to the other. Although he is unlikely to be successful in attempting a formal third-party role, informally he may be able to assist in the communication function for which a third party is needed. Although in this position he is likely to stress shared rather than conflicting goals, he may find ways to help both sides relate to each other significantly and realistically.

The black administrator may assume the most importance in the negotiations process if an agreement has been achieved as a result of negotiations. He may remain as the only active black voice concerned with the execution of the terms. He may participate in administering new policies by joint understanding of the negotiators or be assigned this responsibility by the establishment executives after the negotiations are concluded.

The sketchy data of our cases suggest that it is highly uncertain whether a black administrator who is hired after the dispute brings any significant new role definitions as a black spokesman. As long as there is no continuing organized black constituency to which he should relate and if the immediate pressures have disappeared and it is not predicted that they will return soon, his role remains as ambiguous as those we have studied.

This chapter summarizes and analyzes the experiences of the parties when racial confrontations have developed into negotiations. Even the negotiations and agreement in some of the cases under study could not have been achieved without the supplementary assistance of a third-party intervenor. In a few cases it was also assumed that such a person could play a role in the continuing machinery as projected by the parties. The following section discusses the actual and potential roles of third-party intervenors.

THIRD-PARTY INTERVENTION

Can third parties help to work out a black challenge and help the parties to come to an agreement that concludes a racial confrontation? Can they influence the terms of agreement? Logic suggests an affirmative answer to both questions. If the two sides want to agree but are having difficulty, a person removed from the specific conflict *ought* to be able to help them. In social conflict situations involving labor, commerical interests, and international affairs, a good deal of experience suggests that third parties are helpful in aiding or in coercing settlements of disputes.

The use of third-party intervenors as mediators and/or arbitrators is relatively common in union-management experience. In the data gathered from our cases and from other evidence, however, there were only a few situations in which third-party roles were attempted. Our generalizations, therefore, are even more tentative and speculative than in other aspects of racial negotiations. These speculative conclusions are derived from the roles that third-party intervenors have played in one or another of the cases we studied and from the logic of the negotiating actions and perspectives of the two sides in all of our cases.

This analysis confronts the same problem that has reappeared throughout the study: the differences among sectors. As the previous analysis suggested, potential third-party intervenors may be involved in racial conflicts involving different kinds of establishments and black organizations with different issues, depending on the sector in which the conflict appears. Their potential relation to the existing rules for changing or resisting change will vary, therefore, depending on the sector of the establishment. The speculative analysis that follows can most usefully be viewed as raising some questions about which generalizations are quite difficult.

Any third-party intervenor in racial conflict is pioneering in new territory and cannot operate from a general consensus as to how the conflict should be resolved. In contrast to union-management relations, the protestors have no formally established rights and the establishments are not expected to engage in negotiations or to reach an agreement. In most situations there is not even enough experience and support to establish a climate of expectation and approval for a negotiating pattern of resolving racial conflicts. Even more fundamentally, as the previous analysis suggests, there is no general consensus that substantial changes should be made in establishments to provide representation for blacks or to adjust to specialized black interests.

Characteristics of Racial Negotiations 243

The general approaches of a third-party intervenor are sufficiently known from the logic of social conflict situations and from experience in a wide variety of situations. The effort to analyze the experiences in racial conflict may be built on two sets of generalized propositions: the role of the third-party intervenor is based on what he is *trying* to achieve; the limits of his capacities to help resolve the conflict depend on the situation and on the approach that he adopts. These two general aspects will be discussed next, focusing specifically on what appear to be the racial elements of such efforts in each case.

What Are Mediators Trying to Accomplish?

Not all third-party intervenors operate in the same way. Their variations in mediational styles can be classified according to the purposes that bring them into the racial conflict and guide their actions during the conflict and negotiations. Our earlier analysis suggested that one or even both sides in some racial conflicts may *not* want to negotiate at all. It follows also that such an *anti-negotiations* preference could be the judgment of the person who intervened in the conflict. He might agree with establishment spokesmen that there is no need to negotiate black demands and that to do so would be unnecessarily damaging to the establishment position. He might agree with the black leadership that they should not negotiate because they are not ready and, indeed, might never be. In such circumstances the third-party intervenor may use his skills and resources to aid the nonnegotiating stance of either one or both parties.

In some cases intervenors may judge that it is their responsibility to be neutral, that is, to help the parties conclude their argument on any basis. Thus, the intervenor would remain indifferent as to whether the terms resulted in a capitulation by the establishment that substantially changed its policies in the direction demanded by the protestors or an abandonment of the conflict by the blacks with no gains at all. If there are no gains for blacks, the intervenor may be judged to have "cooled it" at the expense of black needs for change. In any case the only value that guides the intervenor is that peace is important; whether or not establishment practices have changed is not his responsibility. Conceptually, of course, this approach is completely consistent with the idea of one who helps the parties to find their *own* basis for agreement—what each wants, what each is prepared to press for, and what each is prepared to accept as the price for not mobilizing its coercive resources further. Under some circumstances, these neutral activities can be of great help to an inexperienced black leadership and to inept establishment spokesmen in achieving the agreement they prefer instead of continuing the pressure or the threat of pressure that they are seeking to avoid.

The value stance of the neutral in a racial conflict does not necessarily involve *negotiations* at all. In many racial clashes in which third parties seek to help, the conflict may terminate without any real give and take, without a black agreement, and without any acceptance by the establishment that it needs *agreement* with the protestors or is ready to make concessions to secure such an agreement.

A second and different mediating role occurs, however, when the intervenor begins with the judgment that an agreement should be achieved. He feels, in other words, that possible settlement terms should be considered and explored by both sides until they agree that the conflict will be abated, and new policies and/or practices will be initiated. It does not follow, of course, that the parties will achieve an accommodated agreement even with the assistance of a skilled mediator. But, within this category, the important distinction is that the intervenor is using the discretions available to him in an effort to achieve an agreement.

From the earlier case and sector analyses it is apparent that if the black protestors wish to negotiate, their most difficult hurdle is to persuade the establishment to accept them as legitimate representatives of an extended constituency on behalf of the black community. In this speculation it is relevant to consider our earlier discussion of the issues facing the establishment as to whether there *is* a specialized black interest to which establishment policies should be attuned and, therefore, whether a negotiated basis for decision making should be accorded to the spokesmen for that black interest. In addition there is the equally urgent question of whether or not the particular spokesmen of the black community who are making the current demands should be accepted as representatives. If the mediator who is operating within a specific conflict answers both questions for himself in the affirmative, he uses his capacities to achieve an agreement with these spokesmen.

Similarly, in an earlier chapter we also analyzed the problems facing the black leadership: Should it enter negotiations, be prepared to modify its demands, and be ready to accept terms and suspend its pressures against the establishment? If the mediator believes that this is the best course, he will attempt to persuade protestors and establishment spokesmen to negotiate and reach an agreement. In this second category, the intervenor works to achieve the recognition of the black protest leadership and the development of an agreement between the parties—on *any* terms. This is the stance that the pre-Wagner Act labor mediators sometimes adopted and that is generally taken by labor mediators today in areas covered by the Labor Relations Acts, which specify the duty to bargain and the processes for establishing representation.

This stance has a specialized meaning in racial conflict. It is possible for the mediator to judge that dignity, freedom, justice, and independence are terms expressing black rights that are nonnegotiable. With such a view the self-definition of his role would be to aid in finding compromises in the terms of agreement, while preserving the principles that derive from black identity in an American context.

The values of some mediators carry them one step further. They may believe that it is desirable for the establishment to recognize and negotiate with the protestors, that the black leaders also enter into serious negotiations, that the two parties come to some formal agreement, and that the terms result in some changes pressed by the black leaders.

The case data and analyses suggest some particular racial aspects involved in the intervenor's choice of emphasis. When he uses his discretionary capacities to press either party in one direction or another, he is making a choice as to whether resource reallocation or guarantees of continuing participation are more urgent. In addition, this position requires him to predict the terms that might produce a settlement and to judge how future developments will contribute to making one set of terms more productive than another. Of course, the individual who uses the rhetoric of change may, in fact, be operating largely as a neutral helping the partisans to find their own solutions. In this case he is operating as a change agent only to the degree that the partisans have defined their own needs and capacities and are striking a bargain that fits their relative capacities and desires.

The analysis suggests, therefore, that it is posssible and useful to distinguish between a neutral mediator and a mediator-advocate. The distinction is helpful in examining the style and capacities of a third-party intervenor in a racial conflict. Our data suggest that a completely neutral stance in racial conflicts is quite likely to result in temporizing and cooling the conflict. Since power is largely on the side of the establishment, most organizations are strongly against recognizing militant blacks as appropriate spokesmen for black interests, and are determined not to enlarge the decision-making process to include a new, black interest in the requirement for consensus on establishment policies and programs.

Further, the analysis suggests that there is a range of different positions that a mediator-advocate could adopt. His advocacy thrust might even subvert the negotiating process if he took the position that either side should not negotiate, at least at that time. On the other hand, he might make a serious effort to secure recognition of black leadership and a negotiating stance from the two sides. There are, indeed, situations within our cases in which the intervenor advocated recognition and an accommodated agreement and, in addition, established some of his own criteria for the terms he prefered.

To What Degree Can Intervenors Affect the Results?

What patterns affect the possibility that an intervenor can influence the outcome of a clash? The first element to consider is whether the parties directly involved in the conflict want his help. In a number of the cases we reviewed there was no third-party intervenor because either one or both parties did not think it would be helpful. The parties are likely to welcome assistance only if and when they cannot work out a settlement themselves. Intervenors can be effective only if the protestors are willing to negotiate for compromises and concessions within a system whose purposes and functions would be changed only moderately. As the analyses in the earlier chapters suggest, the establishment must be ready to agree that the black spokesmen represent a reasonably powerful black interest or constituency.

Of course, a potential third-party intervenor can function in a racial dispute only if the parties accept the need for such a role and also accept the individual who may be interested and available. The lack of experience with racial negotiations and the uncertainty inherent in the process make this particularly difficult. One could speculate that the intervenor will not be accepted by the black protestors unless he has shown a real understanding and empathy with their position; he may not be accepted by the establishment unless he has shown an appreciation of its role and problems. The intervenor is more likely to be acceptable to the side whose position he appears to favor. On the other hand, the cases suggest that either side may feel a need to work with someone who is most able to move the other side, whether or not he shares their points of view. The requirement that the intervenor understand the position of both sides is relevant, of course, so that he may achieve acceptance and perform necessary communications.

In racial conflicts and negotiations each side has difficulty in seeing the situation through the eyes of the other. If the intervenor comes from outside the situation, he will need to know how the establishment operates, where the sources of power are in decision making, and the organizational flexibilities and constraints. He must understand why there are *racial* complaints about the ways in which the establishment is operating.

Understanding the black side may be more difficult. Deep-seated objections arising from a life experience may be behind the demands and the angry rhetoric, and the white intervenor may either understate or overstate their relevance to the immediate situation. He may also have great difficulty understanding the leadership-constituency relationships, especially of black ad hoc organizations.

An understanding of each side, of course, is the basis for the mediator's second major role—aiding communications. In this role the intervenor cannot be anything more than a messenger boy if he does not have the confidence of each side. He must be depended on to communicate only what each party is ready to share with the other. If the establishment implies a readiness to reach an agreement but really intends to end the discussions by a unilateral decision, the mediator cannot successfully pretend that the black side has been recognized, and that a negotiating pattern has been accepted. If the black leaders have not yet achieved the coercive capacity they need, the mediator who betrays to the other side the uncertainties behind their rehtoric may soon lose his effectiveness. In any conflict situation, but particularly in racial conflicts, the understanding shared between the two sides through the mediator is a delicate and artful mixture.

As we have noted, in the negotiating process the parties operate on estimates of external conditions, including the future consequences to each if they take various bargaining positions. By logical extension, therefore, a third major role of the intervenor is helping the parties with their predictions of the future. Two factors make such a role particularly important but difficult in racial conflicts. The establishment will have had no previous experience with the black leaders and their thrust; the protest leaders will have had little experience with how an establishment may adjust to any new understandings.

Mediating Procedures

The procedures that the mediator can use to aid the parties in their racial conflict negotiations appear to share common characteristics with the negotiations process in nonracial situations. The similarity of these procedural moves may have created the illusion that the mediation process is the same regardless of context. The process includes separate and confidential consultation with each side to explore what each seeks and what responses it intends. Messages are carried from one side to the other so that modified positions can be explored without too firm a commitment by either side. The two sides are brought into joint sessions if and when it appears that some face-to-face contact can advance either their mutual understanding or their readiness to explore alternative moves toward reaching agreement. Not infrequently the two parties require a neutral chairman for these joint discussions to hold emotions within tolerable limits, to keep the group exploring possible areas of agreement, and to suspend the sessions if separate caucuses are appropriate. Discussions may be suspended while a fact-finding process is pursued or some issues are referred to binding arbitration. The skill in selecting and timing these moves is crucially important to the success of any third-party interventions, including those in which racial issues are involved.

Characteristics of Intervenors

Third-party intervenors in racial conflicts appear to have some characteristics that are quite different from those of intervenors in labor or international areas. The black administrator who simultaneously is part of the establishment yet seeks to mediate a dispute between it and the black protestors is an example. Although he appears peripherally in a number of our case studies, he seldom plays a major mediating role. He usually is either not trusted by the black protestors or has too little importance within the establishment to play a significant mediating role in the controversy.

Even if the individual is independent of the establishment, his color identification may be of great importance in the role that he is able to play. In some situations white establishment leaders are anxious to have the services of blacks who can command the confidence of the protest leadership and can understand establishment policies and problems to moderate extreme black demands. Conversely, the protestors may find it useful to have a mediator who is in a position to persuade establishment leaders that black interests can be accommodated in various ways. These two separate mediating perspectives and roles can be combined in a single mediating team made up of a white establishment representative and a militant black if neither are identified directly with the specific dispute and if both are able to work together toward the common objective of satisfactorily resolving the dispute.

The above analysis assumes that the intervenor has no capacity to influence the clash between the parties except through his skill, persuasiveness, and empathy with one or both sides which the two parties use to find their own way to a settlement of their conflict. Our case histories and our general sector analyses, however, suggest that the third party may have a specialized interest in getting the conflict resolved and may even be concerned about the terms of agreement that are adopted to settle the argument. Perhaps the clearest illustration of this within our cases is in the report on the construction case in Chicago (Chapter 7). Although the two conflicting parties were the industry-union on one side and the black community leaders on the other, the mayor and some federal agencies were also involved and concerned about the outcome. Indeed, it appears that there was a settlement only because the two government units needed one and that the terms made little change in the prevailing patterns because the two government units chose to use only a little of their potential supplementary coercive pressure on the union and industry.

In that case, each political unit had coercive capacities that were partly based on laws and court rulings but also allowed considerable administrative discretion. There are many other possibilities of private and government relationships in which the intervening party is interested not only in achieving racial peace in the immediate conflict but also in working toward terms that he values.

In Chapter 2 alternative programs for black advances were dichotomously classified as *either* negotiations or political action. Third-party intervention by a political figure (whether an elected official or an administrator) provides a route for merging the two approaches. If, for reasons not fully analyzed in our cases, the political purposes of that agent are best served by identifying with the black protestors, his mediational intervention can move the establishment further than it would otherwise go. The degree of additional change as a result of such a mediator-advocate role is, obviously, a function of how much coercive potential the political figure has available and is willing to use. It is probably reasonable to speculate that political intervenors have added only minimal supplementary coercive potential to date and that, quite frequently, their role is more supportive of the establishment than of the black position.

In summary, the case materials appear to suggest a number of general conclusions about third-party intervention, despite the fact that the potential for the help of a third-party intervenor is considerably greater in some seectors than in others. First, the way an intervenor operates is a function of his values and judgments. Second, he can help the parties only if they have confidence in his integrity, understanding, and commitment. Third, it takes a considerable range of skills to intervene successfully and only a small part of these skills can be taught since they involve an art that draws on experience and uses very general guidelines. Fourth, if the mediator is to be an advocate he needs "clout," which can be achieved, to some degree, if the parties recognize his skill and his identification with their interests. He can be much more effective, however, if he has an interest of his own in the outcome of the negotiations and tries to manipulate the rewards and punishments available to him to push both sides in the directions he seeks.

There are at least three ways, therefore, in which the experienced labor mediator may be poorly equipped to function as an intervenor in racial conflicts and, indeed, may be at a disadvantage: He may not have an empathy for racial positions; he may not understand the institutional context of the particular racial conflict; and he may fail to bring to the conflict the kind of pressures that are needed to supplement the black coercive positions.

CHAPTER 10

Summary and Conclusions

This chapter summarizes the major findings of the study and draws general inferences from the analyses of sector developments, the negotiations process, and the experiences with third-party intervention. It is important to note that our project began with a set of social values: America needs to make progress toward racial equality; and black interests, now under-represented in our society, must be given greater weight. Since this requires a new and different accommodation between black and other interests, the process of confrontation-negotiation-agreement provides a possible route for correcting these urgent racial imbalances. From these value assumptions we derived the original formulations of the problems on which the research was focused: What are the possibilities for, and the limitations restricting, the use of negotiations to accommodate racial interests?

The data and analyses presented in earlier chapters suggest the need to modify the value assumptions of the study to make them apply to the real world in a more meaningful way. Three modifications appear to be particularly urgent. The first is to understand that progress toward racial equality cannot be measured by the fact that conflicting parties have achieved a settlement of their conflict and have agreed on terms so the overt conflict will not be further pressed. The original design embodied the implied approach of many participants in industrial relations that a negotiated and mutually accepted agreement produced improvements for labor and stability for both labor and management. Thus, management and labor were willing to negotiate agreements because they were reasonably satisfied with the results. By analogy, in our preliminary value formulation the achievement of a settlement would provide the peace that was assumed to be an important ingredient of black goals for racial progress.

But, as the case data demonstrate, racial peace may be reestablished with little or no change in the procedures or the resource distributions of the establishment. The agreement may subvert black needs for changes in the establishment. It may leave black leadership-constituency relationships in such disarray that future pressures for change are less likely. The terms of settlement may have a retrogressive impact on the groups that mounted the confrontation. We cannot assume, therefore, that progress satisfactory to blacks develops just because an agreement has been reached. Within our analysis, settlement, or peace, is an instrumental step that *may* contribute to change, not an independent value whose achievement is itself a desirable end.

This first modification shifts the emphasis in our value pattern from settlement to the degree of change sought by blacks. On reflection, it is clear that racial progress cannot be equated with racial peace. The modified emphasis seeks exploration of the possibilities and limitations of significant change in racial patterns through confrontation-negotiation-agreement.

From this reformulation it becomes clearer that a second modification of our problem statement is needed. We began with the black objective of racial equality and used a simple abstract summary of racial progress to indicate "change toward black interests and away from white racism." As the next section of this chapter explains, however, there are differing judgments about which changes in establishment practices are most important. It is possible to identify a variety of possible changes. There may be different judgments as to how much progress toward equality would develop from various programs. Some blacks give priority to the elimination of specific discriminatory practices; some emphasize improvement in establishment services to black clients; still others place an even greater emphasis on the participation of independent black spokesmen in the establishment's decision-making machinery; others focus on the building of black power and stress the development of black identity and black pride.

There is no single criterion, therefore, that can be used to determine the success of any particular settlement in producing the progress toward equality that blacks seek. Neither is there any precise way to assess *how much* change will develop from the modification of one establishment practice as compared to any other.

The study does not attempt to present an analysis only in terms of one set of these potentially conflicting black values. It does appear, however, that goals of resource allocation and nondiscriminatory treatment are *not* the full measure of changes needed to incorporate blacks into American society. Some methods for self-determination of black interests by blacks is also needed, and this separate black role should be incorporated into the functioning of each institution. It is also important to note, however, that this value does not deny the need for effective functioning of each institution, taking account of other interests as well as those of blacks. This formulation considers the need for an accommodation of numerous interests within each establishment and in the society as a whole, but the direction of change must be toward black interests, as defined by blacks, and away from the structuring of interests and attitudes that has been labeled white racism.

The complexity of these value objectives, however, may frustrate efforts to state the exact degree of change needed in any particular action. Thus, rating the merits of one kind of a negotiated settlement as compared to all others does not eliminate the need for the usefulness of a general change criterion. There is sufficient agreement among black advocates and their white supporters on the general direction of the thrust needed for black progress toward equality so that each incident can be assessed by evaluating the degree of change in establishment practices toward black interests.

The third modification problem is suggested by the final formulation of the second and derives from the relatively narrow time focus of each of the case studies. Although each case analysis has taken account of the emerging patterns of events that gave rise to the confrontation-negotiation-settlement, the description and analysis largely stop there. It is undoubtedly ture that any one incident should be judged within a longer time span so that it can be determined whether the settlement terms and the redefined relationships between protestors and establishment contribute to the kinds of lasting changes with which this study is concerned. Limitation of research resources was one of the most important reasons for the short time period of the research design. It is also true that any one incident is embedded in much wider movements and forces so that its consequences as well as its origin and developments should be assessed in a wider time and institutional framework. The data and tentative conclusions of this study must be viewed as only a step in an understanding of racial conflict and adjustment. The tests of immediate relevance that we affirmed above may be drawn from the data, but wider implications will await more data and an expanded perspective.

The problem toward which these conclusions are directed can be restated as: How much change in white establishments, in the directions sought by blacks, can be made through the processes of confrontation and negotiations when the parties are seeking to achieve an agreement between their conflicting positions?

BLACK AND WHITE ALIGNMENTS

A first step toward answering the question explored by the project is to define more precisely the nature of the racial conflict with which we are concerned. This section seeks to identify the parties and their perspectives. According to the original study design, black leaders and their constituencies are expressing generalized black needs that are in conflict with the positions adopted by a system dominated by whites, a pattern of racial discrimination throughout the society, and specific grievances about the way particular establishments act toward blacks.

This conceptualization assumes that the origins of the racial conflicts under study can be found in the contrasting perspectives on the norms and values of a society of which we are all members, the relation between these abstract norms and the hard realities of social life, and programs for adjustment and change. Such a simplified conflict formulation implies that, despite gradations of views within each of the two sides, there tends to be a consensus among whites in decision-making roles and in power positions, on the one hand, and a different consensus among a large number of blacks on the other. Thus, the studies and the sector analyses have accurately used the phrases "the white side" and "the black side." But these are only abstractions that must be examined in greater detail. Two illustrations drawn from the cases already reported underline the usefulness of the abstractions and provide the basis for the variations with which these studies have been concerned.

The first illustration is drawn from the challenge by black students to The University of Michigan. At the time when students formulated their demands, the university was functioning to provide an education designed largely for white and foreign students and was conducting research and adult extension activities that had little relation to black needs. It was assumed by most of those in decision-making roles that such functions best served national interests and, therefore, black interests. On the other hand, the protesting black students were certain that the university was not performing its proper educational role because they judged that many qualified black students were denied enrollment by inappropriate admission tests and by the failure of the university to provide adequate financial and other supports.

Since white perspectives on how the university ought to function were already built into its operations and its supports, the "white" university became the defender of the status quo. This illustration underlines an additional aspect of the analysis. The primary thrust of the black challenge was not directed toward the performance of the educational function. Rather, it focused on the effort to make those same functions available to more blacks and to expand the number of black graduates who could be as well equipped as whites in the larger society. In that conflict there were important white groupings which also agreed that these educational functions should be available to more blacks, although most of them judged that the black demands were exorbitant and that the pace of change should be much slower.

In the public school cases most of the decision makers were white. When challenged, they defended their work in providing educational opportunities for all and insisted that the high rate of school failures and drop-outs among minority and slum children indicated the students' failure to profit from this education. Most white teachers, school administrators, and members of boards of education supported these views on the purposes of schools and the inadequacy of black children who fail to learn.

Black students, parents, and communities held that resources were unequally distributed so that less skilled and less experienced teachers were assigned to poorly equipped buildings which were located in the black or other poor sections of the city. Fewer books, libraries, laboratories, and physical resources were available. Classes were larger. Students and parents perceived that teachers and school administrators failed in their function because they expected little from black students, demanding obedience but not achievement while retaining the educational techniques and curriculum used in all other schools. Black protestors wanted a flexible curriculum, taught by teachers who understood the life-styles of the students and related realistically to their lives. They wanted educators who would understand and respond to the black students' color, culture, and identify. Finally, some black protestors saw that changed educational patterns could be achieved only if blacks themselves had a voice in running their educational establishments.

In an abstract and symbolic sense, whites and blacks share the idea of equality. However, they differ on the meaning of the symbol and on their perceptions of the degree to which America approximates such an ideal. But within the black consensus and the white consensus, there are gradations of views that affect the confrontation-negotiation patterns of our study. On each side the differences are primarily programmatic.

White Positions on Equal Opportunity

The prevailing interpretations of the ideal of racial equality have been developed within a society dominated by whites. According to these norms, it is desirable for American institutions to merge those of different origins, religions, and races into common patterns by providing equal opportunities for each individual. The decision makers functioning in each establishment in our study tend to consider that their functions should be consistent with the social norms of equal opportunity and tend to say that the relation between the establishment and individuals is, as it should be, regardless of race, creed, or color.

This societal and establishment norm also extends to the standards that guide each individual within the establishment in relating to peers or clients. All establishment relationships with blacks are presumed to derive their meaning not from color differentiation, but from other aspects of personality and capacity.

Not all whites judge reality in the same way, however. Some believe that blacks are inferior to whites (whether by heredity or by environment) and, thus, that equal opportunity is provided even though most blacks may be far below most whites in achievement and social roles. Other whites who recognize the effect of environmental influences but do not believe that blacks are genetically different judge that inferior and superior social statuses are socially created and can be socially modified. Still others focus less on the degree to which blacks conform to white social norms and more on the availability of opportunities for blacks and others to achieve meaningful, self-defined identifications. For this latter group of whites, social reality is tested by the degree to which cultural pluralism is encouraged and aided.

These differing interpretations of reality in relation to a commonly verbalized ideal of equal opportunity give rise to four conflicting positions of white establishment decision makers. One judgment is that, since blacks are inferior to whites, differential treatment by the establishment is acceptable and conforms to the goals of equal opportunity. A second position holds that the norm of equal treatment is frequently violated and that discriminatory actions by individuals and by the establishment are common. Whites with this perspective seek to find ways to require other white individuals and establishments to abandon anti-black discrimination.

A third racial conflict area among establishment whites involves judgments about present consequences of previous individual and institutional discriminatory actions. On the basis of this perception, some whites judge that the establishment should find ways to provide supplementary assistance to blacks so that they could be equipped, as whites are, to take advantage of the equal opportunities that the social norm specifies for each of its members on a noncolor basis. A few whites hold that establishments should make positive contributions to the development of cultural pluralism.

In each of the establishments in the white society's sectors, therefore, there are four possible areas of conflict: (1) the degree to which discrimination exists and the degree of its importance; (2) the kinds of programs that are needed to correct the discriminatory actions of individuals and establishment policies; (3) the appropriateness of compensatory establishment policies to aid blacks in taking advantage of equal opportunity; and (4) establishment functions to further black identity.

The data from the cases suggest that, in each establishment studied, black challenges led to differing white responses on the basis of these alternative perspectives. Despite these differences, however, and probably more important than the disagreements among whites, the establishments adhered to a general policy of treating each individual equally. Moreover, many individuals in each establishment felt that this norm was already largely achieved and that no significant change in policy or practice was necessary.

Black Positions

Among blacks, too, there are significant differences in the perceptions of reality and the appropriate application of the ideal of equality. Those who accept the white-imposed view that blacks are inherently inferior are not prepared to challenge the evaluation and role assigned to them. Although this group was large at some periods in American history, its numbers are now declining. Such individuals and their social institutions play no significant part in the racial conflicts under study here.

Most blacks who agree that many blacks in inferior positions may not have developed adequate capacities to deal with the white society assign the fault to the social system. They believe that, with great personal and perhaps family effort, they and their children can hope to achieve levels equivalent to whites in similar situations. This objective may be viewed as desirable because it permits the achieving black individual to merge with whites and to enjoy the benefits of the white norm of noncolor opportunity. Some holding this view appear in our cases. A few are in administrative roles within establishments. Others are the potential constituents of more militant black leaders.

A third group, although fully conscious and resentful of discrimination against blacks, judges that economic and political discrimination urgently need correction. These blacks seek to participate on a noncolor basis in reform activities in trade unions, political parties, and similar organizations.

A fourth group is convinced that collective black action can move the white-dominated institutions to reduce discriminatory actions and work toward their professed norm of equality for all. Although this view may be shared by a number of whites, the pressure for change based on the demand for equal treatment is likely to originate with and be mobilized by blacks. Many of the constituents of the protest leadership are in this group.

A fifth group of blacks also seeks steps toward equality but holds that blacks must define the reform measures for white institutions. Most of the black protest leadership is found in this (and the sixth) grouping. As with their white reformist allies, these blacks judge that the final goal should be a society in which opportunities are equally available and in which color will cease to be a distinguishing social, institutional, or individual characteristic.

Still other blacks place a greater emphasis on the need for black identity and black pride. They see these as meaningful aspects of their personal and cultural development. Black pride and black identity are, simultaneously, a defense against white postures of superiority and a promise of meaningful affirmative wholeness for each black in his relation to his own past and group. Blacks seek to develop a black unity and to identify aspects of each major institution that should contribute to the development and meaning of black identity and black pride.

Each of the six black perspectives summarized above appears in the cases that have been studied. Despite these differences, all blacks relate to each other in some sense, and, collectively, may think of themselves as the black community. For this reason, leaders pressing various programs are likely to find considerable sympathy and support within the community even from those whose perspectives are different. Those in the first three groupings listed above are unlikely to become participants in group actions that challenge white institutions. Those in the other three categories appear as leaders or at least as potential constituents when conflict develops with a white establishment.

These alternative black positions develop three identifiable black challenges to establishments: (1) correct discriminatory policies and practices; (2) accept black spokesmen and their definitions of goals and priorities in establishment changes; and (3) revise establishment objectives so as to contribute to black identity and pride.

In concluding this section, we return to the question of whether "white side versus black side" is an appropriate description of the racial conflicts that have been studied. Our analysis poses two questions about such a label. In some sense, there is an abstract ideal of equal opportunity which is supported by most whites and blacks. The essential basis for the racial conflict, however, is the enormous contrast between how most whites and most blacks define the meaning of the ideal and assess the reality of its application in American life.

Differences between groups of whites and groups of blacks cross color lines so that some whites support programs desired by blacks and some blacks support establishment positions as defined by whites. Yet the predominant alignments are within the single color grouping. Most white decision makers support the general policies and programs of the establishment, and black militant leaders find their constituencies largely among blacks who protest discrimination more intensely than do their white allies. The preceding analysis, therefore, adds necessary dimensions to the dynamics of confrontation, but, nevertheless, the conflict is so color-related that the abstract description, "white side versus black side" is retained.

POWER RELATIONSHIPS

Building on these generalizations about the differing black and white perspectives, the analysis draws on the case data to suggest some possible confrontation patterns. These data appear to confirm the original hypothesis that if blacks wait for whites and white institutions to reform themselves, change is likely to be slow and minimal at best. Thus, an important step in projecting the outlook for black progress is to assess the coercive capacities of each side because their power relationship profoundly affected the negotiated outcome in each of the case studies. In the subsequent section we will assess the degree to which black power can be used to modify establishment policies and the extent to which white executives may respond to black definitions of the inadequacy of establishment functioning and work out changes with black spokesmen.

The more completely whites judge that the establishments of a sector are already satisfying a social norm of nondiscrimination, the greater will be their internal and community support in resisting black demands. In those sectors in which blacks perceive excessive individual and group discrimination, the black challenge will be greater because there will be greater black cohesion and a greater capacity to recruit white allies. These images, of course, relate less to reality than to the abilities of leaders of both sides to shape the perspectives of their supporters.

Black power appears to be more effective where there is a continuity of individual and group attachment to the same establishment. This effectiveness is illustrated by the involvement of black employees and their union in a continuing relationship with an employer, and black parents and the black community with local public schools.

Black Power

Other general propositions about black and white power also emerge from the case studies. These data suggest how extremely difficult it is to develop and sustain black power. In the case studies, powerful outside help rallied to support local actions only when the black grouping had been a part of an ongoing organization such as the union movement. Some local support came from black politicians, church leaders, and organizations and from white allies who responded to a black call for additional support. If the case selections are at all typical of the situations in the various sectors, it appears significant that only in the San Francisco State case was there an extension of black power through a coalition with other minority groups.

Some blacks who confront the establishment hope that white executives will react positively to calls for justice and equality and will be ready to correct the discriminatory practices that are brought to their attention. Some may hold this view even while they are deeply aware of continuing inequality. When establishment spokesmen do not agree on the extensive changes demanded in the early stages of a confrontation, much of this kind of black support drifts away. A limited number of such adherents remain embittered and angry and even more determined to support the challenges developed by their leadership.

In most of the cases there was no previously established organization or leadership-constituency relationship that focused specifically on the issues of that conflict. Blacks who assumed protest leadership had to develop and refine demands that would speak to specific black needs for changes in a particular establishment. Their call to action usually had two interrelated thrusts. They presented an appeal, usually couched in strong black rhetoric, which would arouse black unity, express shared anger toward the white society, and call for black-defined social goals. Giving focus to this were definite demands to correct specific discriminatory practices and to meaningfully improve the functioning of the particular establishment.

It was difficult for the leadership to employ sustained disruptions because many black clients were wary of risking the displeasure of the establishment. White response was quite likely to be far less than the leadership hoped for, and potential allies frequently were slow to respond to the message of a demonstration or to make substantial commitments to establishment change, particularly if it meant some loss of resources or services to themselves.

Perhaps the greatest weakness in the black power position was that many blacks doubted that the prospects of success were very bright. If the demands were expressed in terms of sweeping changes, the prospects might soon appear to be zero. If the demands were minimal, many might consider it not worth the effort. When a time frame is added to the analysis, it becomes apparent that the greatest long-run weakness of the black thrust was the fact that black organizations were not available to continually monitor and press for further action.

The militant black leader is the key figure in the development and use of black power resources in racial conflict. He builds a constituency by defining the conflict objectives but may be trapped in this process by his own rhetoric. He rallies support by appealing to long-standing reactions to discrimination and by implying that the particular struggle should be supported because it may achieve sweeping changes. He also builds support by defining issues which are to be presented to the establishment as demands. In this process he may make his own task of compromise more difficult for he may have to choose only a few demands on which to concentrate and be prepared to settle for less on any particular demand. On the other hand, this very process of defining issues may increase his capacity to secure acceptance of change since he may be able to define for the establishment spokesmen the inadequacies of the ways in which the establishment is performing its functions as it deals with blacks. This latter capacity, then, may provide the basis for a negotiating pattern in which the establishment, in yielding to some black demands, will have improved its own functioning.

Establishment Power

When blacks can mobilize some coercive capacity to push the establishment to change in ways that it does not wish to change, the next question concerns the capacity of the establishment to resist. The resistance can be based on any combination of four responses: (1) a defense that it is already adequately performing its functions for blacks; (2) a rallying of support from other interests for whom the establishment is performing satisfactorily; (3) a suppression of the black pressures; and (4) an avoidance of the negotiation of demands that are being pressed by black leaders.

The usual first response is to insist that the establishment is already functioning adequately for blacks. This is based in part on the allegation that no change is necessary since blacks as well as others need functions that have already been adequately developed. Individuals supporting this position frequently insist that no racial criteria are appropriated for its functioning. This response may be meaningful and cogent to many white groupings within the establishment, which urge and support resistance to the demands and oppose any concessions that might be contemplated. The appeal is effective for blacks served by the establishment if it appears to summarize the importance of the establishment functions to them, even though they may agree with the militant leadership that it has not been fully responsive to their particular needs.

A second basis for establishment power in standing firm against black demands comes from those other interests whose needs are already served by the establishment and who are prepared to resist either a sharing of decision-making authority with a black grouping or any reallocation of resources. Such resistance may come from professionals (such as teachers or faculties), from other organized elements in the establishment (such as administrators or blue collar workers), from others whom the establishment services (such as white parents), and from publics that provide resources for the establishment (such as legislatures, city officials, and other citizen groupings).

A third establishment power base is the use of suppressive devices or disciplinary actions. If demonstrations or disruptions are available to the black leadership, the suppressive power of police action and/or court injunctions may be available to the establishment. These resources are available if the publics are satisfied with the establishment's functioning and, particularly, if they fear the escalating effects of demonstrations or black power.

On the other hand, each of the power sources summarized here has its own built-in limits. It is striking that the use of the police and the courts to block the pressures of the black militants has a predictable ancillary result that may limit its use: Administrators who judge it necessary to squelch black action are signaling that the interests of blacks are, in fact, being suppressed. These actions may damage rather than protect the images as well as the processes of more rational decision making. Insofar as white polarization develops, it may make the task of reasonable adjustment more difficult for establishment leaders.

The fourth resource available to the establishment when it has decided to reject black pressures for change is refusal to negotiate. The fundamental basis for this position is that the establishment should not recognize a specialized black interest in its functioning and that proper overall policy should be nonracial. There are at least four ways in which such a position can be used to secure support for the refusal to negotiate.

One elaborate tactic is to attempt to persuade potential supporters that legitimate concerns about discrimination have already been taken into account in policies and administration. When blacks are added to an establishment executive hierarchy and are assigned the task of making sure that there is no discrimination, the establishment hopes that some blacks as well as many whites will reject the more extreme positions pressed by the black protest leadership. Some of the profound complications in this dual role for black administrators have been summarized in Chapter 9.

A second tactic that can be used to avoid negotiations is to draw on the specialized assistance of black groups in contributing to establishment purposes. In the Chicago construction case the industry justified its position by using a black organization to recruit candidates for training and employment. This approach also appears in a number of federally financed projects that are designed to enlist black involvement in developing black individuals for the establishment's job criteria.

A third tactic for avoiding negotiations is to provide a mechanism so that black views can be presented and taken into account in any revision of establishment policies. Not infrequently, of course, such a tactic means only that the policy makers go through the form but not the substance of consultation, or that they simply assign a subordinate agent to discuss the concerns of black protestors for later, incidental consideration.

In the last analysis, the capacity of the establishment to refuse to negotiate with blacks stems from the limited degree to which the establishment needs the continued involvement of any group of black protestors. For instance, most power sources in the construction industry of Chicago considered that they did not need black skilled workers or black community support, because they did not control public or private construction money and did not buy houses. A welfare system is not seriously injured if a limited number of black clients refuse assistance from it. Although a school system is supported by the white community on the assumption that it is educating blacks as well as other pupils, school representatives in our cases had little difficulty in persuading their supporters that the boycott of some black pupils was unimportant. Interestingly enough the clout of boycotting black pupils came because of the elaborate and mechanical state aid formula that penalized a school whose pupil days were reduced.

Thus, the relative power of black challengers versus establishment insistence on the status quo will vary within a sector and among sectors. But as a generalization, the data suggest an extreme imbalance—little and probably transitory power available to black protest leaders compared to strong and lasting support for decision makers within establishments.

NEGOTIATIONS

Despite a power imbalance between protestors and establishments, one or both sides may consider it worthwhile to attempt to negotiate resolution of the issues raised by a set of black demands. The questions then become: How is relative power modified by and during negotiations and how is this power translated into change in establishment policies and practices in the direction of black interests? To what degree is such change accomplished? What, if any, parallel interests of blacks and the establishment explain the degree of change achieved?

The data from the cases give clues to the answers to those questions by identifying four major aspects of such racial negotiations: (1) recognition issues; (2) judgments of each side on whether negotiation is an acceptable process; (3) stages through which a negotiations process is likely to go; and (4) the last stage of agreement and possible ratification of terms.[1] In this summary, the concept of negotiations is the same as that used throughout this volume: a set of interactions, usually face-to-face, in which alternate positions and perspectives are explored and in which each side seeks to discover whether terms of settlement can be formulated which are preferred by both sides as an alternative to continuing the conflict.

Recognition

There are two aspects of this question that both parties need to decide in the affirmative, at least tentatively, before negotiations can begin. The first of these is whether there is a distinguishable black interest in the way the establishment is operating that justifies such negotiations. Black leaders who are formulating demands obviously tend to have a clear affirmative answer to that aspect of the question, that is, the establishment is not functioning properly for blacks and can only be expected to change when separate black interests are expressed and pressed.

At this point establishment executives make a decision, which, if not later modified, defines the whole pattern of subsequent confrontations and possible negotiations. Is discrimination such an urgent prob-

---

[1] In this section the sometimes unrealistic assumption that no third parties play any significant part in the negotiations is made. In the following section we speculate about the possible impact of various kinds of intervenors, which differ according to their skills, their understanding of the conflict, their interest in its outcome, and the influence they may bring to it.

Summary and Conclusions 265

lem that it requires new perspectives and approaches? Should the stabilized processes of decision making be complicated further by accepting an obligation to accommodate this new force? In most of the cases, at the first presentation of black demands, the executives choose to refuse to recognize outsiders. Although they admit that the establishment is not fully living up to its own norm of nondiscrimination, they assume that the interplay of assigned responsibilities and internal forces within the organization will make whatever corrections are necessary.

If executives make an alternative choice, the subsequent pattern of negotiations will be strikingly different. Among the alternatives are voluntary acceptance of the protest leadership or mutal reevaluation of the effect of discrimination on establishment functions and a joint search for a balance of interests. Almost surely such positions would produce greater changes in establishment policies than those that occurred through the pressure negotiations that followed in our cases.

The second aspect of the recognition issue poses more urgent problems for each side. It involves the decision of whether the other side is represented by appropriate spokesmen. For the black side this question becomes a judgment as to whether those who speak on behalf of the establishment have the authority to agree to all, or indeed to any part, of the demanded changes. Our study illustrates the reasonableness of such caution. Consciously or unconsciously, in some of our cases, executives laid a trap for the protestors. An administrator was sent to conduct discussions, not with the intention of committing the establishment to any change in policy, but only to hear and report back to his superiors on the black complaints and to explain establishment policies and problems to the protestors.

On the other hand, it is frequently difficult for an outsider to judge authority alignments within an organization. A refusal to bargain with an administrator may lose a negotiating opportunity if he does in fact have the capacity to deliver. In a few of our cases the protest leadership refused to negotiate with establishment spokesmen, whom they perceived as lacking the power to act. In these and other cases, the difficulty of judging the authority of the establishment spokesmen during negotiations continued to plague the black leadership.

Even when executives acknowledge the need for outside help in realigning their policies, they must choose black leaders, all of whom have differing definitions of black needs and, therefore, differing demands, that they will recognize. If there are many black groupings, the establishment may be honestly confused as to who represents the black community. If the black groupings have formed a coalition, the establishment may use the recognition question as a tactic to delay negotiations or to select more amenable negotiators.

In a number of the cases the establishment first decided against recognition. There are several explanations for such a decision. We have already noted that some establishments used a black who was assigned the role of representing black interests within the hierarchy. This role, it was assumed, could better express the black concerns of the establishment because it involved an understanding and adjustment to other administration problems and functions and, therefore, a realistic approach toward such changes. At the same time it was assumed that the black administrator could work out adjustments with all other power elements within the establishment. Finally, the role would include communicating establishment problems to the black community and the reasonableness of adjustments that were being made.

In part this use of a black administrator may have been adopted because the establishment judged that there was no agreement within the black community on how it should function and that to recognize one group of spokesmen was to deny recognition to alternative groupings with diverse views of black needs and priorities. The inside black spokesman is assigned the role of pulling together reasonable black positions, securing the understanding and, hopefully, the agreement of some black leaders, and therefore eliminating the need to deal with other spokesmen and other presumably more unrealistic black positions.

In the kinds of cases that have been explored in this study, the unwillingness of the establishment to recognize the black militant leaders as appropriate spokesmen for change meant that the changes adopted to forestall a confrontation were narrow, limited, and perhaps temporary unless the black threat was sufficiently credible to force an establishment to recognize outside black leaders.

Acceptance of a Negotiations Process

In the cases we studied both sides tended to take nonnegotiable positions. For the black leaders the nonnegotiable phraseology had several different meanings. On some issues it meant that no negotiation was possible, even though accommodated solutions could be found on others. For the establishment nonnegotiable positions had to be abandoned, or at least modified, before a settlement was possible.

During a confrontation and even during the efforts to find agreement between the parties, some black positions are never relinquished. In this sense, they are nonnegotiable. These include the conviction that only blacks with roots in the black community can legitimately speak for black interests. If a compromise on this point is reached, it is only a temporary truce while the black leaders hope to achieve an exclusive role in defining the black interests that seem right and needed. This position is based on the assumption that white policies are discriminatory and that white individuals are prejudiced. Thus, a second nonnegotiable position is that white individuals and institutions must be drastically changed before black equality and black identify are fully achieved. Again, there may be temporary agreements marking limited steps toward equality, but the fundamental position cannot be bargained away.

Black rhetoric also has been used to communicate a firm position on some specific issues. This situation may start with a set of demands whose appropriateness is so clear to the black leaders that no concessions should be considered. However, as the discussions continue, as the blacks get a better understanding of the limited responsiveness of the establishment to their black perspectives, and as their relative power appears to be substantially less than they had originally assumed, black leaders may abandon some demands in order to preserve the pressure for others. They may temporarily accept some changes even though these are much less than they desired. The rhetoric of nonnegotiability on such aspects, then, is essentially a bargaining ploy.

Although establishment leaders strongly object to any nonnegotiating position by black protestors, they tend to take similar positions themselves. These intransigent establishment positions must be modified, or at least circumvented, if negotiation is to follow. In some cases the adjustment of some policies and practices can be labeled an administrative matter about which an administrator is permitted to enter into understandings with blacks so long as fundamental policies are unaffected. In other cases the fiction of nonnegotiation is preserved by a final action of chief policy makers who adopt negotiated changes in policies as though they were unilaterally decided.

The power relationship influences each side on whether they choose to negotiate as well as what the outcome might be. Neither side is likely to choose to negotiate if it appears that the conclusion would be capitulation to the other. Black leaders would be reluctant to negotiate if they saw no hope for meaningful change, and the establishment would be unwilling if it judged that extreme changes were to result. Thus, tested by the prospects for applying coercive power, each side has to see that the results can be expected to fall within an acceptable range before they will begin serious negotiations.

One logical extension of the last generalization has a particular significance for the central question of how much change may be achieved through negotiations. In our cases black leaders had no prospect of compelling general and sweeping changes in policy covering any wide-ranging establishment. Their base was too narrow, and their power too limited. What they did concentrate on, however, with hope for limited success, was some unit within the larger establishment toward which their coercive capacity was greatest for any combination of reasons. Thus, welfare clients organized in small ethnic units could hope to get minor administrative changes but had no prospect of requiring a whole welfare system to negotiate with them. Black pupils and their parents could hope to cause a school unit to change its approaches but did not have enough power to force general policy changes on a whole school board. Black students might hope to change an admissions and recruitment policy affecting blacks or to develop a black studies program, but they could not force a reorganization of the university structure or its teaching or research programs.

The decision of whether or not to enter into negotiations is based on each side's assessment of the advantages that might be gained through negotiations and the consequences of the uses of relative coercive pressures. The conflict, we have noted, is substantial, but not complete. Even when defining the establishment functions with differing emphases and describing them differently, each side has something to gain by working out an agreement.

For the establishment the gain can be the possibility that black perspectives and demands will bring needs for change into focus. These changes can come because chief policy makers have gained a new perspective on their own purposes, or because some groupings within the establishment which are insisting that changes be made have found allies. It is hoped, then, that black pressures will decline or even disappear.

The black leaders develop a confrontation to get some changes. The appeal to enter negotiations is as strong as the priorities assigned to the changes that appear to be achievable. In this process black leaders may also gain a degree of recognition and a strengthening of their relations to a black constituency. This may be viewed as a more important long-run accomplishment of the particular negotiations.

Stages

Another way to consider the possibilities for change through racial negotiations is to abstract the more or less typical stages from which a confrontation may develop. It is striking that in most of our cases the confrontation originated from a rather limited triggering incident. Some relatively small establishment action, perhaps affecting only a few black clients or initiating only a small change in policy, may start a chain of events that leads to a major confrontation. The incident may appear minor to the establishment. For the blacks, however, the incident may be an emotionally charged illustration of long-time frustrations and thus may rally support for a general push against establishment policies. At this point establishment administrators confront a crucial decision. If they accept the justice of the complaints, view the incident as an unfair application or extension of policy, and are able and willing to amend it, the incident may not set off a more general confrontation. If, on the other hand, the administrators hold that a reversal would be unwarranted and risky, a confrontation may well develop.

The next step for each side is likely to be an effort to develop support. For blacks this may be accomplished by convincing constituents of the intransigence of the establishment. For establishment spokesmen it may come about by portraying the threat to established patterns embodied in the sweeping black demands. Black rhetoric plays an important role for both sides. It may rally blacks and frighten whites. The polarization problem first appears at this stage. Black leaders face the danger that anti-black emotion will greatly increase the resistance of the establishment. White leaders cope with the problem that, even if they wanted to, the clashing interests cannot be accommodated.

Coalitions tend to develop in this stage. Blacks may find white allies within the establishment. There may be outsiders whose social values lead them to support the black positions. Other minority groups may be prepared to make common cause with the black leaders on these and allied specific issues. White alignments may perform the same function for the establishment. Outside groupings may perceive the stability of their relationship with the establishment to be threatened if concessions are made to the black militant leaders. Thus, the establishment may rally a whole range of supplementary resources to resist such concessions.

The alternative developments in this second state affect the final outcome and, therefore, the answers to our question about the potential for negotiated change. In a search for allies there may be significant, if subtle, changes in the respective positions of the two sides. More than this, in any formal alliances positions may have to be consciously altered to secure wider support. Therefore, establishment spokesmen may find it useful to be ready to make minor concessions in the interest of peace and stability, while black leaders may find it desirable to shift their priorities to give more emphasis to general issues and less to specifically black complaints against the establishment.

The third stage, usually developed largely around a bargaining table, has the same general purposes as in any other negotiating process, that is, the exploration by each side of the real position of the other. This involves penetration beyond words, which may be intended more to confuse, or even entrap, then to enlighten. Each party judges what priorities exist for its side for each issue and assesses how much power each side could marshal in support of its own position. Black and white spokesmen, however, are much less likely to understand one another's position than is true with present-day union-management exchanges. At this stage there may be so little white understanding of black demands and black power alignments that white spokesmen may seriously misjudge the protestors' positions and their determination and support. On the other hand, the blacks perceptions may be so affected by their own views of right and justice that they misread white positions and white institutional alignments.

Next is the stage in which compromise positions are explored. This, like the previous stage, generally parallels bargaining experience, although it has particular racial elements and consequences. For blacks this stage may require a sorting out of the degree to which they will support one direction of change versus another. During this stage black leaders may have difficulty extricating themselves from the implied promises of their own rhetoric if they decide to abandon demands for sweeping changes and for their more profound black identity demands in order to preserve some pressure for changes in discriminatory policies and practices. At this stage white leaders have to reassess the concessions that will be acceptable within their own organizations and to outside establishment supporters.

As in bargaining generally, it is not necessary for each side to attach the same importance *or* even the same meaning to possible sets of agreement terms. The two sides do not have the same needs and the same solution may contribute differently to their respective interests. A package of possible agreement terms may include some critical elements for one side and different elements for the other. In this connection particularly, some modifications of policy and practice may be interpreted by the establishment as moving toward nondiscrimination, while the black spokesmen may view these as steps toward black identity and the building of black power.

Agreement and Ratification

The concluding stage of a negotiations process is an agreement. In most of the cases analyzed by the study the terms of agreement represented some concessions in the direction demanded by the black leaders. There was some modification of discriminatory practices or the replacement of officials charged with discriminatory actions. The establishment accepted, to some degree, an obligation to provide greater or different services to its black clients, although the general criteria adopted by the establishment for equal treatment was modified little, and there was little response to any demand for supplementary services. The fact that the establishment entered negotiations and reached some agreement with blacks represented a first step in the direction of black involvement in decision making. Long-range predictions, however, were quite uncertain unless the negotiations-agreement process had built an expanded black power base that could be used by black spokesmen in the future. In most cases the terms of the agreements did not ensure an expanded black power base. Most of the agreements did not provide ongoing machinery for the resolution of future racial conflicts about the meaning and application of the terms agreed upon or new issues.

The final stage of negotiations in each case involved a ratification process. As far as the black side was concerned, some form of constituency ratification was used to establish the legitimacy of the acceptance of the terms by the black leaders. The acceptance of the terms signaled that modest changes had been achieved and that, for the moment, there was no capacity to push the establishment further. In some cases concurrence was given by a wider leadership coalition; in others there was the absence of any constituency objection.

For the establishment side the ratification process was more complicated. It usually required a process by which authority figures accepted the commitments of their spokesmen. There still remained, however, the question of how the agreement would be formalized. In a few cases the announcement of agreement was made jointly by black and white spokesmen. In most cases, however, it appeared as a recommendation by establishment spokesmen that was then adopted as policy by the establishment executive authorities who appeared to be acting unilaterally.

THE MEDIATOR'S ROLE IN THIRD-PARTY INTERVENTION

A neutral third party may play a substantial role by helping two conflicting parties to find terms of agreement. This is frequently used in international conflicts and, within narrower patterns, has been developed to a fine art by industrial relations. The mediator arranges the mechanics of negotiations and helps each party to better understand the position of the other. He suggests fresh approaches and imaginative new ways to develop alternative terms for possible agreement. In these and numerous other ways a neutral third party can help in a racial as well as in a labor-management conflict.

There are, however, important differences. It is not easy for an outside mediator, particularly if he is white, to understand black objectives, perspectives, and organizational problems. It is not easy to avoid being trapped by the assumption that, since agreement appears desirable and since the general structure and objectives of the establishment are likely to appear reasonable, any settlement that blacks can be persuaded to accept is appropriate. Thus, a third-party neutral may contribute nothing toward improving the kind of settlement that would be achieved without him and may make successful change less likely.

A mediator may play an additional role. Some of the cases illustrate a third party who seeks to help the parties reach an agreement because he considers that there ought to be black progress toward equality. If he is prepared to define black progress in terms of black self-definition of need, he becomes a mediator-advocate who recognizes legitimate black interests in the functioning of the establishment and the role of black leaders as spokesmen for such a black interest. Under such circumstances his single most important function is to persuade reluctant establishment representatives to negotiate. Even though he may be otherwise uninvolved in one outcome versus another, he has two tools that are specific to a racial conflict. From his understanding of establishment purposes and functions, he may be able to interpret establishment needs for a realignment of policies and practices and indicate some of the ways in which a negotiating process may benefit the organization. He may also make use of social norms of equal opportunity.

The second approach available to the mediator-advocate is to help each of the parties reassess their judgments about the consequences of nonnegotiation and nonagreement. For the establishment this means assessment of the prospect of disruptions and other black coercive pressures. For the protestors it involves an assessment of what might be gained by negotiation as compared to their alternative position if no negotiations are attempted.

There is an additional role for an advocate-mediator if he brings to the negotiations a third-party preference for one outcome rather than another. He may be interested only in the stabilization of the situation—the achievement of peace so that the social and political risks of unrest may be reduced. This appears to have been the principal motivation of President Lyndon Johnson's mediating agent at Memphis. Apparently it was Mayor Richard Daley's principal concern in the Chicago construction case as well. Since that focus involves getting blacks as well as establishment representatives to agree, blacks can use such a concern to press their interests. Beyond this an advocate-mediator may represent those who want more rapid black progress than black pressure itself can produce. Some of the contract compliance approaches under federal contracts have led to pressures for affirmative action in employment that were more elaborate than blacks could negotiate alone. Some maximum community participation pressures have moved administrations in the direction of recognition and of substantive change.

An intervening mediator has to build the confidence of each side while becoming familiar with the position of each and helping to work out an acceptable agreement. On these counts, our limited data suggest that a black mediator may be particularly useful. His insights on the establishment position may be more penetrating and more acceptable to the black leadership. His capacity to interpret and to empathize with black positions may be particularly helpful to the establishment representatives. He may bring to his role not only an understanding that any agreement has to be built on the proper establishment functioning, but also a commitment to black progress. The result of his intervention, therefore, may be greater changes than would have been achieved by blacks without him. More limited data, incidentally, suggest that a team of black and white mediators can be even more helpful.

The changes that can be effected by a mediator, then, are in part a function of whether he brings to his role his own commitments on the kinds, depth, and rapidity of change. The results of the negotiations are affected even more by any pressure that he may be able to exert on the two sides. Obviously, pressure from a third party which is directed toward black advances improves the black negotiating position. The experience to date indicates that this type of influence may contribute to a recognition of black spokesmen. Black challengers are unlikely to get much help from uncommitted mediators toward more extensive objectives unless white fears of social instability or black political power become much greater than they were at the time the study data were collected.

TIME PERSPECTIVES ON THE RESULTS OF NEGOTIATIONS

In the previous section we formulated some general propositions about the possible development of racial negotiations that might achieve some modification of establishment practices by reducing discrimination, improving services for black clients, increasing the participation of black spokesmen in the decision-making processes, and developing black power. Our general conclusion is that it is likely that discrimination will be reduced, which may be viewed by establishment leaders as an improvement. Based on much of the same white perspective, it is less likely, but possible, that services will be improved for black clients. Increasing the participation of black spokesmen and the development of black power are much less likely to occur.

Unfortunately at this point in our analysis we have come to the end of the data on which we could draw. The limited resources available to the project required that the focus of each case study be limited to a specific incident. One may speculate, however, on the possible long-run consequences of the negotiated results of these confrontations. Obviously, a long-range perspective is needed before an evaluation of the process can be given. In none of the cases that we studied were the changes instituted through negotiations extensive enough to indicate that establishments would make additional changes on their own or even retain those that were won by blacks in the confrontations. Thus, there is a real danger that the results of the incidents, when viewed over time, may show the negotiations process to be simply a device that cooled unrest but produced little black progress.

Even within the cases, however, two modifications of that prediction might be warranted. White decision makers tended to worry about prospective black moods. When whites interpreted black moods as likely to lead to further violent clashes with white authorities, they tended to accept some changes that they considered possible and realistic. This fear of potential black attitudes was used frequently by black negotiators to secure greater white support for some changes. Within the short time span between the incidents studied and the final writing of this volume, however, there appears to have been a reduction in white fears about black riots and even about black guerilla tactics. For better or for worse, white fears of black revolts appear to be a declining motivation for white concessions.

There is a second and more affirmative possibility, however. If black leaders and constituencies judge that the results of the confrontation represent real progress toward equality, they may be encouraged to press establishments further in future negotiations.

The union-management analogy suggests an additional alternative. Union agreements usually provide continuing machinery to monitor company policy and administrative actions. Law, precedent, and perhaps even the agreement itself generally provide for later negotiating activities. In those cases in which there are a union and a union-management framework, such continuing machinery is usually of considerable importance in consolidating and extending union gains. Thus, the recognition and dues check-off issues in Memphis, which were compromised in the first agreement, were almost fully achieved in the negotiations held the following year.

Drawing on that analogy, one might predict that if future conditions were favorable for the use of such machinery, results that were affirmative to black interests could be obtained by the same devices. An arrangement could be provided under which black leaders could object to either an executive or administrative failure to live up to a previous agreement. It could permit either two-party discussion or an arbitrator's award. If this machinery were used, it might well protect against retrogression in the black position. If continuing consultative machinery were also provided, perhaps black leaders would increasingly become more unified and more realistic in their demands on the establishment. They might then be able to modify executive perceptions and policies. If the machinery also provided the mechanics for future recognition of black leaders and the negotiations of new demands, it *could* produce favorable accommodation of black and establishment interests.

But there is little evidence from the cases, other than those in which union-management patterns appear, that establishing any such machinery is likely to make a real contribution to black progress. The key aspect of such an analysis is the degree to which continuing black organization outside the establishment has been built and continues to focus on black complaints against these specific establishments. Just as many of the cases began with unplanned triggering incidents, and just as the black leadership-constituency relationships were built on an ad hoc basis, the tendency has been for organizational patterns to disappear after the incident has been resolved, no matter how elaborate or modest the changes that were achieved through negotiations.

CHALLENGING PROBLEMS

Even if all of the speculative analyses drawn from the research data accurately approximate the course of black confrontations, there are many unanswered questions. Some of these are implicit in the data that have been collected but not adequately analyzed. Some might have developed from different times and different situations.

The case studies were all written between 1968 and 1970. Although in some ways white attitudes and institutions controlled by whites change very slowly, some relevant characteristics change much more rapidly. Black expectations and black power have already changed a good deal, just as they changed during the sixties, and black judgments as to important strategies may also be changing. The first question, then, is: Are blacks inclined to use the experiences analyzed here to pursue the same routes more aggressively and with greater sophistication, or are they moving in other and perhaps more elaborately structured political directions?

The second question relates to the sector conceptualization built into this research design. As the chapters have indicated, there are striking differences between sectors in regard to power structures, establishment purposes, and specific negotiating issues. Our resources did not permit an extension of the study to some other areas. It may be that black caucuses within unions and other such institutions may have even greater promise. There are other, perhaps more favorable, areas in landlord-tenant relationships, in police functions, and in the delivery of health services. The questions with which this study is concerned can also be addressed to these institutions.

The analysis suggests that, even for a first confrontation, power is greater if there is some black organizational structure and if it can be extended and reinforced during the confrontation. Further, we have speculated that the meaning and extent of any establishment changes depend less on white good intentions than on continuing black pressure. A much more complete study of the dimensions and dynamics of continuing black power development is urgent.

The possibilities for coalitions among black leadership groups are important to the development of black power organization. These include coalitions between black and white organized units that share specific objectives, between other minority groupings with the same general perspectives, and/or between whites who occupy the same status or client position as the constituencies of the black leaders. We have already speculated that any such coalition tends to modify black protest demands. We have also speculated that, potentially at least, such coalitions may significantly extend the coercive power of the black group. More research must be done on the effects of the mix of these two positions, that is, more power and modified issues.

An additional problem that was identified but not explored by this report involves the intentions of the federal government in affecting directions of potential black progress. Limited government backing of black pressures may signal future trends. Indications that federal pressure is greatly weakened by state and local government power and political structures may support this prediction. On the other hand, perhaps the future holds a much more extensive role for black political power in influencing federal and local governments. Such a change from the present climate could make an enormous difference in the possible uses of the negotiation processes in a specific establishment whose racial positions could be affected by government action.

In our analyses it was difficult to judge the priorities assigned by black leaders to improvements in the services provided to blacks and the correction of discriminatory practices in contrast to the development of black power within the establishment structure. Primarily, we attempted a single, overall generalization, while the black positions varied considerably in terms of different sector characteristics. Although the cases tended to illustrate a clear progression of objectives, the specific negotiating positions were controlled by the practicalities of what could be achieved. The expressions of black militant leaders give some clues to directions; however, they also were attempting to build unity and commitment. It is quite possible that black scholars can contribute more information on this and on many other points than can be concluded from case studies made by black-white teams or from case analyses made by the white director of this research project.

The findings from the original research design and the case and sector analyses indicate that an essential element of the conflict developed from the perspectives of establishments, which are likely to profess commitments to equality and to justify their own policies and practices as contributing as much as can be expected toward such equality. As our analysis proceeded, we found that limited black power used and even depended on the degree to which these perspectives could be changed. If establishments have a clearer perspective on their racist characteristics and a sharper determination to change them, the negotiations process could be much more meaningful for blacks than our cases report. Are such changes likely? They do *not* appear likely from the data summarized here, but if different forces come into play, the prospect for change through negotiation might appear brighter.

Finally, there is the problem of the black administrator. He constantly appeared in the cases, but our research did not bring his functions and dilemmas into focus. This is an area that requires further exploration. The black administrator in our cases was frequently an agent of the establishment. He was often out of sympathy with the specific demands, tactics, and timing of the black protestors. His contacts and perspectives may come from different sections of the black community and from different experiences than do those of the militant leaders of protest. Frequently, he has been selected by white executives to report to them on black moods and has been assigned some authority to intervene within the establishment on ways to respond to black needs. At times the white executives have acted as though their black staff member was the spokesman for the black community.

There were also other ways to describe his perspectives, possible roles, and identifications. He may be much more aware than the white executives of the shortcomings of the establishment in its relations to blacks. He may wish to play a role in moving the establishment further and faster. To that end he may be pressing black interests, whether or not there are concerned protest groups. In addition, he may help black protest groupings to identify the elements of the establishment that are the most likely to support their positions. His knowledge of how the establishment operates may provide realism to the black protest leaders as they build a case against establishment practices and focus on the issues that they hope to affect. He also may be assigned the role of executing the terms that were settled by the negotiations.

Perhaps a more adequate analysis would begin by defining the dilemma of the black administrator. If he wants to see an accommodation of institutional and black interests with extensive changes, he has very limited power, for two basic reasons. On one hand, the administration that has assigned his role usually has not been prepared to give him much authority for making changes in establishment policies or practices. On the other hand, the black constituency to which he can turn for guidance is usually very limited. There is no single black community and no unified black position on specific establishment activities behind which all blacks will rally. Usually there is not even a strong independent organization of blacks who articulate a common, organized perspective on what the administrator's position and role should be. His limited reference to the black community is further diluted since he may believe that the understands the organizational, administrative, and technical problems posed by policy or administrative decisions affecting blacks within the establishment more accurately than black outsiders.

The guidance he gets from the black community is almost entirely limited, therefore, to some vague and general black positions. He has no organized black constituency to guide or support him. Because he is appointed by the establishment, his credentials as an advocate for black progress are questioned by blacks. He performs to the best of his ability and makes judgments in accordance with his own perspectives of what is most useful and meaningful for his black brothers. His is not an enviable position.

CONCLUDING PERSPECTIVE

This research was based on one assumption and two underlying hypotheses. The assumption was that racial conflict, both in real and perceptual terms, exists in America. Nothing in the case data appears to challenge that assumption.

The first underlying hypothesis is that under some circumstances, a negotiating process can be used by the white and the black sides of that conflict. The data appear to support and elaborate that hypothesis. Many of the most immediate and pervasive experiences of black Americans come from their client or participant relationships to specific establishments. In a society whose functions and decisions are decentralized, these establishments are the units where service decisions are made and where power is focused. The establishments with which we are concerned tend to justify their policies and actions by insisting that they are designed to provide equal treatment for all citizens. Conflicts of interest are admitted, but these are described in economic and social terms as conflicts between the "haves" and the "have nots," and the machinery for the adjustment of conflict is based on that description. For black protest leaders, however, these conflicts mirror racist views of white establishments toward a depressed black minority; they are have nots primarily *because* they are black. Indeed, many blacks perceive the attempts by whites to define conflict in nonracial terms as merely another form of racism and as a device used by whites to conceal their racism from themselves.

We are dealing, then, with conflicts that are racial and functional. There appears to be no way for us to isolate these separate factors in our data and to choose one emphasis as against another. The differing perceptions of white executives and black protestors provide their own reality and their own truth. Black perceptions lead to the objectives of the redress of black grievances, black recognition, black dignity, and black control. In some ways the recognition issue most clearly illustrates these differing interpretations. For black protestors recognition includes acknowledgement of the moral rightness of their grievances by whites, the correction of wrongs, and the recognition of their right to designate their own spokesmen and to set up some of the rules by which negotiations will occur. These, in effect, become the nonnegotiable demands that are frequently mentioned. In all of these ways the issue of recognition is more fundamental to the conflict than the usual acceptance of an organization and its leaders as the spokesman for an interest group.

Despite the depth and intensity of such a conflict, we hypothesize that negotiations could be a way to achieve step-by-step changes in establishment practices toward black equality. The hypothesis suggests that some kinds of nonrevolutionary accommodation could be ahcieved within individual establishments and within the total social system through this process.

The case data indicate two sets of variables that are fundamental in determining the degree to which the negotiating process will be used: (1) the degree to which white executives of specific establishments recognize the racist characteristics of their functioning and seek ways to realign their policies toward equal performance for blacks, and (2) the degree of readiness of black leaders and their potential constituencies to take their destiny in their own hands and use specific black complaints and generalized black anger as a basis for requiring establishment change.

The second underlying hypothesis was that important progress for blacks would result from such negotiations. The data indicate, however, that only minimal progress is achieved. To apply such an assessment to the data, of course, requires some scale of values about establishment changes. This project used a hierarchy of values that began with reductions in institutional discriminatory practices and policies and included roles, implementation of independent black definitions of black interests and priorities, and the use of blacks of institutional functions to foster and develop black identity and black pride within a pluralistic society.[2]

The same basic factors that determine whether or not negotiations will be used at all probably also explain the minimal results we have summarized. No great movement exists among whites to reform the institutions for which they are responsible. Perhaps the clearest indication of the weakness of reformist pressures is the inability of so many whites to even identify their racist characteristics. Blacks feel disenchantment and frustration as black pressures succeed in making establishments change just enough to bolster their claims of non-discrimination of a kind of tokenism, but not enough to really change their relationships with black citizens.

We are also placing the burden of reforming America on blacks, who have been held in second-class status for 300 years. Our data demonstrate the difficulty of such an assignment. White resistance is strong while independent black protest organizations are still very weak. The devices of tokenism and co-optation have constantly been used to drain support and leadership. Commitment to a black cause

---

[2] It is recognized that others may adopt different values or arrangements of the value scale. If one uses different values or a different assignment of priorities, the data yield moderately different evaluations.

must be profound before its power can be felt. There are enormous social pressures on blacks to conform to a melting pot idea rather than pressing for an ideal of black identity within cultural pluralism.

An evaluation of the negotiations process is complicated by the fact that many of the normal tactics of negotiations are subject to differential interpretations in a racial conflict. Are the negotiations judged to be a tactic designed to cool a situation or do they constitute good faith bargaining? Such judgments depend primarily on the past experiences of blacks in dealing with whites and on the personalities of the negotiators. It is possible to speculate that the degree to which minimal gains in a first negotiation are implemented will control whether blacks will again be willing to use the process, and here the burden is clearly on the white establishments.

The larger implications of our findings lie in the future. Presumably, black expectations and determination are rising. Perhaps we are in a period where white America is moving toward equality in institutions such as schools and public accommodations. White concern for the reform of schools, universities, and other institutions is growing. Even if these trends develop, however, blacks and their white supporters may find their maximum effectiveness through the political process. Of course, the negotiating process is frequently used to accommodate conflicting interests in politics. If this is the case, the conceptualizations rather than the specifics of this study may assume primary importance.